Nationalization in France and Italy

Nationalization in France and Italy

>>>>>>>>>>>>>>>>>>>>>><<<<<<<<<<<<<<<<<<<<

MARIO EINAUDI

MAURICE BYÉ

ERNESTO ROSSI

Cornell University Press

ITHACA, NEW YORK

PRINTED IN THE UNITED STATES OF AMERICA BY THE
VAIL-BALLOU PRESS, INC., BINGHAMTON, NEW YORK

Foreword

THIS volume is the fourth, and for the moment the last, of a series devoted to the political, economic, and constitutional problems of postwar France and Italy. The series is part of a "French-Italian Inquiry" undertaken at Cornell University in 1949 in the belief that the changes brought about by fascism, revolution, and war in these two countries were sufficiently significant to warrant the attention of students of comparative government.

The first three volumes have dealt with the political ideologies of communism and Christian democracy and with the evolution of constitutional government in France since 1945.[1]

The present volume deals with one of the issues that, not only in France and Italy but throughout the democratic world, have been the source of much political debate in the first decade since the end of World War II—nationalization of the key sectors of the economy. Few questions of public policy have attracted the attention or raised the hopes that nationalization policies have. Here they are discussed in the colder light of the aftermath.

A study of French and Italian policies has also seemed important because, in contrast to the relative wealth of materials on British nationalization, not much has hitherto been available on Continental developments. In the variety of their origins and in their subsequent political complications they add many interesting new aspects to the traditionally received image of nationalization.

---

[1] Mario Einaudi, Jean-Marie Domenach, Aldo Garosci, *Communism in Western Europe* (Ithaca: Cornell University Press, 1951); Mario Einaudi and François Goguel, *Christian Democracy in Italy and France* (Notre Dame: University of Notre Dame, 1952); François Goguel, *France under the Fourth Republic* (Ithaca: Cornell University Press, 1952).

v

The publication of this volume has been delayed in the hope that France and Italy would carry out the promised reforms in the administration of their nationalized industries. The reforms are for the most part yet to come, but certain significant changes took place in 1953, thus enabling our account to reach a logical concluding point. While 1953 is the terminal date, an effort has been made, wherever it mattered, to bring up to date statistical and other data.

Like the first volume of the French-Italian Inquiry, this volume too is the fruit of the collaboration of three authors. Each author, however, is responsible only for his own contribution.

In the first part, the issues of nationalization of industry in France and Italy have been viewed within the larger framework of the Western community, and those parallels and contrasts have been singled out that appeared most important for an integrated study of government intervention in the two countries.

Maurice Byé, a distinguished French economist, has, as a member of some of the new institutions and political movements of the French Republic, the Conseil Économique and the Mouvement Républicain Populaire, contributed much to the clarification of French economic problems. In the second part, he gives us a documented and detailed analysis of nationalization in France.

In the third part, Ernesto Rossi reviews nationalization in Italy. He does this largely through the vicissitudes of IRI, the government agency which until recently has summed up most of that country's experience in the field.[2] After more than twenty years in the forefront of the struggle against fascism, Rossi is today playing a leading role in Italian political life as a journalist and prototype of that administrative class whose strengthening he advocates.

The Inquiry has been made possible by a grant from the Rockefeller Foundation to Cornell University. Eve Benda, Joyce Gee, Ina and Gerhard Loewenberg, Steven Muller, Win and Roy Pierce, John Roche, and Melvin Wachs have given me invaluable assistance in the various phases of preparation of this volume.

MARIO EINAUDI

Cornell University, April, 1955

---

[2] The publication of a more detailed version of Ernesto Rossi's study was first arranged in Italy, under the title *Lo Stato Industriale* (Bari, 1953).

Contents

Part II by Maurice Byé
NATIONALIZATION IN FRANCE

Part III by Ernesto Rossi

NATIONALIZATION IN ITALY

Part I by Mario Einaudi
≫≫≫≫≫≫≫≫≫≫≫≫≪≪≪≪≪≪≪≪≪≪≪

A COMPARATIVE STUDY OF

NATIONALIZATION POLICIES

I

Some General Issues

THE SHIFT TO DIRECT CONTROLS

In all their variety, the policies developed by the Western countries in the last decades to cope with urgent economic matters appear to have one element in common, their greater reliance on direct, than indirect, controls.

Indirect controls are applied through such time-honored devices as monetary policies, whereby governments seek to direct the volume and direction of investments and the rate of economic expansion, and the control of credit facilities, to prevent excessive cyclical variations in the course of economic life. They include as well relatively new fiscal policies, which in Great Britain and in the United States have become major instruments of governmental power.

But more and more the emphasis has shifted to semidirect or direct means of control, such as the enforcement of antitrust legislation, the payment of subsidies, or the formulation of plans for the channeling of investments into specific fields which public authorities consider either to be lagging behind the rest of the economy or to have acquired a particularly important role in the nation's economy. Perhaps the outstanding example of the latter is the postwar French plan for modernization of equipment, which selected a number of specific areas, some public, some private, within which an especially intensive effort toward reconstruction and development had to be carried out by direct state intervention. These areas were initially coal, electricity, steel,

3

cement, agricultural machinery, and transportation. Fuel and nitrogen were added later.

These large-scale interventions, the scope of which went much beyond the traditional indirect approaches, failed, however, in many European countries to satisfy either the new political pressures or the new economic needs, alleged or true. Since the end of World War II, governments have, to an increasing extent, accepted the premise that in order to achieve certain vital aims of public economic policy it was necessary to place not only control but outright ownership of economic assets in public hands. The tides of human affairs move slowly, and in a century that has seen the idea of private property modified and qualified and private property rights subjected to frequent restrictions and interpretations the ancient belief was kept alive in many political quarters that government was still confronted by an unchanging and rigid concept of property rights, and that the only way to go forward was to deal with title deeds as if they still had the fearsome strength given them by the Napoleonic codes.

The argument was more impressive in some countries than in others, for the substantive content of those title deeds varied a great deal. In France there was a spirit of rebelliousness against public power on the part of some private owners, which made indirect controls difficult to assert. In other countries, such as Great Britain, there could never be any question of the authority of the government to assert itself over economic power, which was still formally private. But the argument in favor of the assumption of direct ownership by the state had a certain plausibility about it, especially when the zeal of the reformers coincided with harsh crisis conditions, and there is no question that the most significant moves of the last twenty years have been made in that direction.

Even so, these moves have not been made in a uniform manner. In the United States direct ownership by the federal government has been established, as in the case of the TVA, on a regional basis. That is, public ownership has been considered as a useful tool to set up certain standards of comparison and not as an instrument to liquidate a whole class of private businessmen in the name of the general welfare. The general welfare could equally well be served by measuring the performance of the surviving and chastised businessmen against a public yardstick of clearly limited scope. Elsewhere, as for instance in France and Italy, there was from time to time some experimentation with mixed corporations in which both government and private owners participated, with the government the dominant factor but with private stockholders permitted to have a share in management as well as to nourish the hope that ultimately they might recover full control of the enterprise. Finally, and perhaps most typically, public ownership has meant the taking over, on a national scale, of all the enterprises within a given sphere of economic activity. This is what is generally meant by nationalization.

THE MEANINGS OF NATIONALIZATION

The concept of nationalization is not, however, free from ambiguities. Different meanings have been attached to it, depending upon prevalent traditions, the role of political parties, or the type of governmental structure.

Sometimes the political conditions which existed when nationalization took place and the economic causes which led to it have continued to determine to a large extent the course of subsequent events. This is probably truer in Italy than in any other country. Nationalization occurred there almost a quarter of a century ago under a cloak of mystery and without public discussion, since this was of the essence of the conduct of economic, or any other, policies under the Fascist dictatorship. An elaborate propaganda went on for years to persuade the country of the virtues of the corporativistic structure, which remained, however, an empty shell. But no steps were taken to inform the people of the shift in economic power that occurred when the government took over about one-quarter of the industrial and financial assets of Italy.

While nationalization was very much the private concern of the ruling Fascist élite in the beginning, it has been kept away from the limelight to the present day, for no postwar government has yet had the courage to face up fully to the problems of nationalization. Since all sorts of "privatistic" slogans are still used in the conduct of what should be a public business, it is not surprising to see the nationalized sector sometimes exploited as a convenient shield behind which to transact private business. Nationalized industries may thus be used for experimental purposes in hazardous activities whose more profitable by-products are then taken over by private business, or they may frankly be regarded as a public pound of varying contents into which sick enterprises are cast but out of which, whenever possible, the profitable ones are retrieved.[1]

This is a concept of nationalization which can survive only in an atmosphere of scant public awareness of the issues involved and in a business system which as a matter of principle refuses to admit that its activities are a matter of public concern. But one should add at once that the private rather than public purposes to be served by this approach to nationalization need not be those of the business community only, but can also be those of other groups, such as political parties.

A good example of nationalization as a powerful instrument of party warfare is found in France in the years from 1945 to 1947, when the Communist party was a government party. Thanks to the legislative provisions of the main nationalization acts and to the quasi-revolutionary role played in those years by the Communist party, some French nationalized industries, such as coal, started to become the private domains of a political organization, the Communist party. What nationalization was achieving under those conditions, therefore, was the transfer of basic national economic assets from certain private interests to other private interests. That such transfer from private to even more private hands did violence to the fundamental and almost literal meaning of a policy of nationalization was a criticism not readily accepted in all quarters, and certainly not by the Communists. They advanced the view that nationalization in a democratic sense must mean the liquidation of the private owners, who are then replaced by the

1 Cf. Rossi, below, pp. 230–231.

people. In the case of industrial nationalization the "people" are the workers, and the workers are logically to be represented by their strongest trade union. That the strongest trade union was controlled by a political party was in effect claimed to be the sheerest coincidence, and not to affect the validity of the principle in question.

The crisis was brought to a head in France, however, because the party in question was the Communist and because, soon after 1947, the French people and government realized that the formation of private economic Communist empires that would have subverted and divided the French state could not be tolerated. The Communist control or dominant influence over nationalized industries was broken through a complicated and painful process of amendment and interpretation of the nationalization acts.[2]

But yet another concept of nationalization made its appearance at that point. As if by reaction to the extreme risk of autonomy under Communist auspices, the agencies administering nationalized industries gradually were merged into the traditional and dull landscape of the other departments of the central government. The prevailing mood refused to take into account the unique problems posed by nationalization, the need for separateness, for flexibility, for decentralization, for objective and skilled technical management. More and more public action seemed to be based on the principle that these requirements could be satisfied along with the varied other activities that in the course of centuries had been thrust upon the government, and in the same manner.

In a country such as France where there is no clear balance between the power exercised by the people's representatives and the power exercised by the executive, the role of the civil servant is difficult to define. The lines of accountability, of limitation of power, of acceptance of the policies laid down by the politically responsible bodies, are often confused. Nationalization, then, if it becomes the province of self-perpetuating and uncontrollable

[2] Cf. below, passim.

civil servants, runs once more the risk of assuming characteristics that are contrary to those national, public, and responsible policies which ought to be associated with it.

It is in Great Britain that a concept of nationalization more in keeping with its "ideal" definition seems to have found haven at last. The satisfaction and pride which pervade Professor Robson's "General Conclusions" in his *Problems of Nationalized Industry* [3] are justified from this point of view. For in Great Britain fair play, intelligent and independent management, public controls, defined national objectives, are present in a measure which ought to quiet all but the sharpest critics of nationalization. The contrast with the Continent could not be greater.

It should be made clear, however, that this was not the result of an automatic or self-evident process, even though the issues, insofar as there were any, were settled quickly. The position of the Labour party, the most important political group pressing forward on a broad front in the field of nationalization, had been for a long time in favor of the adoption of workers' control as the key to nationalization. It is true that the party theoreticians and pamphleteers were more vocal in support of this view than were the solemn official organs of the trade unions and of the party, which by 1944 had abandoned their earlier position. But the influence of the constitutional framework, in this as in so many other aspects of British government, should not be underestimated. The Labour party, upon assuming the responsibilities of office, became first of all an instrument for the fulfillment of policies that stood for the common good and the general welfare. The Labour government realized that a policy of representation of workers' interests applied to nationalization would not fulfill the requirements of a national policy and would greatly slow down the realization of urgent production needs. Those could be met only by establishing the most efficient type of management, capable of operating not in the interest of the workers alone but of the entire community, and allowing the industry the freedom of movement it needed. Nor were the principles of accountability

[3] Ed. by W. A. Robson (London, 1952), pp. 275–367.

to the Cabinet and through it to Parliament to be lost sight of. The public corporation, which British tradition had developed over a period of time into a successful instrument of administration, became the chosen instrument of the Labour government. After a number of necessary and desirable changes, primarily aimed at strengthening political controls, the public corporations emerged, in the words of Professor Robson, as an "invention of high significance in the government of modern countries" and as the tool through which the avowed ideals of nationalization could be best realized.

NATIONALIZATION AND PLANNING

Nationalization is frequently equated with planning. The different meanings which can be concealed behind the simple word "nationalization" are forgotten, the former private owners are without further questioning classified as nonplanners (is not a "free-wheeling private enterpriser" the enemy of planning?), and the allegedly self-evident conclusion is reached that planning is guaranteed by nationalization.

The experience of Western Europe is more complex. Planning in itself is not an obvious concept. It does not mean the type of public investment that merely replaces private investment or that becomes available in fields where no adequate private investment is available. If railroads are nationalized because private capital is no longer in a position to maintain what is still considered an essentially public service, we do not use "planning" to refer to the subsequent public investments that are made as a matter of necessity in order to keep the railroad system going. If the steel industry is nationalized, we do not use "planning" to refer to the public investments that are made to replace the private investments that would have been made had the industry remained in private hands.

National planning must be related, it would appear, to at least some of the following elements: (1) the process of modernization and the merging of numerous and stubbornly independent private enterprises into larger units, (2) the integration of the investment and development policies of different economic sectors moving in haphazard and mutually detrimental directions, (3) the coordination of major economic activities by a central board, with a view to fulfilling national policies of defense, to maintaining standards of living and of consumption, and to expanding foreign markets, (4) the adoption of radically new techniques, which, because of their cost and risk, were avoided by private business.

Nationalization in postwar Europe had relatively little to do with any of these four areas, with the exception of the first. Indeed, nationalization and planning were not conceived as a single task, as planning proceeded outside the scope of nationalized industries.

In Great Britain the compatibility between nationalization and planning can best be seen in the power and coal industries, where mergers were carried out and goals established which appeared hopeless under private ownership. In the field of transportation no such relationship is apparent, and systematic underinvestment of a type that would disqualify any planning board is the main characteristic of the first decade of nationalized railways. The expansion of the iron and steel industry after nationalization is largely the fruit of plans laid down by private industry as a result of firm government prodding, and before nationalization. The history of the iron and steel industry in Great Britain seems to prove the contention that, with strong governmental leadership and policy on such issues as modernization of plant and production targets, planning goals may be achieved just as well without nationalization and conceivably even better. A parallel may be found in developments in the United States under the Truman administration. The federal government, in the years following the end of World War II, presented the steel industry with the alternatives of either greatly expanding its production capacity by private means, or of suffering the consequences of competition by new plants built with the financial support of the government. Even though the outlines of the controversy were blurred and the anxiety of private industry to meet the consumption needs of

America was authentic, the thinking and planning of the industry were decisively influenced by the openly stated goals of public policy. A strong government, with a clear vision of what the common good requires, does not have to destroy the foundations of private property in order to reach the substance of its purpose.

This view is borne out also by the British handling of the banking problem. The justification of the British decision not to nationalize the great private commercial banks is found in the confidence of the government in its own strength. There could be no doubt that, the Bank of England having been nationalized, the private banks would follow its broad lines of policy.

Modern private enterprise in the Western world is increasingly reluctant to flout the directives and the assistance or outright participation in its activities of governmental power. If there are valid goals that can be achieved through planned and concerted activity transcending that of a single individual or corporation, then those goals can often be achieved more readily through the formulation of clear-cut and strongly supported public policy than through the transfer of property rights. The idea that in order to plan we must nationalize is a survival of the belief that ascribed superhuman and uncontrollable powers to private property. If, on the other hand, we consider property rights as social and limited, then many of the goals of planning may be reached without altering property relationships.

After looking at the experience of several countries, one is tempted to say that nationalization is an escape from planning. For, having nationalized, the politicians feel they can sit back and say that they have fulfilled their duty of slaying the dragon, when in effect nothing has been achieved and the conditions of the industry affected may be deteriorating as fast or even faster than before. Nationalization is always a beginning and never the end, but the temptation in Europe has been to consider the reverse as true. France succeeded in part in escaping this temptation, but the history of the inception and the development of the Monnet Plan is good proof of the unrelated ways in which nationalization and planning can proceed. The Monnet Plan was set up as a result of the failure of nationalized industries to meet the goals of the planners and because of the fact that the goals of the planners extended beyond the area that had been nationalized. The Monnet Plan took under its wing both private and public sectors of the French economy. The two sectors had common problems that had to be solved by the intervention of a higher authority. The fact that both private and public industries were under the jurisdiction of the Plan was in essence a merely formal matter which did not affect the formulation of planning policy.

Finally, in Italy, the top government corporation which owns and manages nationalized industries, the Institute of Industrial Reconstruction (IRI), has not been so far, for all its elaborate structure, a planning body. This may have been due to the peculiar difficulties of the Fascist and postwar periods. However this may be, no planning has been in evidence because nationalization did not succeed in calling into existence a planning fervor that was not there. It might be countered that the reconstruction and fresh growth of the IRI-owned steel industry are proof of the identity of nationalization and planning. This is not the case, however, since the expanded and renovated steel industry is due to political and international decisions arrived at without taking into the slightest account the legal status of the industry. The Italian steel industry would have been the object of far-reaching United States and Italian government plans even had the industry been in private hands. The decisive factors involved were the need to restore steel production and to modernize the country's steel plant, so that by producing cheap steel Italy could impart new vigor to a multitude of secondary and tertiary industries which needed low-cost crude steel. Against these major economic and political considerations, the question of public or private ownership becomes almost insignificant.

THE SOVIET UNION AND THE WEST

If the complexities, the vagaries, and the inventiveness of Western economic policies are borne in mind, the remoteness and irrelevance of the Soviet experiment as far as nationalization and planning in Western European countries are concerned should not be too difficult to establish. Ever since World War I all the major industrial nations have had to face the economic issues confronting them with local means and by drawing upon domestic traditions. There is little support for the assumption that in these matters Soviet planning has been a dominant factor in Western thought and that the method of physical transfer of industries from private to public ownership has been influenced by the Soviet example.

Rather has it been apparent for some time that the influence of Soviet planning on Western thought has been negligible. This is due primarily to the essential differences in concept and method of planning and intervention when applied to an agrarian and industrially underdeveloped country, such as Russia, and when applied to countries which, since the eighteenth century, have undergone intensive economic development and have attained a state of advanced industrial maturity. It is hardly necessary to point out today that the problems the Soviet planners have attempted to solve, regardless of economic or human costs, have been those of the most complete industrialization of their country in the shortest possible period of time. The key elements of Soviet planning have from the beginning been: (1) the establishment of a firm scale of priorities as to the types of plants to be built and goods to be produced and the provision of the means necessary for its fulfillment; (2) decisions concerning the geographical location of the industries to be created; and (3) solution of the difficulties caused by the population transfers which had to follow.

In the second place, the Soviet experiment, applied as it was to an economic framework vastly different from the Western one, was totalitarian in its political implications as well. Not only did it move toward rigid ultimate goals of economic output, it also moved within the rigid boundaries of the Marxist-Stalinist ideology, founded upon the rule of the Communist élite enjoying the absolute right to guide the mass of people under its control and to dispose of their lives and hopes.

These two fundamental features of Soviet planning, the decision to build from almost nothing one of the strongest industrial societies in the world and the total lack of freedom, were of course understood in the West. When Carr wrote in 1947, "Certainly, if 'we are all planners now,' this is largely the result, conscious or unconscious, of the impact of Soviet practice and Soviet achievement," [4] he was claiming for the Soviet Union an influence greater than he himself could subsequently demonstrate. The verbal similarities between the Soviet Five-Year Plans and the so-called Three- or Five- or Seven-Year Plans announced or carried out elsewhere are too inconsequential to be taken seriously into account. In all instances, non-Russian plans have dealt with problems different from those faced by the Soviet planners. In democratic countries, such as France, the task faced by the Monnet Plan was that of tying together schemes of reconstruction and development, to be carried out in various combinations of private and public endeavors, in order to give a great unified purpose and impetus to investments that otherwise would have stretched out over a somewhat longer period of time. Directly affected were a selected few key areas that could in turn influence other industries left out of the plan.

In the totalitarian interludes of Germany and Italy, the plans, when there were any, were the consequence of political dictatorship, war planning, and nationalistic suicidal tendencies, all superimposed upon fully or fairly developed industrial systems. The parallels with Soviet Russia which exist here derive from common political premises and are not the result of Soviet economic influence.

The plans for the development, mostly through state-owned plants, of the heavy industries of countries such as Brazil and India are of course related to the worldwide drive for intensive industrialization—a drive which has been a general phenomenon of the twentieth century, not one brought into being by the Soviet revolution.

The only direct Soviet influence in economic planning has been

[4] Edward H. Carr, *The Soviet Impact on the Western World* (New York, 1947), p. 20.

seen since 1945 in those countries of Eastern Europe which have fallen under the direct political control of the Soviet Union. And even there the techniques and the goals differ from those of the Soviet pattern. Only China, with its immense population, a predominantly agrarian economy, and an almost total lack of industrialization, could become an important area for the testing of Soviet planning policies. But there is no certainty that it will, owing to the extent to which Chinese Communist leaders appear determined to take into account the requirements and peculiarities of China itself.

If Soviet planning is so much the result of the unique economic characteristics of Russia and of the unique totalitarian features of the regime which governs that country, it is hardly surprising that none of its features is relevant to the experience and the needs of Western society. Not even in the enforced savings and the "discipline" of production of the Soviet state, which some economists have seen as susceptible of fruitful application elsewhere, can one see ideas applicable in the West, for they are both based on the premise of repression of individual choice and freedom. The political essence of Soviet planning dominates the issues. The acceptance of Soviet planning must be based upon a prior political decision—and one that would sanction the triumph of Communist totalitarianism over Western democratic and constitutional systems.

To say this means of course to restate the concept of the primacy of political life over economic life, of political decision over economic policy. The accumulated historical evidence of the last generation supports the validity of the concept and affords some consolation to those who, in the gloom of successive depressions, revolutions, and wars, have resisted the conclusion of the inevitability of tyranny because of the adoption of certain collective economic policies. The political climate of each country has everywhere proved to be the decisive factor.

Thus the seizure of political power by the Bolsheviks led to totalitarian economic and agricultural planning, and not vice versa. The same is true of Germany and Italy, where near—or half

—totalitarian economic policies were imposed only after the establishment of political dictatorship. There is nothing to show that the birth of the complex political, psychological, irrational, nationalistic phenomena of fascism and national socialism was due to previously inaugurated policies of public economic controls. A much better case can be made for the thesis that the political failure of the German and Italian ruling classes led to the failure of their economic policies and thus paved the way to dictatorship. In France it was the moral and political climate of the immediate postwar period that led to nationalization and planning.

In Great Britain statesmen and not economists have been in control of the problem of government ownership of industry, first in fixing the boundary line between private and public, second in choosing the instrumentalities of public management, last in deciding upon the shifting of the boundary line once more to the advantage of the private sector. Throughout, the primary decisions have been political. The influence of Soviet planning, the ideological schematisms of nationalizers, the doctrine of workers' control, the alleged inevitability of a steady progression toward a larger and larger area of public ownership, the "one-way" character of nationalization, in brief, the entire ideological baggage of those who either out of fear or out of faith were convinced of the superiority of economics over politics and of the inevitability of the surrender of the latter to the former has proved unreal in a society such as the British, one which has known how to keep itself politically free.

Whatever may be the inevitabilities of history, they cannot be proved in economic terms. It is true that the economic patterns of the nineteenth century are changing. But the transformation is taking place in a number of different directions according to the general political and social orientation prevailing in each country. To say that capitalism is dying is as unhelpful as to say that the trend toward universal acceptance of Soviet planning cannot be stopped. What matters is the defense and vitality of constitutional and democratic systems which can control the instruments of public economic policy.

To deny the influence of Soviet planning on the broad economic movements of Western society and on the strivings for a fuller development of non-European countries does not, of course, imply that the massive increase in Soviet economic strength is casting no shadows across the world today and is not prompting nearly every nation to a reconsideration of its future outlook and plans. No great shift in power can take place anywhere without causing deep repercussions and the birth here and there, in weaker communities, of imitative policies. But to say that in 1955 the Soviet Union has become a major factor in the economic thinking of all those responsible for public and private economic policy is vastly different from saying that Keynes's doctrines could be accepted partly because the minds of his contemporaries had been prepared by a contemplation of the planned economy of the Soviet Union.[5] In 1936, when *The General Theory of Employment, Interest and Money* was published, there was little to contemplate, except the ruthless political excesses of Stalinism. It would be more in keeping with the real autonomy of Western history to point out that the ground had been prepared by List and Barone, by Lloyd George and Rathenau, by World War I and the great depression. Whatever trends the future may show, the past is our very own.

[5] Cf. Carr, *op. cit.,* p. 34.

II

French and Italian
Nationalization Policies

THE INDUSTRIAL SCENE IN FRANCE AND ITALY

It has been the purpose of the French-Italian Inquiry to analyze those areas of the political and economic life of the two countries which by virtue of certain common issues or similar traditions lend themselves to a more integrated analysis than has been usual in the past. Indeed, until recently there was a greater readiness to emphasize the contrasts, than the similarities, between France and Italy. The longer history of French democracy and parliamentary institutions, the deeper crisis revealed by Italian fascism, the obvious difference in economic strength and international power, appeared—and at times were—plausible reasons for a sharp differentiation between the two countries.

But after the end of World War II, certain underlying long-range realities began to assert themselves and to create conditions leading to related, if not identical, developments. France and Italy emerged at the end of the war bearing common scars due to fascism and Nazi occupation, though French fascism lasted a much shorter time than did Italian fascism and Nazi occupation was the result of different circumstances. But the parallels were greater than the contrasts. Both Pétain and Mussolini had become the visible symbols of a common crisis of parliamentary and democratic institutions and left equally bitter national cleavages. The occupation and the Resistance which followed it were, in 1944

and 1945, to produce reactions and to give rise to political conflicts and movements which in both countries colored and affected
the course of events for the next decade, setting off a series of repercussions which has yet to come to an end.

Since 1945 the maintenance of a democratic political society,
the difficulties of stable government amid the confusion of a multi-
party system, the divisions caused by the best-organized, strongest,
most aggressive Communist parties within Western society, and
the goal of giving substance to newly written constitutions have
raised the same issues in the two countries. The readjustment to
sharply reduced circumstances, the striving for a better realization
of economic justice, and the enforcement of certain principles of
taxation have been the source of similar frictions and difficulties
in both states.

The previous studies on the major political currents of communism and Christian Democracy were inspired by these considerations, which apply equally to a study of common economic
problems, among which nationalization policies are central.

In looking at twentieth-century French and Italian industrial
systems, the political scientist is attracted less by their obvious difference in size than by some of the common characteristics and implied economic doctrines of those systems. In a study of modern
industrial societies, the question of size is only one, and not the
most interesting, of the issues that confront the researcher. More
significant appear to be questions of distribution of ownership between private and public sectors, of monopoly, of rapidity of
technological change, of attitudes to domestic and foreign markets, of reliance on family traditions, of relationships among
managers and owners and workers, as well as between owners and
the state. In many of these areas France and Italy offer striking
parallels.

Particularly since the end of World War I have French and
Italian businessmen seemed more anxious to keep and protect
what they have built than to continue to expand and renovate
and run the risk of continuing change. They did not look anxious
to act on the basis of that fundamental law of capitalistic develop-

ment which is constant revolutionary transformation. Thus there developed a common tendency to foster protected and limited markets and to rely on governmental power and support to keep the industrial system going. The growth of strong managerial groups capable of handling the difficulties of modern industry in a modern way was hampered by continuing traditional family controls as well as by the existence of strong pressures applied from below as the working class developed some of the habits of the owners themselves, such as reliance on public power or on political parties to give them a more sheltered position. As a result, in the quarter of a century from 1925 to 1950, France had failed, unlike other major industrial countries, to raise the volume of its output, while Italy, owing to Fascist policies, had deflected a great many energies into unproductive and costly enterprises.

The frustrations of the owning and managerial classes had engendered a mood of recrimination and a negative attitude that made them reluctant to accept the far-reaching transformations that alone would have meant progress. At the same time those classes maintained an ill-concealed feeling of hostility toward the working class, made stronger and easier to justify by the equally strong class hatreds nourished by a majority of the Communist-organized workers.

The paternalistic attitude of industry toward the workers led also to a proprietary attitude toward the state, which was seen by many of the more important representatives of industry as nothing but an instrument for the defense of their interests. These most vociferous of all the critics of the Marxian theory of the state and of society were themselves perfect proof of the validity of Marxian contentions whenever their policies were successful. For what was the state in their hands if not the executive committee of the capitalistic class? There could be no doubt that the authentic anti-Marxist position was defended by those who wanted to resist the pressures of industrial groups and permit the state to function freely as the agent of the community.

Nationalization was, at bottom, an attempt to express the uneasiness of the public, made increasingly resentful of certain attitudes and policies toward the public good and welfare. This was clearly the case in France in 1945, when to the old issues were added those created by the revolutionary atmosphere of war and Liberation. In Italy the breakdown of the system in the great depression was the immediate cause of nationalization, but even there the postwar climate was similar to that of France.

To maintain the necessary clarity in presenting the fundamental outlines of nationalization of industry in France and Italy, it will be necessary to proceed separately to an analysis and appraisal of the contrasts and parallels of those policies. To have stressed so far the similarities of the developments in the two countries does not mean, of course, that all the concrete public issues emerging from them are the same. Both in the beginning and in the unfolding of events there are important divergences that need stressing.

CONTRASTS

1. Nationalization began under different circumstances: in Italy, amid the secrecy imposed by the Fascist dictatorship trying to avoid public scandal; in France, in the rush of the glittering hopes created by victory and liberation.

Italian nationalization occurred in 1933 in the form of emergency action taken by the Fascist government to deal with the crisis of the financial and industrial system of Italy. If the lack of public discussion was a typical feature of totalitarianism, the policy itself had some precedents in similar, if less important, pre-Fascist government decisions. The evil habit of calling upon the government to rescue private enterprise from threatened bankruptcy was compounded by the evil of the absence of any public awareness with respect to an undertaking whose scope exceeded anything that had occurred in the past.

The Fascist government decision of 1933 to take over, through the IRI, what in the end was found (perhaps to everybody's surprise) to amount roughly to one-fourth of the total financial and industrial assets of the country, was essentially a negative one. After ten years of Fascist rule, which had maintained itself in power to the accompaniment of an unceasing propaganda concerning the virtues, political and economic, of the new regime, it was painful to admit that the Italian banking system was suffering from the "freezing" of some of its more important assets and that most of Italy's heavy industry and a great many of its secondary industries were in as great trouble as the industries of the much-criticized and supposedly inferior capitalistic countries. Not only was the sheltered economy of Fascist Italy in a crisis as deep as that of the unprotected American economy, but, had that fact become widely known, the Fascists would have been forced to admit that they had no policies which could attempt the type of recovery that was then the major goal of Roosevelt's New Deal.

The "planned" corporative state had no plan. Its policy became that of taking over direct responsibility for the bankrupt section of Italy's economy and then, having avoided open collapse, hoping for the beneficent consequences that a world-wide recovery from the depth of the depression would ultimately have on Italy.

Nor should one forget that the years from 1933 to 1936 saw the growth of a quite remarkable divergence between theory and practice. That such conflicts should develop in a democratic and pluralistic state, where the formulation of the theories (if any) and the realization of the practice are the task of many and separate groups and institutions, is to be expected. But they are worthy of special notice when they appear within the monopolistic structure of the totalitarian states, claiming to bring together ideology and power.

Those were the years when the Fascist critics of capitalism were decrying the ineffectiveness and shortcomings of a corporative system which, to control the flow of economic life, relied on the bringing together of capital and labor under the protective aegis of the state. According to them, the stage was now set for an actual transfer of the instruments of production to the state, for this was to be the direction of the inevitable transformation of the economy in the twentieth century and fascism was to lead the way. As the theoretical discussion progressed and widened, supposedly lending to the drab police state the excitement of ideas freshly discovered on the speculative frontier, it became increasingly evident (alas! only to the very few who had any inkling of the matter) that the theoreticians were unaware of two developments:

The first was, of course, that the much-discussed transfer had actually already taken place in some key sectors of the economy, thanks to IRI's rescue operations. The levers of command already were in the hands of the state. The distant goals of which the philosophers of fascism were still dreaming were already a reality. It was regrettable that the dictator should have forgotten to provide proper notification of the event.

The second was that, ever since practical developments had caught up—perhaps unexpectedly—with theory, the machine of the dictatorship, in complete disregard of the wishes of its thinkers, had ordered that as soon as possible as many as possible of IRI's units should be sold back to private business. Having reached the Fascist paradise, the dictatorship was silently getting ready to descend once more into the capitalistic purgatory as quickly as it could.

That it was not altogether successful in its plans was due first to the scarcity of private investors and secondly to the growth of the regime into an aggressive military machine. And it was only because of this that, on the eve of World War II, a certain sense of direction was imparted to the economic enterprises of the Fascist state. IRI became a positive instrument of Fascist policy, aimed at the achievement of certain specific military goals. Nationalization, which had initially been a by-product of the dictator's fear of public opinion, became later an instrument of imperialistic aggression.

How different the atmosphere and the circumstances under which nationalization took place in France, immediately after the end of World War II! In the imagination of politicians and statesmen, scholars and propagandists, nationalization became the touchstone of the new morality and the new democracy, the chief test of the redemption of French political life from the sins of the past. Nationalization was to break monopoly, to punish the trai-

tors and collaborators, to achieve industrial democracy, to produce abundance and prosperity for all. Nationalization was the
magic formula which would make France strong and free. It was
a policy framed and nurtured in the long night of the Resistance
by those bravest of men who were fighting against the Nazi oppres-
sor and the strongholds of capitalistic iniquity at home. It was a
policy which could not properly be resisted by anyone since its
beneficence was claimed to be self-evident. Criticism was indeed
small. Few could be found in the Constituent Assembly to vote
against nationalization, which had become the new common de-
nominator of postwar France.

This explains why nationalization was put through with such
tremendous speed. Twelve years earlier, in secret, fascism too had
moved with great speed. With the open publicity of a democratic
Assembly elected by the people, the French moved with equal
speed. France was not going to be hampered by painful and pro-
longed attention to detail, procedures, and administrative problems as British socialists were to be for the next six years. The
future would take care of itself, and the essential question was not
to delay by one day the advent of the new era.

2. A second contrast is to be found in the scope of nationalization policies. In both countries major commercial banks are
nationalized. In both countries communications, radio, and television are a public monopoly. Major airlines and shipping lines
are equally government property. Coal is nationalized in France,
and the same is true of whatever coal industry there is in Italy.
The aviation and automobile factories that have been nationalized in France find a rough counterpart in the engineering and
shipbuilding plants that have become government property in
Italy.

But here the parallels end. Since in France nationalization was
a planned operation intended to achieve certain results, public
utilities were nationalized as they ususally are whenever a democratic country embarks upon a policy of this type. Public utilities
are monopolies controlling the use of natural resources and occupy position number one in the nationalizers' programs. Since

fascism had no plans in 1933, only those public utilities which happened to be within the scope of the salvage operation (because they were bank-owned) became public property, and this was less than one-quarter of the total.

The reverse happened in the case of iron and steel. This is an industry which is also at the core of all theoretical discussions of nationalizaton, for iron and steel is the heart of any industrial system; and, if the purpose of a program of nationalization is to transfer the center of economic power from private to public hands, then iron and steel should be nationalized. This was, to be sure, the intention of France in 1945. But the initial rush did not have the strength it needed to carry this formidable stronghold of private rights. As the tide receded in 1946 and in 1947 with the realization of some of the consequences of the nationalization program (chiefly in terms of the advantages it offered to the Communist party), iron and steel could never again be brought within the scope of the nationalizers' influence. These difficulties are not surprising, because even in Great Britain iron and steel was the last of the industries to be nationalized by the Labour government and since 1952 it has provided the decisive test of the possibility of denationalization.

On the other hand, the bulk of the Italian iron and steel industry was among the assets taken over by IRI in 1933. It remains today the only iron and steel industry in the Western world to be largely government owned.

3. A third set of contrasts flows from the manner in which these financial and industrial assets were handled, once they were nationalized.

In Italy, the policy which has been maintained without a break for the past twenty years has been that of retaining for nationalized enterprises as many of the characteristics and appearances of private business and of conferring on them as few of the features of public corporations, as possible. This has been called the "privatistic" approach.

Initially nationalization simply meant the taking over of the industrial securities portfolios of the three largest Italian banks.

(With these portfolios came also a majority of the stock of the three banks themselves.) These blocks of shares were handed over to IRI, conceived as a government investment trust. Certain consequences followed from this broad legal picture.

a) Only seldom did IRI secure all the stock of a given company. And as no efforts were made to secure full control where this was lacking, surviving private stockholders were not disturbed. Many of the stocks continued to be listed and traded on the stock exchanges. Thus, in effect, mixed corporations came into existence, with the government the controlling stockholder.

b) The old managers were not liquidated. Of course over a period of more than twenty years many changes have now occurred. These have been gradual, however, and the decision to retain the services of former managers has never been abandoned. The critics of the system point out that this has retarded the formation of a group of public-spirited managers capable of administering public assets with an eye to the public welfare.

c) The names of the old corporate entities were kept in every instance, so that the industrial landscape of the country was not in any way altered on the surface. In France this policy was adopted only for the banks, and in Great Britain only for iron and steel. In Italy it was the generalized approach, meant to stress the "private" character of nationalization.

d) These decisions were favored by the shaken business community, which needed, it is true, the helping hand of the government to lift it out of its current difficulties but which nevertheless hoped that when better times came around it could recover control of the more profitable pieces of the fallen empire. The hoped-for process of future denationalization would be made simpler if the government introduced as few legal and managerial changes as possible.

In France, these preoccupations and premises were generally absent. Nationalization had come to stay. The public character of nationalized enterprises was to be made clear wherever desirable, and some variety could be introduced in their administration. Banks and insurance companies were allowed to maintain their previous corporate identities. Customer relations, international transactions, competition with banks and insurance companies still in private hands, would be better if the traditional setup was retained. On the other hand, in the areas in which nationalization brought about a total transfer of industrial activities to the state, such as in coal, gas, and electricity, a basic rearrangement of the old corporate structures took place which eliminated old firms' names and brought everybody under the protective and generic bureaucratic wings of the coal, gas, and electricity boards. Finally, in the case of the Renault motor works, an experiment was tried which remains without parallel outside France. This was a profit-sharing arrangement whereby the workers were to divide evenly with the government the profits made by the plant. Some question has been raised as to whether in the calculations of "profits" the management of Renault has not shown an excess of optimism calculated to increase the total amount available for sharing with the workers beyond what would have been considered prudent and legitimate under private or traditional governmental operation. Profits can become an elastic concept once organized workers' pressure is applied,[1] and the Renault plants are not only one of the important concentrations of French industry but are also one of the main seats of Communist power.

PARALLELS

In spite of these differences, a major area of parallel development exists in the extent to which nationalized industries continued to be subject to undue political influences. With the vagaries and uncertainties of French and Italian political life, this has meant in practice an increase of bureaucratic power, the only power capable of asserting itself with continuity. While one of Great Britain's important problems of recent years has been to prevent the growth of too autonomous centers of economic power

[1] The nebulous character of the "profits" that are distributed may perhaps be deduced from the fact that the 1951 government share had to be retained by the Renault management to meet urgent operational needs.

(and this in spite of the fact that in all post-World War II nation-alization acts the influence of Cabinet ministers over the long-range policies of public corporations has been increased), the issue in Italy and in France is to relieve public enterprises from the excesses both of political pressures and of bureaucratic con-trols.

In post-Fascist Italy, IRI has properly come under the over-all control of the Cabinet. But the president of IRI has not been al-lowed to acquire the power he should have to face the conflicting tendencies of coalition Cabinets and the divergent trends of the various wings of the ruling Christian Democratic party. A ma-jority of the members of the board of directors are merely repre-sentatives of various government departments, appointed by the heads of those departments and removable at will by them. Thus the board stands exposed to the twin influences of politicians and of bureaucracy, the latter asserting itself to an increasing degree as the former becomes more confused.

In France there has been a shift from the extreme of allegedly autonomous national enterprises managed by boards of directors representing the more important interested parties (the workers, the consumers, and the state) to the other extreme of the full as-sumption of power by the central government.

The original position was an untenable one. Interest representa-tion is not a concept that can usefully be applied to the manage-ment of public national assets. By definition, the representatives of given interests, specifically appointed to represent those inter-ests, cannot act other than as defenders of the partial and narrow point of view they represent.

But the retreat from that exposed position has been so com-plete as to raise the question as to whether it has not created issues just as serious. The initial stage of the retreat from the interest representation position can be seen in the wonderfully intricate and twisted formula of the decree of June 12, 1947, which reads, "Each member of the board must be independent of the interests he is not representing." The need for this startling provision was of course due to Communist appropriation and perversion of the interest representation doctrine embodied in the French legislation of 1945 and 1946. Until the spring of 1947 Communist Cabinet members, having the power of appointment of representatives of the state to the boards of nationalized enterprises, had proceeded on the theory that to be a representative of the state all that was needed was to be described as one. Thus the defense of the interests of the community could be properly entrusted to a Communist party organizer lacking any visible qualification provided he carried a label which identified him as "state representative." Hence the Communist conquest of the nationalized industries.

Hence, too, the revolt of 1947 and the strange proclamation of the independence of interest representatives from the interests they did not represent. But in saying that a Communist trade unionist could not, by definition, represent the state, the decree of June 12 was also implying that among the groups representing the contrasting interests of state, consumers, and workers a great gulf is fixed—that hostility and conflict are the normal conditions of life of interest boards.

Once these admissions were made or implied, the retreat was bound to go farther. The terminal point of this transformation can best be seen in the decrees of 1953, discussed in their proper sequence by Professor Byé but of such importance as to warrant mention at this point.[2]

Their significance can best be seen by looking at the changes they bring about in the composition of the boards of directors of coal, gas, and electricity. Under the original legislation of 1946 all three boards were composed of eighteen members, of which

[2] Cf. Byé, below, pp. 103–105 and 113–118.
The decrees in question are those issued during the months of May and August in 1953 by the governments of René Mayer and Joseph Laniel. They refer chiefly to the organization of the boards of directors of nationalized enterprises, to the appointment of their presidents, to the powers of the government with respect to the policies and decisions of nationalized enterprises, and finally to procedures of control to be exercised by the government. They bear Nos. 53412, 53413, 53415, 53416–53420, all of May 11, 1953, published in *Journal Officiel, Lois et Décrets*, May 12, 1953, pp. 4329–4334, and Nos. 53707 and 53708, both of August 9, 1953, *ibid.*, August 10, 1953, pp. 7051–7052.

six represented the government, six the consumers and the local communities, and six the workers. Boards selected their own presidents. This arrangement placed the state representatives in the minority. By the decrees of 1953, taken on the authority of the delegation of powers to the Cabinet included in the law of August 17, 1948, the representatives of the state are placed in the majority. The boards of directors are reduced from eighteen to twelve members, four representing the state, four appointed by the Cabinet on the basis of their technical competence in industrial and financial matters, and four representing the workers. The president of the board of directors is appointed by the Cabinet from among the members of the board and after consultation with it Even though two of the four technical members are to represent the consumers, the government can count on a minimum of six members out of twelve. The law provides that in case of a tie the vote of the president shall be decisive. Since the president is most likely to be chosen from among the four representatives of the state, the state has a guaranteed majority even under the most adverse circumstances.

In the justification which accompanies these revolutionary decrees, the government carefully avoids saying that their chief purpose is to give to the state the decisive voice in the management of most nationalized enterprises. The reason given for what is mildly called an "amendment" to the legislation of 1946 but is in reality a basic alteration in the balance of power, is that a board made up of twelve members is a more manageable and effective tool of administration than a board made up of eighteen members. It is further pointed out that the representation of the workers is maintained in the same proportions fixed by the original laws, that is, one-third of the total. There is no open admission of the fact that, because of the new expert members and of the Cabinet-appointed president, the post-1953 boards bear no resemblance to the 1946 ones.

Nor is this all. The decree of May 11 establishing the limits of current Cabinet controls over the management of nationalized enterprises (coal, gas, and electricity) provides also that a government commissioner is to be appointed to be present at the meetings of the board of directors and of the technical and consultative committees. The government commissioner communicates to the board of directors the views of the government on the matters before the board, and he also informs the appropriate Cabinet members of the deliberations of the board. The commissioner has the power, within three weeks, to ask that any decision that appears to be contrary to the general interest be suspended. The decision of the board becomes effective unless within eight days the Minister of Industry requires its modification.

The decrees of 1953 provide also for a system of control of the operations of nationalized enterprises which to some extent replaces that exercised for a period of about three years by the Committee for the Verification of Accounts of public enterprises. Control commissions have been appointed whose heads must devote their full time to the task of verifying and controlling the activities of public enterprises. The powers of the commissions are not limited to the verification of the accounts and of operating results. They have the added power of intervening in current decisions and operations of public enterprises and to suspend those decisions which are described as having a notable financial significance. Whenever this happens, the competent minister must render a decision within twenty days.

Many of these provisions follow the general outlines of a bill introduced as early as December 31, 1948, by the government but never brought out of committee to the floor of the Assembly. Despairing of legislative action, the Mayer and Laniel governments decided to use their decree powers to achieve the objectives of the 1948 bill. The original dreams of "socialization" and "autonomy" have yielded to the most complete bureaucratization of nationalized enterprises. Circumscribed on all sides by a multiple tier of control agencies, French nationalized enterprises have become the victims both of bureaucracy and of politics to an extent that even the excesses caused by the extravagant legislation of 1946 do not seem to justify.

III

French and Italian vs. British
and American Experience

POLITICS AND ECONOMICS

GREAT BRITAIN carried out its nationalization program after a general election had turned power over to a political party which had made that program the foundation of its postwar platform. Eight nationalization acts were seen through Parliament over a period of five years from March 1946 (the nationalization of the Bank of England) to February 1951 (the nationalization of iron and steel). The whole process was a good example of British method, proceeding from certain broad political premises, through careful legislative debate and work, to the attainment of certain specific goals of public policy. The British government had a program sanctioned by public opinion and carried it out in proper constitutional manner. It was a political program which gained added strength from the economic realities of the industries that were being nationalized.

On balance, British socialism managed to compromise the vaguer motivations of nationalization policy such as social welfare and workers' democracy with the demands of industrial output. For a party which was still a working-class party, even though it had been put in office by the newly won votes of the middle classes, this was an effort of no mean proportions. How easy it would have been for it, having gained political control of the nation after a wait of half a century, to move forward on the broad popular fronts of increased wages and benefits, of more power to workers, of realization, in brief, of all the aspirations of democratic socialism. Instead, in the government's appraisal of what the nationalized industries needed, the hard economic facts of productivity, investment, and the survival of Great Britain as a major industrial nation, even its defense needs, were the primary factors taken into account. British nationalization remains to this day a unique example of orderly, deliberate, and reasoned expansion of governmental power. That this was in keeping with British traditions in other fields does not detract from the importance of the achievement, for the field was new and treacherous and the temptations many.

The two Continental countries which are the object of the present study moved along different paths.

Although French socialism even before World War II had spoken out, in somewhat confused fashion, in defense of the right of the working class to take over capitalistic monopolies in key industries, it had no chance then of realizing its program through the normal processes of coalition governments. The majority against large-scale nationalizations (apart from such special issues as the taking over of railroads and aircraft factories) was a decisive one. Under normal prewar conditions, nationalization was far too big an ideological issue to be solved in the prevailing atmosphere of uncertain compromises and of inaction, bred by the weakness of both executive and legislative powers.

Thus nationalization in France is linked to World War II in a way in which British nationalization is not. It is true that Labour came to power in 1945 and that the war played a definite role in that event. But the social transformation of Great Britain, the disappearance of the Liberal party, the shift of key middle-class groups to Labour, were phenomena that had developed over a long period of time. The war added the final push to a transformation that was under way and that would have occurred even without the war. In France, it was the war, and the war alone, with its dual experience of Vichy and Nazi occupation, which brought about in the days of the Resistance and of the liberation an extraordinary measure of national agreement on certain fundamental economic policies.

The policies that developed as a consequence of these exceptional circumstances were characterized by both strength and weakness. They had the strength of an ideal of political renovation of sufficient intensity to bring together socialists, Communists, Christian Democrats, de Gaullists, and Radical Socialists on legislation which did extreme violence to the traditions of private property and individual rights of the French Republic. No decisive economic argument, as in Great Britain, could be adduced for the nationalization of French coal mines. Mines had been consolidated and modernized; productivity was high and manpower adequate. But the problem was a political one, that of punishing an industrial class which had collaborated with the enemy and of removing from private controls groups which in the past had moved against the free operation of parliamentary government.

How different in conception were these policies from the British ones, which looked in a realistic and almost pedantic way to the technical problems of how to run a complex economic structure efficiently. To the Frenchmen who had suffered through the war, the image that had presented itself was that of an ideal economic republic, independent and free from the shackles of bureaucratic controls. Nationalization was to mean the birth of working-class democracy, of autonomous structures within the French community directly responsive to the interests and rights of the social groups concerned. The French idea represented a vision of a political nature, to be carried out all at once without waiting for the forces of evil to reassert themselves. It was as if the planners were themselves afraid, and anxious, therefore, to proceed as fast as possible.

There was a program, but its scope, while clear in the minds of those who during the Resistance were constructing the future institutions of a modern France, could never be fully realized. This was due to the political and emotional overtones of the program and to the uncertainties of that approach. The most conspicuous shortfall was the failure to nationalize iron and steel, one of the oldest of industries, one in which a high degree of obsolescence was present, one in which concentration and quasi-monopolistic conditions tend to prevail, and one in which heavy investments were necessary—an industry, finally, in which abuse of private power could certainly be feared. But because of the complexity of the problem nationalization was delayed long enough for the political fervor, which was a vital ingredient of French policy, to die out. In the cold light of post-1946 politics iron and steel could no longer be nationalized.

On the other hand, the near-revolutionary climate of those years was sufficient to bring about the nationalization of most of the physical facilities of the French press, an area which, except in totalitarian countries, has been carefully excluded from the scope of nationalization programs. What happened here, despite the pious assertions of the need to punish newspapers for collaboration with the enemy (assertions that were not accompanied by any effort to discriminate between those which had and those which had not collaborated), was an attempt by the mass parties, both old and new, which then dominated the French political scene—the Communist, socialist, and MRP parties—to gain control of the physical means needed to print their party newspapers on the scale and in the quantity which their increased influence and following seemed to require. In devious and complicated ways the consequences of the nationalization of the press are now being gradually undone. As the influence of the mass parties declines, some of the injustices of the press nationalization law of April 16, 1946, are being corrected, both by legislative measures and by the pressure of the public, which, by refusing to buy extreme partisan newspapers, is hastening their liquidation. But even if we may now be allowed to describe the 1946 press law as an episode, its crucial significance in the evaluation of the climate which produced nationalization in France will remain.

The dominant influence of politics on French nationalization is further proved by the extraordinary speed with which nationalization acts went through the legislative process. Against the five years needed by Great Britain, four months were enough in

France. Paradoxically, a country that habitually uses the legislative process with great deliberation and gives a full chance to anyone interested in using delaying tactics surprised the world with a show of legislative efficiency and speed which has not been repeated since. If no time was wasted, no time was allowed for proper formulation of the legislative thoughts that were being enacted into law. It should be remembered that nationalization became a chief activity of the first Constituent Assembly, whose primary duty was that of writing the new constitution. As it happened, the constitution which it drafted was rejected by the people, so that the nationalization acts remain as the only lasting monument to the work of an Assembly which otherwise failed to win approval for its work.

In conclusion, British nationalization, which was of course the result of a fundamental political decision, was carried out with constant regard for the economic necessities of the program, while French nationalization remained from beginning to end largely the expression of political anxiety and conflict.

In the case of Italy, as has been pointed out before, nationalization initially took place in response to the decision, unclear and unspoken, of the Fascist dictatorship to do what was necessary to avoid economic chaos. The government's permanent, or long-range, policies in matters of industrial ownership were never publicly clarified or defined.

This initial vice has continued into post-Fascist Italy. Steps are taken in response to localized and concealed pressures. The boundaries of nationalization may be casually expanded because of a forceful administrator who is successful in increasing his sphere of operation and has sufficient political strength to carry the government with him. While IRI is still the biggest agency in the field of nationalized industries, new agencies are being formed outside IRI, thus creating rival centers of government economic power.

An example of this is afforded by the rapid growth since 1953 of ENI (Ente Nazionale Idrocarburi), the public corporation that has become the holding company for most of the government interests in the fields of natural gas, oil production and refining, and pipeline transportation. There has been no clear government or parliamentary decision to set up another vast area of governmental operations outside IRI, nor has there been any over-all decision as to the proper role of public ownership in the field of such natural resources as oil and gas, which have suddenly acquired great importance following the discovery of natural gas in the Po Valley and of oil in Sicily. These are matters still under sustained discussion, linked as they are to problems of foreign investment and of the role of major foreign oil companies. In the meantime, ENI is expanding, assuming monopolistic characteristics and adding a political role to its economic functions as it reflects the views of particular political machines within the Christian Democratic party. It may very well be that ENI represents an admirable solution to the question of the exploitation by Italy of its oil and gas resources. But this is not the point at issue. The question is whether ENI should be allowed to entrench itself as a government monopoly, when no fundamental, and fully debated, political decision on the matter has been reached by constitutional means.

In December 1954 a first report, covering the year 1953–1954, was made public by ENI through an unusual resort to full-page advertisements in a number of newspapers. The statistics offered by the report confirmed the importance of ENI as the producer of 90 percent of Italy's natural gas and as a seller of 25 percent of all oil products sold in the country. (Italy is not yet a significant producer of crude oil.) Exploration was being carried out throughout Italy, including Sicily, and seventy-three successful wells were drilled during the year.

The report contains a curious mixture of defensive and aggressive or boastful language. ENI rejects the charge that it has a "private enterprise" outlook and states that its drive for efficiency and profits has been carried out within the framework provided by publicly stated national economic goals. Whether these rather mythical goals also sanction the vast expansion which ENI's report announces in petrochemicals, nitrogen, synthetic rubber, and many other areas of the chemical industry, which is glitteringly and breathlessly described as the "apex of achievement of any country which is undergoing industrial development," is left unsaid. The assumption is simply made that this extension of the boundary line of the nationalized sector is logical and inevitable and does not have to wait upon any discussion and decision by the constitutional organs of the state.

There is no way of evaluating the reality of the "profits" claimed in the report. ENI is a holding company whose main function is to finance, through advances and stock purchases, the exploration, production, refining, distribution, and industrial activities of its subsidiaries and to receive in return from them interest on the advances and dividends on the stocks. It is impossible to say whether the 7.5 percent rate of interest charged by ENI is justified (ENI is paying no interest to the state on the endowment fund out of which loans are made), or whether "dividends" are paid by affiliates after the amortizations and reserves which are proper for young, rapidly expanding, and speculative enterprises.

The even more general question should be raised of what "profits" are proper in a nationalized enterprise, in the light of the optimum rates of expansion of production and of increase in consumption that presumably have been set. More likely, however, no long-range policies exist, and no such delicate issues of rate making or allowed profits have been raised as have concerned the Tennessee Valley Authority, the Federal Power Commission, or other United States federal or state regulatory agencies.

The net resulting impression is that ENI is a powerful and expanding industrial empire, managed by able and ambitious people, anxious to assert total power over large economic areas, and only appearing to act under the guidance of publicly established policy. The links that tie the ENI management to certain groups within the Christian Democratic party are clear, since the general manager, Enrico Mattei, is a young and vigorous member of the northern party leadership. ENI is an instrument of political power, used as such by the dominant political party and to be judged as such.

If the full story of the last twenty-five years is taken into account, the conclusion is inevitable that nationalization policy in Italy suffers from serious economic and political handicaps. Its economic objectives have remained clouded, while politically it is, and has been, deeply influenced and at times corrupted by partisan considerations which often cannot claim for themselves either the redeeming qualities of the ideals which supported French policies or the constitutional sanction received by British nationalization.

COMPENSATION OR EXPROPRIATION

The question of compensation or expropriation should be linked to the larger questions raised in the preceding sections.

In Great Britain, the premise of full compensation was accompanied by measures which did, in effect, carry it out. The British government and Parliament, having agreed without effort on the principle that nationalization was to be accompanied by full compensation, were further agreed on the effective practical steps to be taken so that the principle could be translated fully into reality. After a fair valuation, government bonds were issued carrying a rate of interest that bore an appropriate relationship to the prevailing conditions of the money market. Thus if a rate of interest of 3 percent was needed to maintain at or near par the bonds exchanged for the stocks of the private companies that were being nationalized, the rate of interest would, in effect, be established at 3 percent, and not at 2 or 1 percent. Since 1945 the bonds of nationalized industries have fluctuated in accordance with the fluctuations of the money market, and at the end of 1954 their average price was close to parity. It should further be noted that the policies of both socialist and conservative governments have tried to maintain an economy free from strong inflationary currents, so that not only the market value but also the purchasing power of the securities issued would remain substantially unchanged from year to year.

In France, no serious thought was ever given to proposals for punitive nationalization without compensation. There was expropriation only in limited instances, chiefly for newspaper enterprises and for the Renault automobile works, in spite of Communist insistence that compensation should be paid in the coal industry only to small and "patriotic" stockholders. The difficulties involved in using the elusive concept of patriotism to decide whether indemnities should or should not be paid were recognized, and the principle of indemnity for all former owners was eventually accepted. This victory proved to be more significant in principle than in practice, for the computation of the indemnities and the methods chosen for paying them reduced the legitimate claims of the owners.

For the shares of the Bank of France, Article 2 of the law of December 2, 1945, provided that the indemnity was to be equal to their liquidating value but not higher than the average market price of the shares between September 1, 1944, and August 31, 1945. This average price was 28,000 francs per share. The normal liquidating value was later found to be about 70,000 francs, but this was reduced to 44,000 francs on the basis of an evaluating procedure of dubious validity. The stockholder, of course, received no more than 28,000 francs. For the four great commercial banks, Article 8 of the same law provided that the indemnity was to be based on the average market value for the period from September 1, 1944, to October 31, 1945, a period during which the nationalization of the banks had become a certainty.

In the case of power and coal a different method was followed. The government decided first what percentage of increase to allow over the average stock market prices of 1938, proceeding next to the selection of a base period that would yield such an increase. The initial decision was to pay the stockholders of the electrical and gas industries by multiplying 1938 values by 3.33 and those of the coal industry by multiplying the same values by 4.2. These proposed payments the finance commission of the Constituent Assembly found too low. Since the finance commission had exactly the same political color as the Constituent Assembly as a whole, as well as of the government, one is forced to conclude that its defense of the interests of the owners was due to the fact that they met in the rooms where once Caillaux ruled. Thanks to the finance commission's efforts, the ratios were increased to 3.98 for electricity and gas and to 4.46 for coal (excluding the mines of Lorraine). For the power and coal companies whose stocks were not quoted on the stock markets, the indemnity was to be on the basis of the liquidation value of the enterprise, which was to be calculated on the same rigid basis as that used for the Bank of France.

Fifty-year amortizable bonds or stock have been used for the payment of indemnities. For the Bank of France the law of December 2, 1945, provided for 2 percent bonds. This was soon found to be too low, and a law of April 8, 1946, raised the rate of interest to 3 percent. For the commercial banks the law provided for the distribution of variable dividend stock, the dividend not to be inferior to that of 1944. The subsequent law of May 17, 1946, provided that the dividend could be no less than 3 percent and that this was to be guaranteed by the state. The same solution was adopted in the case of insurance companies.

A more complicated solution, and one more favorable to former owners, was adopted for power and coal. Here the principle of participation by the bondholders in the possible future growth of the industries was accepted by a provision that in addition to a fixed payment of 3 percent for both power and coal a certain percentage of gross total revenues—not profits—was to be distributed each year to the bondholders. For power, the percentage was to be at least 1 percent of total revenues but could be more; for coal, on the other hand, the percentage was fixed at 0.25 percent.

Thus the French situation, as a result of political pressures and variables, fluctuates between the extremes of partial expropriation due to low valuations and inflation and of provisions which, if fully applied in the case of electricity, might result in interest payments to the former owners higher than is warranted by their present riskless status.

In Italy, nationalization took place before World War II, at the depth of the great depression, and it was carried out with monetary units which bear no resemblance to the present currency, which has in the meantime lost between 98 and 99 percent of its 1933 value. Generally speaking, one can hazard the statement that, since the government paid for those assets in 1933 lire, it acquired them at no present cost to itself, as is always the case whenever a purchase of physical assets is followed by violent inflation. The real problem is whether the assets that were acquired for nothing were worth anything. The answer must be that some of the assets were and still are exceedingly valuable, such as the banks, the utilities, and the telephones, while others, such as the mechanical, engineering, shipping, and iron and steel plants, had little value by the end of the war. Most of the latter assets have a substantial value today (this is true of the new steel plants), but their present value is value that has been added since nationalization as a result of investments made in the last seven or eight years. Thus the Italian problem should be stated in terms, not of compensation or expropriation, but of the important benefits that have accrued to the government, thanks to the inflationary pressures resulting from the war.

MANAGEMENT

To some extent post-1945 nationalization acts in Great Britain show the influence of Labour party views. The powers of the minister have been increased, financial autonomy has been reduced, and certain other changes have been made in keeping with socialist ideas of stronger central controls. But by and large the fundamental concepts that had grown around the public corporation in the twentieth century have remained unaltered. The chosen instrument of British public economic management has continued in its slow evolution without giving up the belief that the autonomy of impartial administrators is of central importance. The powers of the minister to determine the terms of office and the other conditions of tenure of the members of the boards of nationalized industries are valuable in establishing the principle of the ultimate responsibility of nationalized boards to the Cabinet and the House of Commons. But within this broad political frame of reference the freedom and responsibility of the managers who are chosen to do the job have so far been secure.

If the experience of the first decade of nationalization is thus reassuring, there is no certainty that in some of the more politically and economically exposed areas, such as railroad transportation, pressures may not develop that will in the end threaten the principle of the boards' managerial responsibility and independence. The practice of appointing *ad hoc* courts of inquiry when the problem appears to be a politically delicate one may indeed lead to a weakening of the public corporations. This has been true as to the Court of Inquiry appointed in 1954 by the Minister of Labour to deal with a threatened strike of railwaymen. One of the principal conclusions of the Court was that "the Nation has provided by statute that there shall be a nationalized system of railway transport, which must therefore be regarded as a public utility of the first importance. Having willed the end, the Nation must will the means." This concept, if accepted by the Transport Commission and the government, must mean that questions of efficiency and costs should be put aside and that the statutory obligation of covering expenditures by receipts, taking one year with another, is no longer applicable, since the means must be provided to attain nationally willed ends.[1] In the long run this approach could undo many of the policies of the past and start in Great Britain that intrusion of politics upon the management of nationalized industries which has been such a serious source of weakness on the Continent. While politics —in its democratic and constitutional expression—should preside at the start of nationalization, it should later hover in the background and allow to responsible administrators the freedom of action they must have.

In France, the solutions found for the problems of how to manage nationalized industries and of how much freedom to give the managers have changed with the changing political atmosphere and with the changing intensity of certain political pressures. Even now, after nearly ten years, there is no real agreement.

[1] Cf. "Means to What End?" *The Economist,* January 8, 1955.

Certainly the extreme doctrine of representation of interests has been abandoned, if not on paper, then in reality. Representation of interests as interpreted by the Communists meant rule by the Communist trade unions. If representation of interests means the right of groups of consumers, users, and other interested parties to be heard in a consultative capacity, it need not be abandoned at all; but this is a view far removed from the original Resistance idea of workers' democracy and autonomy. The gap between the initial dreams and the point of arrival, which finds power concentrated in the hands of general directors and managers appointed by Cabinet ministers and deprived of any freedom of decision both in matters of long-range operations and of day-to-day activities, measures the distance traveled by France in her restless search for a solution. There is widespread recognition in France that the present system is ill adapted to efficient administration of vast enterprises and that a way out may be found along lines not far removed from those of the British public corporations.

There has been no comparable transition in Italy from party-controlled "autonomy" to control by the central government. Policy has always been controlled from Rome, even though its realization has often been left to the same managers who directed operations under private ownership. Thus to the influence of politics has been added the influence of private interests, certain of a receptive hearing before friendly public managers. As in France, the pressure for reform and uniformity has been great, but the results have been negligible so far because of the absence of a clearly formulated doctrine of the public interest.

FINANCES

Certain financial obligations rest on British nationalized industries. To quote the typical provisions of the Coal Act: "The Revenues of the board shall not be less than sufficient for meeting all their outgoings properly chargeable to revenue account (including interest and contributions to reserve fund) in an average of good and bad years." Thus the operating accounts must be balanced over a period of years. The borrowing powers of the boards are outlined in the acts, and the conditions under which a Treasury guarantee may or may not be granted are stated. The initial clarity of purposes and policies has called forth, on the whole, a keen sense of financial responsibility. Full publicity and regular publication of financial reports and accounts have been the practice in Great Britain since 1945. This combination of good management and well-ordered financial operations carried out in full view and according to generally understood book-keeping principles has produced financial results which are generally satisfactory. On the average, accounts have balanced and so far there has been no hidden subsidy of operating losses by the Treasury, even though, as has just been pointed out above, difficulties may be incurred in the future in the case of transport, where the financial problem is most serious. Whatever the future course of events, the fact remains that carefully drawn-up accounts regularly published at annual or even more frequent intervals will continue to furnish the data from which a public estimate of the costs and of the profits and losses of nationalized enterprises will always be possible.

In France and Italy, any analysis of the costs involved in the operations of nationalized enterprises is to this day a difficult task. Not only have reports been published only after considerable delay, but they have included incomplete data and have been based on bookkeeping procedures that are not easy to evaluate. While the nationalization acts in France and Italy speak boldly of the utilization of profits, the common problem has been to meet the operating deficits. French and Italian practices have often been such as to lend support to the traditional popular view of the inefficiency of all government economic activities. Decisions on current operations have sometimes been made on political grounds, prices have been fixed to meet political situations, and, worse still, the flow of new investments and the use of funds obtained through public borrowing have been dictated by noneconomic considerations. Therefore, estimates of relative efficiency and comparative costs have not been possible. As Pierre Mendès-

France said in the course of the first investiture debate before the National Assembly on June 4, 1953:

> The financial decisions and the investments of nationalized enterprises must not be formulated in scattered, planless fashion. A measure of coordination is necessary in order, as we have seen, to avoid having relatively less urgent expenditures made in some areas while other expenses of a more important character are eliminated. There is involved here a matter of choice which requires the presence of an arbiter. . . . If nationalized industries are the servants of the public interest, the government which represents this public interest must be placed in a position to know and to control their investments. What the new government will try to establish will not be, however, narrow and uncertain controls. Rather than on any a priori formal controls, we shall attempt to rely on a system where clear-cut responsibilities will be followed by both rewards and sanctions.[2]

Mendès-France was pleading for the application to nationalized industries of a system that would first establish the financial responsibilities of the managers within the framework of clearly fixed public policy—in terms of investment goals, costs to be suffered, prices and rates to be charged—and then enforce this responsibility not by setting up vexing formal controls but by requiring an accounting that would make possible a public overall evaluation. This approach combines the two principles of clear policy framework and full publicity, which have so far seemed to escape the grasp of Continental statesmen.

YARDSTICK: PUBLIC OR PRIVATE?

The "yardstick" concept is not necessarily a part of nationalization policy. Certain conditions must be present before it can be applied, and frequently those conditions have been absent in Europe. First of all, nationalization of a given economic sector must not be total, in order to allow the possibility of competition between the public and the private sector, a competition to which presumably the yardstick policy will become relevant. If nationalization of an industry is complete, then one can speak of

[2] Cf. Pierre Mendès-France, *Gouverner C'est Choisir* (Paris, 1953), pp. 98-99.

comparisons between private and public costs only in a general manner. Secondly, even if nationalization is complete, there must be a belief on the part of the managers of public enterprises that they can operate at a higher rate of efficiency than private business. If nationalization has occurred in areas that are gravely affected by economic obsolescence, by systematic underinvestment, or by political pressures seriously hampering efficiency and the freedom of management, even a general yardstick concept can hardly assert itself.

But wherever possible, the yardstick policy should be an important factor in public economic policy.[3] Surely the rescue of bankrupt industries or the punishment of politically guilty private owners must not be the sole purpose of nationalization in democratic countries. Together with a desire to weaken private controls of certain excessively powerful and monopolistic industries we should find the determination to provide superior performance. A democratic society with an expanding economy will not tolerate for long the presence of inefficient and high-cost public economic areas.

This view seems to have been best appreciated in the United States, where the Tennessee Valley Authority offers the classic example of a public yardstick policy. The policy can be summed up, in the case of the TVA, as one intended to demonstrate that over a period of time, given an adequate regional foundation, the application of modern mass-production methods to the field of electric power can bring about substantially increased production and decreased costs. At the same time large and real profits (not mere bookkeeping profits) should accrue to the public agency itself, so that the taxpayer will not only suffer no losses but in the end will gain important advantages.

Objective students no longer doubt that the TVA has been able to provide a successful demonstration of that policy over a period of twenty-one years. As a result of power rates that are far below those of neighboring areas (this is a general statement including both TVA rates and the rates of distributing municipalities

---

[3] But see, for somewhat different views, Rossi, below, pp. 237 ff.

and cooperatives whose rates are controlled by TVA), consumption has increased far above that in comparable markets. Profits on net power investments, after all expenses, full amortization, and payment of local taxes, averaged 4 percent for the twenty-one years of TVA operations. Had TVA, to satisfy the Edison Institute, been charged with an average federal income tax of 50 percent of net profits (or rather more than what private utilities have been paying), the profits would still have been 2 percent, a high return considering TVA's very low power rates, the fact that TVA only produces but does not distribute power and thus is cut off from the more profitable part of the power business which it leaves to the cooperatives and municipalities, and the worldwide, direct and indirect, benefits caused by TVA to the principles for which the United States stands.

Were TVA to charge normal rates, such as are considered proper for private utilities, and were it to become a monopolist from dam to kitchen stove, as all private utilities are permitted to be, its profits would be so high as to call for the drastic intervention of regulatory commissions.

A yardstick policy can be said to be successful only if it is adequately reflected in the policies of the private sector which it is presumably to influence. A yardstick which operates in a vacuum and has no repercussions for the outside economic world would seem a rather pointless yardstick. Enough evidence has accumulated over the past twenty years to show that the TVA's yardstick has influenced power rates of private utilities in direct ratio to their geographical proximity to the Tennessee Valley. The influence of the yardstick decreases as one moves away from the Valley and as private public utilities become less and less concerned about the possibility of an extension of TVA into their areas.

If the purpose of the creators of TVA was to prove that, by large-scale integrated modern operations and by the full exploitation of the market, consumption would increase, costs would decrease, and profits would go up, that purpose has been vindicated. The example of TVA has provided the private utilities with the constant anxiety and stimulation they needed to abandon their cautious power policy and to transfer to their production activities some of the boldness they were never slow in demonstrating in their financial operations.

It would be difficult to expect such range and success for the yardstick theory in Continental Europe. Generally speaking, in France entire industries were taken over, and certainly questions of efficiency were not among the paramount initial preoccupations of public managers. If here and there in both France and Italy a limited application of the yardstick policy has become visible, the terms of the problem have often been reversed. When only the larger French insurance companies were nationalized, a comparison might have been made over the course of years of the efficiency of the public and private sectors. Presumably the public sector could, by coordination and the elimination of certain unneeded costs which the competitive structure required, drive down expenses and provide cheaper insurance, thus forcing the private companies to follow suit. But if the yardstick concept was ever taken into account, it was meant to be applied in the opposite direction. The private companies were to be the models of efficiency. The Finance Committee of the Constituent Assembly said that by leaving a part of the industry in private hands, the public sector would be constantly goaded and prodded by the clearly admitted superiority of the private companies.

Now a private yardstick theory makes nonsense of the doctrine of nationalization in economic terms and reduces the issue to a political level, which, as we have seen, has been the controlling factor in European developments. But purely political nationalization represents an implicit admission of weakness on the part of the governing classes. For if politics is the only key to their actions, then it should be possible by a proper application of political power to obtain the desired deconcentration of corporate power, or any other desired change in corporate behavior.

It is possible that a fairly significant example of a public yardstick will be made available over the next few years in the Italian steel industry, which will by then be the only nationalized steel industry in Western Europe (assuming that the British government will be able to denationalize, in full, the steel industry). By 1955 the nationalized sector of the Italian steel industry represented about 60 percent of total capacity and was made up of the most modern steel plants in the country. It should therefore be able as a result of its weight and its efficiency to cause important changes in the policies of the private steel firms. A successful public yardstick policy would have notable advantages for the entire Italian economy. If, however, the European Coal and Steel Community makes the progress that is expected of it, the limited national yardstick might give way to a much longer European yardstick wielded by the Luxembourg High Authority. Before long Italy should leave the provisional shelter which the Steel Community has allotted to her in recognition of her special problems, and the decisive influence should become that of the European Community as a whole.

IV

Looking Ahead

THREE problems seem to call for a great deal of thought as one tries to visualize the future of nationalized industries in France and Italy. The first is the reorganization of the industries' administrative and managerial procedures, together with a clarification of their relationships to the state. The second is a more accurate redefinition of their boundary lines. And the third is their integration with the supranational agencies that Europe has started to create.

ADMINISTRATIVE REORGANIZATION

For reasons linked to the conditions of political life peculiar to France and Italy, the organization of nationalized industries has suffered from the uncertainties of politics and of statesmen, from the drive for power of civil servants, and from the pressures of businessmen. The results are far from satisfactory, and in the constant shifting of the past years we find evidence of a continuing search for a final solution which could do justice both to the national interest and to the requirements of effcient industrial management.

In Italy the so-called "privatistic" approach still dominates IRI. But the claims that can be made on its behalf, such as the greater flexibility and speed of operations which it induces as well as the more generalized adoption of normal business practices which it makes possible, are not enough to counterbalance the hidden influences which are brought to bear on IRI on behalf of bureaucratic power and private business, which either shares in the ownership of the "mixed" corporations or hopes to obtain certain advantages from wholly government-owned industries. The IRI policy of setting up a number of major subholding companies, each controlling as completely as possible a separate sector of industrial activity, a policy which has been realized in the case of telephones, shipping, iron and steel, public utilities, and engineering, could lend itself to the organization of autonomous public corporations in each of these fields. All other state economic enterprises, beginning with ENI, should be similarly reorganized and brought under uniform over-all controls of a planning and financial character, exercised by a politically accountable general board, whose duty it would be to explain to government and parliament and to the country the lines of action and the results of public economic policy. (Whether IRI could be so changed as to be able to carry out these functions, or whether some successor body should be created, is not of the essence of the problem.)

This is not a plan whose realization should present undue difficulties, for it is legitimate to hope that the most serious wartime and postwar obstacles will soon have been largely overcome, so that by vigorous management and some judicious pruning of marginal activities fairly modern industrial complexes might be established. The banks, the telephones and the public utilities, and the iron and steel industry should be profitable and should find it possible to finance themselves on the open market. The shipping and engineering sectors might still offer some difficulties, but here again conditions should be sufficiently clarified, so that the amount of public subsidy still required could be circumscribed and known.

In France, the completion of development plans for the new coal fields and of large-scale modernization of the gas and electric power plants should quickly establish these public enterprises on a sound operational footing. Banks and insurance companies present no serious problems, leaving shipping and transportation the only doubtful areas.

The full retreat which has taken place in France from the Utopian economy of 1946 to the exceedingly rigorous Cabinet controls of 1954 could well be modified in part by a return to the more efficient and expanded nationalized enterprises of some of the freedom which should be theirs once nationalization does not mean conquest by the Communist party. Again the public corporation appears, as in Great Britain, as the proper vehicle for governmental control of nationalized industries. For what is required is a body sufficiently free from day-to-day interference by Cabinets and bureaucratic machines, yet accountable to the politically responsible organs of the country and staffed by both experienced civil servants and industrial and economic statesmen so as to have under one roof, as far as it is humanly possible to do so, both efficiency and impartial administration. These are goals not easily attainable if there are not many men qualified to occupy these positions, men both trained in the complexities of modern industrial life and aware of the meaning of public service. But if confusion and corruption and, therefore, in the long run, economic decline, are to be avoided, there is no other way out.

ADVANCE OR RETREAT?

Before these goals can be attained a review and redefinition of the area of nationalization ought to be undertaken. Pressures for both its expansion and its limitation are present, and since no urgent atmosphere as that of 1945 exists today, if only because of the lessened expectations placed in this particular form of government intervention, no move should be made in either direction without considerably more care than was shown ten years ago.

For the moment the only country in which a serious examination of the issue has been made is Great Britain. In 1952 the Trades Union Congress asked its General Council to review the British experiment in public ownership with a view to extending its scope. In a resolution approved at Margate the Congress called upon the Council "to formulate proposals for the extension of social ownership to other industries and services, particularly those now subject to monopoly control." The Congress also asked for the formulation of general proposals "for the democratization of the nationalized industries and services calculated to make possible the ultimate realization of full industrial democracy."

In its *Interim Report on Public Ownership,* presented at the September 1953 Trades Union Congress, the Council disposed briefly of the question of industrial democracy, which it found to be a minority point of view representing the syndicalist conceptions prevalent in the early part of this century, but dealt in considerable detail and with great care with the basic question of the extension of public ownership. Implicitly admitted is the more intensive use by the government of a number of devices, such as the Capital Issue Committee and taxation, which, by influencing investments, can bring about full employment and planned economic development just as the more direct weapon of nationalization would be expected to do.

But the Council is ready to consider whether further nationalization would be desirable for each of four main industrial categories: (*a*) industries providing basic commodities and services; (*b*) industries of a monopolistic character; (*c*) industries where rapid development is required; (*d*) industries where improved organization and methods are needed.

Among the basic industries and services only two are listed: water supply and investment institutions, since most of the basic industries have already been nationalized. Concerning water supply, the report concludes that "there is a clear case for the complete public ownership of the industry in order to provide a universal service and eliminate waste." The investment institutions are the insurance companies, the investment trusts, and the joint stock banks. The findings of the Council are that the record of the banks and insurance companies since the war has, on the whole, been good. They have, in effect, supported investments in essential industries and agriculture. And "whether conformity to national needs can be secured within the present framework or whether further measures are called for, are questions which can only be answered by further detailed study."

The main monopolistic offender is the chemical industry. There is excessive concentration, too, since 48 percent of the workers are employed by the three largest units. But the troublesome fact is that the chemical industry has boundaries which are difficult to define, since the industry is constantly branching out in new directions; hence monopoly and concentration are not sufficiently firm slogans to permit its seizure. The Council examines earlier proposals of the Labour party for a substantial degree of public ownership of the industry, but the only recommendation it feels should be made is that "in view of the difficulty of obtaining full information about the operations of the industry, the next Labour government should institute an inquiry into the facts of the industry before a final decision is taken on the nature and extent of that control." The alternatives to be considered might then be either ownership of the whole industry or of one or more of the largest firms or supervision by a public board of control without any change of ownership.

Among industries requiring rapid development, the Council recommends the establishment of development agencies for machine tools, motor vehicles, and shipbuilding. For aircraft the Council says that "it would be unwise to commit the trade union movement at this stage to any specific measures of public ownership or further measures of public control in the aircraft industry." Apparently the present cooperative arrangements for research and financing between the industry and the government are found to be adequate.

Finally, for industries in need of improved organization, such as the wholesale and retail distributive industries, the Council recommends further study.

With such a display of caution, one is forced to the conclusion that the Trades Union Congress, having approved the report, feels today quite hesitant about pushing forward the boundaries of nationalization, with the lonely and undramatic exception of water supply. The TUC is clearly anxious to consider carefully forms other than public ownership and to use more fully existing tools of public policy to bring about the desired goals of socialism.

It would therefore appear that, apart from the possibility of re-nationalization of iron and steel, the contours of public ownership are not likely to change much from now on.

About the same conclusion might be reached for France. It is by now probable that steel will not be nationalized unless there is a radical change in the political climate. And even though the French climate has begun to change since 1954, it is changing in a direction that favors the general strengthening of the role of the state rather than further nationalizations. On the other hand, some of the inroads made in the airplane and the automobile industries might well be considered too pronounced under present conditions. It is unlikely that the old pre-1914 outcry about gun merchants could be raised again. French military policy is going to be influenced more decisively by the extent and the nature of the powers that will ultimately be given to Western European Union than by the government's retention or return to private industry of airplane factories. Similarly, there is no valid reason why the Renault automobile works should continue to be owned by the government. But these are relatively small matters. In all other major public sectors—coal, public utilities, railroads, shipping—there does not seem to be any possibility for a return to private ownership. Either private capital is not available or the transformations that have taken place since nationalization and the public investments that have been made do not make the transfer feasible or desirable. The public commitment is a permanent one, and the only issue is that of fulfilling it in the best possible manner.

Greater readjustments may have to be carried out in the case of Italy, where the dividing lines between private and public economic activity are both shifting and clouded, owing to the unique conditions under which nationalization took place and has continued to develop. As in France, a retreat of the frontier of public ownership might be suggested for the mechanical and engineering industries (not to mention the many other minor and purely fortuitous instances of government ownership). In the case of steel, the present situation of preponderant nationalization need not be disturbed since it appears to have brought about a proper balance between public and private interests. Government-owned steel plants have been rebuilt with public funds, and there is no foreseeable way of disposing of them to private interests without an unwarranted sacrifice of government investments. It seems also preferable that government should continue to dominate this field, given the past history of the industry.

The most difficult of the problems confronting IRI is that of telephones and public utilities. Telephones are at present 60 percent nationalized, and the nationalized sector is without question the most efficient one. Public utilities are nationalized to the extent of only about 25 to 30 percent, and here the private sector is the most efficient. But the case for the total nationalization of the telephone system is stronger than that for the full nationalization of public utilities. And before any new policy is undertaken in the field of public utilities, the role and position of the state, through ENI, in the production and distribution of natural gas ought to be determined. The many points of friction and of collusion that exist today are bound to increase the need for a clearly fixed national power policy. Therefore Italy should welcome a full political and legislative debate of the issues, so that the policies and boundaries of nationalized industries may be given democratic sanction. The power complex of Italy's various public economic bodies is too much the fruit of fascism and of chance and the result of political and personal manipulations to be long tolerated in its present structure.

If the problems of nationalization are submitted to the type of clarifying debate that has occurred in Great Britain, it is possible to forecast that nationalization will lose in relative importance and will not again appear, as it did after 1945, as the one essential key to economic salvation and democracy. As governments regain authority and power in more stabilized and prosperous economies, it is quite likely that nationalization will take a subordinate position among the many instruments of public economic policy. A bolder and more steadily applied taxation system, the better operation of national planning agencies, the growth of private

investments, the fruition of United States grants made in the past
ten years to facilitate the recovery of Europe—all will play their
proper part. Nationalization in the ultimate analysis is an instrument of despair and an admission of defeat, unless justified by exceptional circumstances. In the phase which one may hope is now
beginning, nationalizations should either be kept at their present
level or reduced within narrower boundaries, as in Great Britain,
while the main efforts of governments should be applied to the
task of achieving the maximum measure of expert and autonomous administration.

EUROPEAN INTEGRATION

The final issue is that of the relationship of nationalization to the
supranational agencies that exist or have been planned for Western Europe.

The European Coal and Steel Community possesses important
powers in all the fields which, together or separately, have justified
nationalization. The Community stands for freedom of movement
of goods and men to make available throughout the common
market adequate quantities of the commodities it controls. The
Community has power to determine prices as well as the volume
of production in periods of either prosperity or depression for
the protection of consumers' interests and the realization of
orderly economic policies. These are the admitted goals of nationalization too, as it seeks to replace anarchical private action
with the planned wisdom of public bodies.

The Community has strong powers to control the flow and direction of investment and, therefore, the rate of modernization
and expansion of the European coal and steel industries. Through
its prestige and credit standing and its international borrowing
capacity, it can make available to capital-starved European industries the funds needed to move forward. These are also the goals
of nationalization, as it seeks to replace the weakened investment
abilities of exhausted private owners with the abundant means
available to the state. The Community can deal sternly with the
problems of monopoly, restraints of trade, and cartels and can

break the practices which presumably are interfering with the growth of production and the lowering of prices to the consumer. The goal of nationalization also is to replace private power with public ownership, which, even though monopolistic, is presumed to act in the name of the general welfare.

The Community has very much at heart the protection of the rights and welfare of the workers; it is supposed to increase their standard of living and to provide for housing and other facilities which are at present inadequate. Nationalization, too, has as its highest purpose the improvement of the conditions of life of the working classes.

The ideas then which preside over the work of the first of the supranational European communities and guide the policies of nationalized industries are essentially the same, prescinding as we must do today from the sometimes obscure and divergent historical origins of nationalization. If nationalization is to be justified in current terms, it can only be in terms of the purposes which have been outlined above. Those are the purposes of the Coal and Steel Community. Three questions arise.

1. The first is whether national or supranational agencies are better qualified to achieve what has just been described as a common purpose. The answer does not seem to be in doubt, and the superiority of the Coal and Steel Community in bringing about over a period of time the more rational development and the fullest possible expansion of its two industries, with consequent advantages both to the workers and the consumers, is certain. For the Community has the power to deal with the central problem, which is that of the establishment of the common European market, while no nationalized enterprise, by definition, can deal with that issue. It seems reasonable, therefore, to expect that, if the Community is successful in the creation of an authentic common European market, its ability to deal with the other related problems that affect the future of coal and steel will be greatly enhanced.

It should not be assumed, of course, that the Community has been successful, as of the end of 1954, in the establishment of an authentic common market. The difficulties which beset the work of the High Authority appear to be related just as much to the existence of objective obstacles that lie in the path of the common market as to the emergence of conflicting viewpoints between the Authority and certain national governments. But if progress is to be made, it can only be through the firm pressure on particular interests exerted by the Authority with the support of member governments.

This does not mean that national policies, whether they be governmental, private, or of nationalized industries, have no role to play, as the progress of the Community will be assisted and not hindered by modern and enlightened national policies. If the High Authority could deal only with bankrupt and phantomatic governments, its chances of success would be limited. The incompatibility which was thought to have come about in 1954 between the supranational goals of the Community and the recovery efforts of the French government was mostly imaginary. What a closer analysis revealed, was the existence of a fresh determination on the part of Mendès-France to redress certain unfavorable aspects of the French domestic situation in such a manner as to make a significant contribution to the ultimate success of the community.

2. The next issue is whether the possibility of conflict between the Community and national industries is greater if the national industries are nationalized. According to the Community treaty, the High Authority has acquired the power of taxation. Its tax rolls include about one thousand taxpayers. Each taxpayer is directly liable to the Community for its tax payment. Therefore if coal, as in France, or steel, as in Italy, is nationalized, the taxpayers are, in effect, the French and the Italian governments. If pressures are brought to bear by the Authority on coal and steel producers on matters of cartels and trade restrictions, the pressure is aimed directly at governments, if governments are the owners.

The November 1954 report of the High Authority to the Common Assembly of the Community lists in detail, for the first time, some of the actions which the Authority has pending for the ap-

plication of Treaty Articles 65 and 66 relating to cartels and concentrations. In some instances the offenders are member governments, as in the case of ATIC,[1] the French government coal
import monopoly, which is the result of French nationalization
of coal. A modification of ATIC policies will therefore represent a
change of government policies. One may perhaps expect a greater
readiness to alter policies and plans on the part of small and
private producers than on the part of governments. While a government can help the Authority in trying to persuade the recal-
citrant private owners to abide by the Authority's decisions, the
situation is more complicated when a government is directly involved in a conflict with the Authority. Although in principle the
ultimate success of the Authority must rest on the cooperation of
the participating governments, it still appears true to say that the
Community would be better off in dealing with a large number
of operators rather than with a few powerful ones, as the treaty
itself implicitly recognizes in its cartel and concentration provisions. In the face of the expanding power of supranational
agencies, the role of nationalized industries, those carriers of national pride and egoism, should decrease.

3. The third question is that of the possible expansion of the
supranational approach to govern areas other than coal and steel.
There are at present no indications that any such expansion will
be forthcoming in the near future, at least not without the amendment of the terms provided by the Schuman Treaty. There are
hints, however, of the probability of such a trend in the future,
especially in the field of power. There already exist international
agreements, chiefly among countries whose boundaries touch the
Alpine mountain chain, for the exchange of hydroelectric power
across national boundaries. Austria, Germany, Switzerland, Italy,
and France are all more or less involved in arrangements of this
type. Gradually these agreements are bound to increase in scope
and might require the setting up of a European Power Community to regulate the flow of power and of investments in the field.

[1] In full, Association Technique de l'Importation Charbonnière.

When that happens, the question of the subordination of national policies to the supranational agency will present itself, and the considerations discussed above will apply here.

Of even greater importance may be the future application of atomic energy to the production of power. Atomic energy would seem to require the establishment of a supranational agency to distribute special nuclear materials, once the materials become available for general distribution among European countries. Here the obsolescence of national policies is obvious.

If nationalism is on the decline, then the merely national economic policies that have been the object of this study must be on the way out too. Tomorrow they will perhaps be considered as a temporary phase in the painful and all too protracted adaptation to modern needs of the industrial society of the nineteenth century.

Part II by Maurice Byé

NATIONALIZATION IN FRANCE

>>>>>>>>>>>>>>>>>>>>>>>>> <<<<<<<<<<<<<<<<<<<<<<<<<

V

Introduction

THE purpose of this study [1] is to examine the sector of the French economy which is owned by the national government. This sector will be referred to as the "public sector of the economy," [2] and it may be most easily defined by a process of elimination. It excludes enterprises that are entirely operated by private individuals or groups. It also excludes economic enterprises that are owned by governmental units inferior to the national government, like the departments and the cities, and public services performed by agencies of the national government whose purposes are not mainly economic, like defense, education, and the administration of justice.

Problems of definition still remain, however. The frontier between state capitalism and private capitalism is not always clearly distinguishable, as in a mixed corporation, where the capital stock is shared between the state and private owners, or in a case where a private industry holds a concession from the state involving a subsidy, which was for a long time the situation of the French railroads. Moreover, it is difficult to classify an industry owned by the national government, like the Compagnie Nationale du Rhône, whose operations are of local importance only. The

[1] The author wishes to thank M. Vincent, of the Paris Institute of Applied Economics, for his valuable aid in the preparation of this study, especially in connection with the problem of price policy and with the operations of the coal and power industries.

[2] Some statistics use the term "public sector" to describe the noneconomic public services, in contrast to the term "nationalized sector."

public sector will be defined for purposes of convenience as including only those enterprises [3] in which over half of the capital stock is owned by the national government.[4] This has the advantage of corresponding to the basis of classification of the inventory prepared in 1946 by the then Minister of Finance, Robert Schuman.[5]

[3] "Public enterprise" and "nationalized industry" will be used interchangeably in this study, although some persons distinguish between them.

[4] This study will deal only with the nationalized industries of metropolitan France. There are many public enterprises functioning in the extrametropolitan areas of the French Union, especially in the form of mixed corporations.

[5] Ministère des Finances, *Inventaire de la Situation Financière (1913–1946)* (Paris, 1946).

>>>>>>>>>>>>>>>>>>>>>> <<<<<<<<<<<<<<<<<<<<<<<

VI

The Beginnings of Nationalization

LARGE-SCALE nationalization of industry in France is essentially a product of the peculiar political atmosphere of the post-Liberation period, although state ownership and operation of industry on a smaller scale and in a less systematized fashion is by no means a recent phenomenon. On the contrary, such activity in France belongs to a tradition which extends from prerevolutionary France to the last years of the Third Republic.

THE PUBLIC SECTOR BEFORE 1936

Before the revolution of 1789, the king undertook to carry out certain economic activities as a result of political, military, and financial necessities, as well as of the mercantilist conception of the role of the state in this sphere. The postal service dates back to Louis XI, who reigned in the fifteenth century, and the old monarchy created the network of "royal highways" because it was essential for the unification of the country. Colbert, the Finance Minister of Louis XIV, was responsible for some of the royal manufacturing operations that still continue today, like the production of Gobelin and Beauvais tapestries and of Sèvres porcelain. The creation of a state monopoly on the processing and sale of tobacco goes back to another mercantilist period, that of the First Empire.

As early as the nineteenth century there were people who asserted the rights of the nation over certain sources of wealth and who claimed that it was the duty of the state to promote the development and control the operation of certain public services. But the prevailing doctrines of liberalism led to the granting of concessions to private companies for the exploitation of this wealth and the operation of these services.[1]

Occasionally, however, accidental situations arose which led to the creation of public enterprises, although not without doctrinal disputes. Sometimes the French government found itself the sole owner of properties which had been turned over to it by a foreign state and which it wished to retain. This was the case with the Alsace-Lorraine railroad system, returned to France by Germany in 1919. L'Office National Industriel de l'Azote was formed in 1924 for the purpose of exploiting the Haber process, the rights to which were received as reparations from Germany. The liquidation of the assets of German nationals in Alsace-Lorraine left the French state in control of the companies that had exploited most of the Alsatian potash beds; the companies were bought in 1924 and organized as the Mines Domaniales de Potasse d'Alsace in 1937.

Often the state took over the property of bankrupt private enterprises. Two considerations were decisive in this respect. There was, on one hand, the necessity of continuing the operation of certain industries which were regarded as "public services." In this case the government preferred public operation to private operation supported by subsidies, which it considered less rational and more costly. Thus in 1878 the state bought the small and unprofitable Centre-Ouest railroad system. Later, in 1907, the lines of the Ouest, which was in financial difficulties, were similarly acquired by the state.

The second consideration was the protection of the interests of a large number of people with small savings threatened by the prospects of bankruptcy of a private corporation. Here the government preferred to nationalize rather than to try to set the corporation back on its feet. Especially after the 1929 crisis, while some government attempts to aid private firms succeeded in en-

---

[1] Statutes of 1810, 1859, and 1919 regulated, respectively, mining, railroad, and hydroelectric concessions.

abling them to overcome their difficulties (as in the case of the Banque Nationale de Crédit), other attempts ended in the creation of mixed corporations. For example, after having subsidized one of the major French shipping companies, the Compagnie Générale Transatlantique, for a long time, the government, faced with new financial difficulties, reorganized it in 1933. The state became the owner of 87 percent of the capital stock of the company, with ten of the nineteen seats on the board of directors and a government commissioner at its head.

While the steps taken by the French government before 1936 in the direction of public ownership of economic enterprises were not negligible, they were, on the whole, largely *ad hoc* measures. This does not mean, however, that there was no doctrinal consideration of the problem. On the contrary, groups were at work trying to prepare the ideological foundations for large-scale nationalization.

Traditional French liberalism, represented at the end of the nineteenth century and at the beginning of the twentieth century by men such as Gustave de Molinari, Paul Leroy-Beaulieu, and Yves Guyot, had been opposed to any state intervention in economic affairs. More than any other school of liberalism, French liberalism had demonstrated its hostility to any economic activity on the part of the state. Most of the political groups classified as the Right until 1945 drew their inspiration mainly from this tradition and indicated their hostility to nationalization in any form.

For the Socialists, however, the ultimate goal to be achieved was the collectivization of the means of production. The major problem that faced this group was to determine how collectivization should be carried out. The French Socialists who at the end of the nineteenth and at the beginning of the twentieth century considered themselves to be the most faithful representatives of Marxist orthodoxy were openly opposed to a process of nationalization by degrees. If nationalization were accomplished by purchase, it would be a rescue operation for the threatened capitalist interests. Moreover, the domination of a "capitalist state" over vast groups of workers would only retard their emancipation. Collectivization, therefore, would be acceptable only through the prior advent to political power of the "working class."

This attitude, which was held as early as 1883 by Jules Guesde,[2] was challenged at the Socialist party congress at Saint-Quentin in 1911 by another thesis supported by Edgard Milhaud and accepted by Jean Jaurès.[3] These men held that the purchase of the railroads by the state would be a step on the road to socialism. The congress took no stand on the issue, but the later action of the Socialist party made it nevertheless apparent that the party generally regarded nationalization favorably.

While the movements which favored government intervention in economic life, like Social Catholicism and Radical Socialism, were not opposed in principle to specific nationalization acts, they did not place any peculiar and exceptional value upon nationalization. They regarded it merely as one method among several of ensuring social justice. It was not until World War I that a serious and systematic doctrine of nationalization emerged; this doctrine was the product of Revolutionary Syndicalism.

The syndicalists of the Confédération Générale du Travail (CGT, "General Confederation of Labor"), led by Léon Jouhaux, had been associated with the government during World War I and after the war they considered it their duty to lay down the broad outlines of a program for the economic reconstruction of the country. The program of the CGT prepared in 1918 stated that the nation must reassert "its social right to the ownership of the collective wealth and the means of its production and exchange." [4] The nationalization thus envisaged was quite a different thing from the producers' cooperatives, symbolized by the slogan "the mines to the miners," which had often been considered before the war as the syndicalist ideal. It was also to be sharply distinguished from tight state control of industry, for the new organizations were to be administered autonomously.

---

[2] Jules Guesde, *Services Publics et Socialisme* (Paris, 1901).

[3] Alexandre Zévaès, *Histoire du Socialisme et du Communisme en France* (Paris, 1947).

[4] Cf. Jean Montreuil, *Histoire du Mouvement Ouvrier en France* (Paris, 1947), p. 337.

This formula was readopted and clarified at the CGT congress at Lyon in 1919, and again in the course of the work of the Conseil Économique du Travail, which was of syndicalist origin. The resolution voted by the congress merged Léon Jouhaux's doctrine with a similar one that was gaining international currency.[5] Nationalization was admitted to be useful even before socialism's advent to power; and the management of the nationalized industries should be based on the tripartite formula of "cooperative administration" by representatives of the state, the workers, and the consumers. Throughout all its vicissitudes between the two World Wars and in spite of a schism and later a merger with Communist trade unions, the CGT remained faithful to this doctrine.

The managerial plan formulated by the CGT was adopted under the name of "Régie Coopérative" by different groups of theorists. Some of them were originally Socialists, like Edgard Milhaud, who founded and published the *Cahiers de l'Économie Collective;* some came from the cooperative school, like Bernard Lavergne, with his *Revue des Études Coopératives.* A few new enterprises in France, especially the Compagnie Nationale du Rhône, which was created for the purpose of improving the whole Rhône basin from the triple point of view of electrification, irrigation, and navigation, followed this management formula.

On the other hand, the 1919 program did not succeed in bringing about the nationalization of any private industry. The Conseil Économique du Travail presented Parliament with two nationalization plans for the mines and the railroads. The elections of 1920 favored the right-wing parties, however, which were disturbed over attempts to hold a general strike, and a strong antisyndicalist reaction set in. Nothing came of the nationalization proposals.

FROM POPULAR FRONT TO LIBERATION

The depression that followed the crash in 1929 led the unions to make a number of proposals for recovery, including suggestions

[5] The work of the Austrian Social Democrat, Otto Bauer, had been translated in 1919 under the title, *La Marche au Socialisme.* It listed the industries that should be nationalized—transportation, mining, electricity, and banking—and recommended regulation of producers and consumers.

for revising the industrial structure. The CGT Plan, prepared in 1934 under the leadership of Léon Jouhaux and adopted by the congress which re-established trade union unity at Toulouse in 1936, demanded the nationalization, according to the lines laid down in 1919, of the "instruments of economic command." Another plan published in 1936 by the Confédération Française des Travailleurs Chrétiens (CFTC, "French Confederation of Christian Workers") also called for the nationalization of industry, although it differed from the CGT plan on the question of compensation to be paid to private owners.

After the elections of 1936, the Popular Front coalition of left-wing parties took control of the government. These parties were bound by a common program adopted in 1935, but its nationalization plans were much less ambitious than those of the CGT, since the Popular Front's majority contained only one party, the Socialist party, which openly advocated large-scale nationalization. The other two parties of the majority were lukewarm on the question: the Communists for opportunist reasons and the Radical Socialists for doctrinal reasons.

Between 1936 and 1939 a limited nationalization program was enacted, by far the most important part of which was the nationalization of the railroads in 1937. At that time part of the French railroad system was operated by the state, as a result of the acquisitions noted above. Most of the railroad lines, however, were operated by five large private companies.

Relationships between the railroad companies and the government were governed by the agreements of 1921. According to these agreements, all important decisions had to be approved by the Minister of Public Works, after having been submitted for recommendations to the Conseil Supérieur des Chemins de Fer. Thus a dual control was established.

The companies were linked financially by the establishment of a common fund into which the profitable companies paid their surpluses and which was used to meet the losses of the unprofitable companies. If the common fund became exhausted, the companies could issue bonds on which the state guaranteed both interest and principal. The Minister of Public Works could also raise rates "to the extent compatible with the general economic situation."

The seemingly successful operation of the 1921 agreements came to an end with the 1929 crisis and the intensified competition of road transportation. Demands on the common fund multiplied; rate increases were no longer automatic because of the reluctance of the government to resort to measures which would have serious repercussions upon the rest of the country's economy; the burden on the public treasury grew steadily. In 1937 every company was losing money, and loans guaranteed by the state exceeded 30 billion francs.

The agreements of 1921 had been severely criticized right from the start,[6] and perhaps it might have been possible, by coordinating the transportation system and revising the agreements, to maintain private operation of the railroads. The government, however, did not think so, and by the agreement of August 31, 1937, the railroads were nationalized.

Since January 1938 they have been operated by the Société Nationale des Chemins de Fer Français (SNCF), a mixed corporation. The new corporation, with a capitalization of 1,419,412,-000 francs, turned over 1,391,024 shares of class A stock to the old companies, while the state held 1,447,800 shares of class B stock. From the start, therefore, the state held a majority of the stock, and it also had a controlling position on the board of directors. The position of the state was to be progressively strengthened since it was provided that the state should redeem the class A stock annually according to a plan that would leave none outstanding by 1983.

This solution, which was arranged while the railroads' franchises were still in force, their expiration dates being between 1950 and 1960, did not hurt the interests of the stockholders. It received little criticism from the traditional opponents of nationalization; on the contrary, the greater criticism came from the traditional

[6] Especially by Jean-Marcel Jeanneney, and many economists of whom François Perroux should be cited individually (see his "Chronique annuelle des chemins de fer" in *Revue d'Économie Politique*).

advocates of nationalization, who found the arrangement to be too favorable to the old railroad companies.

Another measure taken during this period immediately prior to World War II was the nationalization of part of the armament industry, in particular the Creusot plants and the aircraft industry. This step was held to be necessary to prevent excess profits and to end the abnormal situation of private industries working exclusively for one client, the state.

The Bank of France was reorganized by the law of July 1936, but there was no nationalization as such involved. The Bank of France which, unlike the Bank of England, had never had the character of a completely private institution, because its operation was quasi-governmental even though its capital was privately owned, remained in private hands after 1936. In practice, however, its management was supervised by representatives of the state. Later, in 1940, the distribution of seats on the general board was slightly modified, but no real change in the bank's management was brought about.

Another development during this period was the establishment in July 1939 of the Régie Autonome des Pétroles, which was to develop the field Saint Marcet in Haute-Garonne. Production consists mainly of natural gas, distributed by pipeline throughout southwestern France.

THE POST-LIBERATION NATIONALIZATION ACTS

The National Council of the Resistance, because of the necessity of giving social significance to the liberation of the country and because of the preponderance of left-wing elements—Christian Democrats, Socialists, and Communists—in "Fighting France," recommended in its program "the return to the nation of the great monopolies of the means of production, the fruits of the common labor, the sources of energy, the mineral wealth, the insurance companies, and the banks." [7] Similarly, at Algiers on March 18, 1944, General de Gaulle announced that France would

[7] Program of the National Council of the Resistance, published at Algiers, 1944.

erect "an economic system designed to develop and improve the national resources, and not for the profit of special interests; one in which the great sources of common wealth would belong to the Nation." [8]

It was to be expected, therefore, that these principles should be voiced after the Liberation by General de Gaulle, who became chief of the Provisional Government. "The State," he said on March 2, 1945, before the Consultative Assembly,

must hold the levers of command. Yes, tomorrow it will be the task of the State itself to ensure the development of the great sources of energy: coal, electricity, and petroleum, as well as the principal means of rail, maritime, and air transport and the means of communication on which all the rest depends. It will be its role to bring the major branches of metallurgical production to the necessary level. It will be its role to control credit and to direct the nation's savings. . . .[9]

The three parties associated with De Gaulle in the Provisional Government, the Mouvement Républicain Populaire (MRP), the Socialists, and the Communists, supported these views. They were accepted by the great majority in the First Constituent Assembly, which passed the main nationalization acts. Thus the nationalization of credit and of the banks was passed by 521 votes to 35; the nationalization of electricity and gas by 512 to 64; and the nationalization of insurance by 487 to 63. The nationalization of the coal industry was beyond debate, and it was not even given a roll-call vote.

The nationalization acts passed after the Liberation can be divided into two broad categories. There were a number of incidental nationalization acts, important enough for the interests they affected but without any major implications for the entire economy. On the other hand, there were a number of major nationalization acts which corresponded to the demands for "structural reforms" made at Algiers and which were based on a doctrinal foundation.

[8] Speech before the Provisional Consultative Assembly, reprinted in Charles de Gaulle, *Discours et Messages* (Paris, 1946), p. 422.
[9] *Ibid.*, p. 573.

The incidental nationalization acts were punitive measures aimed at former owners who were accused of having collaborated with the Germans during the Occupation. The Société Anonyme des Usines Renault was transformed in 1944 into the Régie Renault after the holdings of the company's founder and chief stockholder, Louis Renault, had been confiscated. The Société Gnôme et Rhône, which manufactured airplane engines, was nationalized in 1945 and transformed into the Société Nationale d'Études et de Construction des Moteurs d'Avion (SNECMA) under a mixed form of ownership. The Société Anonyme des Automobiles Berliet was nationalized and used as an experiment in workers' control of management. Later the company was returned to Berliet's heirs. Other punitive nationalizations involved the film industry (Tobis Films and Alliance Cinématographique Européenne), a chemical factory (Société Francolor), and the Société Nationale des Entreprises de Presse (SNEP), to which were turned over the assets of a large number of newspapers which had continued to appear during the Occupation.[10]

Many different solutions were adopted for the management of these enterprises, ranging from the direct state administration of the Renault plant to the mixed control of the film companies. The decisions made in these matters were not based on a consistent doctrine. In the case of many businesses that had been sequestered and temporarily confided to the Administration des Domaines, it

[10] The Société Nationale des Enterprises de Presse was created by the law of May 11, 1946. Its establishment had two causes. It appears, first, to have been the consequence of punitive action taken against those newspapers and other publications which continued publication during the Occupation. In this respect it is little different from the nationalization of the Usines Renault, for instance, or of the Société Francolor.

In view of the extreme importance of the measures called for by the law, however, it appears that a second, more radical motive contributed to the creation of the SNEP. This can be discovered in the avowed aim of the resolution introduced by the Socialist deputy Defferre to "prevent rotten journalism from returning in its old form or in some new guise." There can be no doubt that the law had the purpose, unacknowledged but unmistakable, of consolidating the advantages gained by some parties in the distribution of the new newspapers which appeared after the Liberation. The political character of the law therefore seems obvious.

took a long time to decide upon their final disposition, and this meant, in practice, that most of them were turned over to their former private owners for management.

The first of the major nationalization acts was carried out right after the Liberation, in December 1944, when the government took over the Houillères du Nord et Pas-de-Calais, the main French coal beds. This act was modified two years later to bring it into the framework established for the entire nationalized coal industry.

The other important nationalization acts were passed by the First Constituent Assembly soon after the war had ended. These acts were the law of December 2, 1945, nationalizing the Bank of France and the four main commercial banks (as well as establishing state control over business banks [11] and general credit controls through the Conseil National du Crédit); the law of April 8, 1946, nationalizing electricity and gas; the law of April 25, 1946, nationalizing the major insurance companies; and the law of May 17, 1946, nationalizing the coal industry.

These nationalization acts were supported by a great variety of arguments.[12] In the first place, it was argued that in some industries nationalization was necessary for a rational reorganization. At the beginning of 1946 there were no less than 1,730 enterprises exclusively engaged and 970 partially engaged in the production, transmission, and distribution of electric power. In 1942 there were 153 coal-mining companies in France, although it is true that 23 of them furnished nine-tenths of the total production.

There was also much insistence on the need for capital for the modernization and expansion of productive facilities. Such ex-

---

[11] The main distinction between commercial and business banks is that the former operate, as typical United States banks do, mainly in the fields of short-term credit, while the latter make long-range investments of a type that in the United States is left to the financial houses that sell bond and stock issues to private investors.

[12] Although this study relies chiefly on French documentation, mention should be made of the article by Mario Einaudi, "Nationalization of industry in western Europe: Recent literature and debates," *American Political Science Review*, March 1950.

pansion would require enormous investment in the industries whose plant and equipment, regarded as obsolete before the war, had been badly damaged by the war. Many people believed that if public funds were used, the people as a whole should benefit, and not private capitalists.

These arguments, however, were not basic to the question, but were used by the proponents of nationalization to fit certain specific cases. There were doctrinal principles of more permanent significance at the origin of the major nationalization acts, although they were not always made clear because the majorities which voted for the laws were far from homogeneous.

The Communist party certainly viewed nationalization as a process that would help it gain power in France. The nationalization acts were passed at a time when the Communists were participating in the government, holding the Ministry of Industrial Production, the key command post of the nationalized sector.[13] Moreover, the Communists controlled France's largest union, the CGT. The extent of their efforts to exploit participation in the boards of directors of the nationalized industries, as well as to monopolize the production drive that the Communist leaders and union spokesmen undertook at that time, leaves little doubt about the political importance which the Communist party attached to nationalization.

The doctrine of the Socialist party, as it had been restated by Jules Moch in 1933, made equally clear that the Socialist party was in favor of the nationalization of industry as a way to achieve collectivism. But the position of the other parties which endorsed the nationalization acts, and the position of General de Gaulle himself, certainly did not stem from a favorable disposition toward the creation of a thoroughly collectivized economy. Because of this

[13] Marcel Paul, a Communist, was Minister of Industrial Production when the main nationalization acts were passed. An inverse proof of the importance attributed to nationalization by the Communist party while it participated in the government is furnished by the indifference with which it views nationalization now that governmental conditions have changed. In a speech made in 1950 at the congress of Gennevilliers, Paul said: "I am opposed to nationalization because it can be a capitalist weapon."

difference in basic outlook, the "structural reforms" enacted in France were fundamentally different from those which were being pursued at the same time in several countries of central and eastern Europe. While nationalization of industry in France was extensive, it was not complete. The Constituent Assembly that passed the nationalization acts was governed by the idea expressed at Algiers by the Provisional Government, which envisaged an eventual economic structure consisting of three main sectors: a private sector, a controlled sector, and a nationalized sector. The latter was to embrace the "economic public services."

The concept of a public service industry has been the subject of a great deal of controversy.[14] The most common definition of a public service in the United States involves two criteria: the industry must be a monopoly and it must be a "key" industry. If there is no effective monopoly, there is no risk of conflict between the interests of the owners and the general interest; if the industry does not occupy a key position, the risk can be run without serious danger.

But what is a key industry? French administrative theory defines a key industry in terms of the necessity for its uninterrupted operation; furthermore, it must always be ready to respond to any variation in demand. The statement of intentions of a bill introduced by Pierre Schneiter [15] defines a key industry in similar terms: an activity is "indispensable to the life of the nation" if it is an "activity the suspension of which, even if only momentarily, would quickly cause, either directly or indirectly, the cessation of the very life of the country." It should be added that a public service must be "universally available" and treat all citizens alike.

The criterion of key industry alone would have led to extensive nationalization, since the Monnet Plan, which was prepared in 1946, listed six categories of key resources: coal, electricity, iron

[14] A good French study on the American concept of public utility is that by F. Trevoux, "Du service public de droit public au service public économique," in *Mélanges Lambert,* II, 405–406. See also the articles by P. Waline, Georges Vedel, and François Luchaire, published in *Droit Social.*

[15] He was proposing a general reform of the nationalized industries (*Assemblée Nationale, Proposition de Loi,* No. 1522, May 30, 1947).

and steel, cement, agricultural machinery, and transportation. Only three of these industries have actually been nationalized. The operation of a key industry by private enterprise was allowed where no monopoly was involved.

The general criteria were greatly modified in their application. It may be true that the production and distribution of electric power were natural monopolies, but certainly it would be arbitrary to pretend that the iron and steel industry was less monopolistic in France than the coal industry, or than the insurance business, which was characterized by a multiplicity of competing companies. In fact, from the very beginning, some parties, especially the MRP, chose to interpret the word "nationalization" in the broad sense of control by the nation. These parties, for example, refused to nationalize the business banks along with the four large commercial banks.

After the major wave of nationalization acts in April–May, 1946, the First Constituent Assembly came to the end of its term of office. The Second Constituent Assembly, elected in June 1946 and less oriented to the left, indicated a desire to pause in the drive toward nationalization and to submit the experiments already undertaken to the test of experience. It did, however, say, in the preamble of the Constitution of October 27, 1946, "All property and all enterprises that now have or subsequently shall have the character of a national public service or a monopoly in fact must become the property of the community."

The new Parliament, elected in November 1946, in which liberal economic tendencies began to be reasserted and in which, after April 1947, collectivist influence was greatly diminished due to the departure of the Communist party from the government, took no further steps in the direction of nationalization. One can even say that, especially after the senatorial elections of 1949, hostility to nationalization began to appear, a process that was reinforced markedly by the general elections of June 1951. The programs and propaganda of certain political groups which grew in parliamentary strength after these elections, like the Radical-Socialist party, the Independents, the Peasants, and the Rassemblement du Peuple Français (RPF), constantly emphasized criticism of the nationalized industries. There has never been, therefore, any serious possibility since 1946 that nationalization would be extended to industries like iron and steel or road transport, which earlier had figured in nationalization plans.

In general, however, it can be said that, while the criticism aimed at the electricity and coal boards can bring about reforms in their management, there seems to be no serious prospect of a wholesale transfer of the nationalized industries back to private ownership. In this connection, a 1951 speech by Edgar Faure is significant. Faure, then a minister from the Radical-Socialist party, which is well known for its liberal economic doctrine and its often violent criticism of public intervention, said: "If the Radicals have passed no nationalization acts since they have been in power, they nevertheless believe that the State is capable of operating large industries. There is no doubt that a private railroad company would have to face the same managerial problems as the SNCF." [16] The RPF also, while it criticizes the operation of the nationalized industries and proposes that they be organized similarly to private corporations, does not intend to turn back the clock on the major nationalization acts. Accordingly, and despite the attitude of certain conservative members of Parliament, the major nationalization acts do not seem to be threatened with repeal. Undoubtedly the serious complications of such a step act as a powerful deterrent to any denationalization attempt.

THE AREA OF NATIONALIZATION

The Schuman *Inventaire,* published at the end of 1946, revealed that the number of publicly owned industrial or commercial companies and mixed corporations of which the state owned a majority of the stock grew from eleven at the end of 1935 to thirty-one in August 1944, and rose to 103 by December 1, 1946. Since that time certain changes have been made. Senator Marcel Pellenc estimates that the public sector embraces 214 public bodies, of

[16] Speech before the Radical-Socialist congress of Bouches-du-Rhône, December 17, 1951.

which 109 are of an industrial or commercial nature, while 105 are administrative agencies.[17] As each one of these agencies was created by a special law that bears the stamp of the epoch during which it was passed, the public sector is extremely varied.

The *Inventaire* contains a list [18] of the major public enterprises which reveals that they involve most areas of productive activity: power, transportation, manufacturing, chemicals, the press, motion pictures, and so forth. From this list, two functionally different categories can be formed and, in fact, proposals for the general reorganization of the nationalized industries almost all draw a distinction between two types of enterprise. Sometimes the distinction is drawn between monopolistic and competitive industries; sometimes it is between a public service industry and a purely industrial operation. The first distinction is the more common and the easier to draw. It is not, however, the most accurate. Several businesses which obviously must not be managed on a purely commercial basis, like banking or insurance, are not entirely nationalized and are far from being without competitive features, whether the competition is between autonomous public enterprises or between public and private enterprises. But the existence of controlling agencies, like the Conseil National du Crédit, enables common rules to be imposed on the entire body of public and private activity alike.

Accordingly, the two sectors, which might well be called *A* and *B*, will, for the sake of convenience, be defined in terms of whether or not the industry is a public service, however vague this term may be.

Where there is no public service involved, as in the case of the Régie Renault, which manufactures automobiles, the public enterprise should be operated as much like a private enterprise as possible, and it definitely should not be granted any administrative, fiscal, or banking privileges.

[17] Marcel Pellenc, *Le Bilan de Six Ans d'Erreur* (Paris, 1950), p. 5. The 109 industrial and commercial agencies correspond to those listed in the *Inventaire*. The others do not directly affect economic life.

[18] The list is reprinted in Marcel Ventenat, *L'Expérience des Nationalisations* (Paris, 1947).

Where there is a public service, on the other hand, the management must be guided by the general interest. The intention of the men who passed the nationalization acts was to use the public sector of the economy to direct and control the economy as a whole. The investments made in the key industries, which could be more easily supervised and oriented if these industries were nationalized, would permit general direction of the economy. In addition, state control of the prices of the public services would put the state in a position to control market prices generally.

It is unquestionable that the scope of the nationalization acts has placed the public sector in a dominant position over various markets. It dominates the industrial market because it furnishes both power and transportation to all industries, and it dominates the financial market, where either directly or through the inter mediary of the state it is one of the largest borrowers.

It does not appear, however, that the government has wanted or has been able to use this position in the way certain people at first hoped it would. It is true that the lag in the prices charged by the public enterprises must be attributed to the desire to check inflation, but a systematic and coordinated policy does not seem to have been applied in any field except banking. The empirical choices which have been made between precipitating general price increases by raising prices in the nationalized industries and, on the other hand, burdening these industries by keeping down their price level—both undesirable alternatives—have never been based on an over-all view. If there have sometimes been subsidies, in the coal industry especially, there has never been a deliberate policy of deficit operations based on a serious study of prices. The only official goal has been to achieve budgetary equilibrium in the public enterprises by means which allow little room for consideration of the economy as a whole. And even this goal has not always been pursued in practice.

Once a decision has been made to nationalize a given economic activity, the problem still remains of determining how large a portion of this activity should be taken over by the state. In other words, should the entire industry, or only part of it, be nationalized? France has followed both alternatives. In the banking field, only four of the commercial banks were nationalized: the Crédit Lyonnais, the Société Générale, the Banque Nationale pour le Commerce et l'Industrie, and the Comptoir National d'Escompte, which accounted for 54.6 percent of the assets of all commercial banks in 1947. In the insurance field, thirty-four companies were nationalized, representing 62 percent of the total French insurance business.

The criteria used to determine which banks and insurance companies to nationalize were imprecise. The legislators did not want to employ a numerical criterion. In the case of insurance, for example, the importance of the groups to which the companies belonged was taken into consideration—something of an anti-trust approach—but those companies also were singled out which "constituted a danger because of their political influence." On the other hand, certain companies were exempted because they were profitably carrying out activities abroad.

The coal, electricity, and gas industries stand as completely nationalized, but even here there were some exceptions. In the coal industry, enterprises "of secondary interest" were exempted from nationalization and were merely placed under the control of Charbonnages de France. Actually, the output of these small mines is less than 2 percent of the total production. The exemptions are much more important in the electricity and gas industries. The law exempted from nationalization electric companies producing fewer than 12,000,000 kilowatt hours and gas companies producing less than 6,000,000 cubic meters annually. These maximum limits were raised considerably by the law of August 2, 1949.

One other problem that faced France's legislators was determining, within each firm, the precise limits of the property to be nationalized. In certain cases, such as banking and insurance, it was not necessary to state specifically the property to be transferred, for the state simply substituted itself for the private stockholders. But the problem was not quite so simple in other important industries, such as electricity, gas, and coal. Here there were assets, belonging to the larger firms, which were not devoted to the production of coal, gas, or electricity. A commission had to determine which assets would be nationalized and which would not. In short, the scope of the nationalization acts was defined in terms of economic process and not simply in terms of property ownership.

In spite of the application of this principle, the nationalized industries fall heir to a number of subsidiary undertakings and miscellaneous property. Moreover, and more significantly, they have themselves tended to develop subsidiary companies. They were at first encouraged to do this by their own needs, in order to give complete financial autonomy to certain operations that they considered useful, for example, the road transport system of the SNCF. But it must be acknowledged that the interpretation of these necessities has been liberal.

The nationalized industries have also been motivated by the desire to establish reserves to protect themselves against monetary fluctuations, the desire to integrate their suppliers or their clients within their own system, and even, perhaps, to create a certain amount of confusion in their books, as deficits must be covered by the state.

As a result there has been a veritable proliferation of subsidiary companies and of participations. Air-France has 17 subsidiaries; Havas 44; Électricité de France 75; the SNCF 23, and it participates in 57 other companies. Électricité de France operates mines, a vineyard, a hotel company, and a garage and owns real estate. The SNCF has an interest in a company which delivers packages from door to door, in the Compagnie Française du Tourisme, the Groupement Auxiliaire de la Sidérurgie, the Consommateurs de Pétrole, and other organizations.

The complete list of all the partial interests of the big nationalized industries is not officially known. The confusion surrounding this area is one of the commonest grounds of attack against the nationalized industries. The practice of acquiring partial interests outside the legitimate boundaries of nationalized activities threatens private enterprises with the permanent danger of a sort of privileged imperialism because of the large financial means of the nationalized industries. At the same time it threatens the public treasury with the constant menace of concealed and greater losses. Although some of the comments made on this subject have, perhaps, been exaggerated, it would seem desirable for some new system of control to bring about the clarity that is necessary.

VII

The Organization of the Nationalized Industries

T HE French administrative system was developed at a time when the state conducted economic activities only in exceptional cases. As a result it has not been an easy matter to adapt the concepts upon which this administrative system is based to the new facts of large-scale nationalization. For example, the concept of public service is well known to French law and French administration, but some contemporary writers claim that it cannot be applied to the entire public sector without depriving that concept of almost all its meaning. If this were the case, the nationalized industries could not logically be organized in the same way as the public services. Nor would it be appropriate to apply to the industries which unquestionably are public services, like electricity and gas, but which developed as private enterprises, the same legal principles that apply to publicly owned organizations like universities and hospitals. Consequently, the new publicly owned industries have been absorbed into the framework of the French administrative system only by creating important exceptions to the traditional principles of that system.

The organizational structure of the nationalized industries is far from uniform. This fact is amply explained by the diversity in origin, age, activities, size, and operating conditions of the various public enterprises. The variety in organization has been increased by the variations in the prevailing climates of opinion at the different times when the individual enterprises were acquired by the state, as well as by the procedure followed when the most recent nationalization acts were prepared. While some of the acts, such as the one for coal, were the object of serious study and profited from the lessons of experience, others, such as those for electricity and gas, were drafted hastily. Their authors even admitted that the legislation is badly in need of clarification on a number of points.

In fact, a general reorganization of the nationalized industries is necessary. A general statute should have been drafted to simplify and standardize their organization, at the same time leaving room for adaptation to particular situations. The Council of State pointed out the need for such reorganization as early as 1945. The following year the Committee on Administrative Reform attached to the office of the Premier recognized the same need. Three private bills calling for the adoption of a general statute have been introduced. In 1947 the Economic Council debated the matter and drafted a report. In 1948 a government bill was introduced. The report on this bill prepared by the National Assembly's Committee on Economic Affairs was itself followed by a new private bill, which modified the government bill at several major points. But from year to year, parliamentary discussion of these measures has been delayed. The Control Commission of Public Enterprises (Commission de Vérification des Comptes des Entreprises Publiques) has pointed out the urgency of an over-all reform of the nationalized industries in all its reports.[1]

Only minor changes have been made in the original nationalization acts. It is therefore important to sketch the broad outlines of these laws, in all their diversity. It will be noticed that each variety corresponds to the current fashion of the period of its adoption; that varied forms and purposes masquerade under the same names; and that the laws take their meaning from the way in which changing governments have chosen to interpret them.

[1] Three reports have been issued so far: 1949, 1951, and 1952. (For the most recent one, see *Annexe Administrative, Journal Officiel,* October 3, 1952.)

OLDER FORMS OF PUBLIC ENTERPRISE

The Régie and the Public Office

A *régie* is a public agency operating under direct governmental control. In the nineteenth century it was the organizational structure used for all the public services that were not carried out by private concerns under government franchises.

When the economic activities of the state expanded, however, the systematic use of the régie presented serious difficulties. New methods became necessary. The need for new methods was felt first in the financial sphere; this is why the theory of separate budgets for economic enterprises was advanced during the early years of the twentieth century. It was anomalous and confusing, it was argued, for the receipts and expenses of industrial operations to be included in the budget submitted annually for parliamentary approval. It was impossible under these circumstances to evaluate the administration of a publicly owned industry, to organize its long-term finances, or to float loans to secure funds for its operation. Thus certain public enterprises received separate financial status, entitling them to a special budget and giving them the right to borrow. This was the system used for the state railroads from 1882 to 1926, and it is the system still used for the postal, telegraph, and telephone service (on the basis of a 1923 statute).

But still Parliament had to vote these separate budgets annually, a procedure which gave very little satisfaction to the partisans of a really businesslike system of management. The need for such management having been widely emphasized after 1918, a drive for greater autonomy developed. It found organizational expression in the "public office," which grew in popularity between 1918 and 1936.

The formula of the public office was applied not only to state industrial activities but also to many administrative services, like the Wheat Office, the Immigration Office, and the Exchange Office.

All the offices are separate administrative agencies of the state, endowed with a special task, which means that they are public corporations (*établissements publics*) within the meaning of French administrative doctrine. They all have autonomous budgets which do not require parliamentary action and which are drawn up by their own boards of directors and simply submitted to the appropriate minister for approval.

Many offices, however, especially the industrial offices, had certain characteristics different from those of ordinary public corporations—characteristics which foreshadowed the nationalized industries of 1944 and later.

The Office Nationale de l'Azote, for example, has an eighteen-member board of directors, including nine representatives of the various interested ministries, a president designated by the Minister of Public Works, seven representatives of various "interests" such as agricultural associations, chambers of commerce, and producers of electricity and coal, and two specialists. The board fixes prices, salaries, and wages; it can carry out all commercial operations; and it can even enter into an agreement with its private competitors.

But state control is heavy-handed. The approval of the appropriate minister is necessary not only for the budget but for any decision on policies going beyond current operations. The distribution of profits is decided by the minister. The balance sheets and statements are supervised by an accountant named by the minister and, since 1935, by a *contrôleur d'état*. The administration is under the control not only of the Cour des Comptes but also of the Inspection des Finances.

As a result, the industrial offices were subjected to two contradictory types of criticism. They were, on the one hand, reproached for enjoying excessive autonomy. The complaints directed against the industrial offices in the period of budgetary deflation from 1930 to 1939 were, for that matter, valid for the whole group of offices, whose multiplication was a matter of concern and a source of uncertainty for the Minister of Finance. As a result, several acts, especially the decrees of October 30, 1935, and March 20, 1939, tightened financial controls, abolished many offices, and prescribed that in the future only those would be maintained whose autonomy "is justified because of their origin or their economic, social, professional, intellectual or artistic role."

On the other hand, the representatives of the offices complained that the statutes conferred upon them an autonomy that was more formal than real, and that they could not operate in a businesslike manner because of the multiplicity and the type of controls to which they were subjected.

It should be pointed out that these two types of criticism converge at one point. The bureaucratic character of the offices, which deprived their directors of initiative and responsibility, could not fail to transfer to the state, in law or in fact, the difficulties accumulated by a management lacking both incentives and material means.

The Mixed Corporation

After 1930 there was a renewed attempt to follow as closely as possible the forms and practices of private business.

The simplest solution seemed to be to make the state a stockholder "like the others," the holder of shares in a corporation which would thereby become a mixed corporation. The existence alongside this stockholder of other private stockholders did not appear to be an obstacle to the "sane operation" of the business, but actually appeared to be its guarantee. It satisfied all legal requirements while leaving in positions of control persons with a direct interest in the profitability of the business. When the state holds a majority of the stock, it can theoretically follow any policy whatsoever, even one which produces no profits, although it would then run the risk of frightening the private stockholders. Even minority participation has the advantage of giving the state a right to examine the administration of a business, which may possibly become the yardstick for the industry. In this sense, the mixed corporation can be a useful instrument of economic leadership.

Just as the offices, based on the norms of administrative law, had to adopt the different practices of private business in order to satisfy different economic requirements, the mixed corporations, which are theoretically identical with private corporations, follow a very uneven pattern.[2]

In the first place, for many, and the most important, of them the "mixed" nature of the corporation is only a façade. How can one count on the intervention of the private stockholders when the state, with the four Sociétés Nationales de Constructions Aéro-nautiques, owns from 90 to 98 percent of the capital stock?

The state, by its very nature, cannot be a stockholder "like the others" and "like the others" risk the nation's capital. A mixed corporation must be established by law. The corporation must set aside certain administrative posts for the state and submit itself to the external control of state commissions. Moreover, when the state is a minority stockholder or when it is a bondholder, the laws applying to each corporation give the state powers which do not exist in private corporations, like a veto power over directors' decisions.

Although the mixed corporation is more closely related to state capitalism than to nationalization with tripartite management as envisaged by the CGT, the influence of the latter conception was felt in the nationalization acts of 1936 with the introduction into the corporation structure of "interest" representation, as in the SNCF.[3]

The mixed corporation met with so many criticisms that it was not adopted as an organizational form when the chief nationalization acts were passed after the Liberation. It has been said that it encourages indiscriminate and excessive state participation in economic affairs and multiplies the waste of public funds. When

[2] The degree, too, of state participation in the forty mixed corporations existing at present varies greatly. It ranges from 4 percent in the case of Hispano-Suiza to 99 percent for Continental Films.

[3] The Société Nationale des Chemins de Fer Français is the most important mixed corporation. Since 1944 the board of directors has consisted of twenty members: five represent the old companies and are named by them, five represent the workers, and ten are representatives of the state, appointed by the Minister of Public Works from certain selected groups of high civil servants. The president, who is appointed by ministerial decree, must be one of the representatives of the state. A government commissioner also sits on the board. The state's influence, therefore, is dominant.

the state is a minority stockholder, it is involved in a system which alone deserves the name "state capitalism"; when the state is a majority stockholder, it provides surviving private interests with a degree of security on which they did not count when they entered the business and, in practice, often confers upon them powers—directly over the enterprise and indirectly over public funds—which are more extensive than the letter of the law might lead one to believe. In this connection, the organization of the SNCF in particular has been attacked because of the very large role it leaves to the old companies.

The most serious difficulties arise when the state, holding a majority of the stock, as in the SNCF, really transforms the mixed corporation into a sort of office, differing only from a genuine office by being camouflaged with the trappings of private business, and linked to the state budget by agreements that make the state responsible for unlimited deficits.

The state is then forced to multiply controls. In addition to the controls established by pre-1939 legislation and those bequeathed to it as a result of past abuses on the part of the companies, the SNCF found itself suffering from the new controls created after 1948 because of the general reaction against nationalized industries. A 1951 report points out that the SNCF is subject to fifteen different types of control: the control of its own accounting officers, the technical control of the Ministry of Transport, the financial control of a permanent commission, the control of the Commission de Vérification des Comptes, and the whole body of administrative, governmental, and parliamentary controls which apply to all public enterprises.[4]

CHIEF CHARACTERISTICS OF THE NEW INDUSTRIES

The discrediting of the offices, which were considered to be too bureaucratic and not sufficiently flexible, and the attacks on the mixed corporations, which were regarded as binding the state to

---

[4] *Journal Officiel, Avis et Rapports du Conseil Économique,* No. 8, December 13, 1951, p. 277.

an undesirable economic system, were to lead the First Constituent Assembly to seek new formulas. There was, however, a certain amount of continuity between the pre-1944 and the post-1944 formulas.

Like the offices, the new public enterprises have individual legal status and financial autonomy, but in contrast with the offices, they do not as a rule have to prepare a budget. They are not subject to the administrative and financial controls established in 1935 and 1944. They are exempted from the rules of public accounting. More often than not they have their own capital, distinct from that of the state but subject to the regulations that protect state property. Borrowing is done, theoretically, in the same way it is done by private enterprise. No employee has the status of a civil servant; the president of the board himself can be and is chosen from outside the ranks of officialdom.

The new enterprises are more like mixed corporations, especially those in which the state owns almost all of the stock, than the offices are. But the ultimate operative principle is, in theory, different: the representatives of the state are not the spokesmen of "state capitalism" but of the general interest.[5]

Despite this legal ambiguity, two principles stand out as the chief ones underlying the new public enterprises, for they are in evidence in all the postwar nationalization acts. First, there is a desire to have the industries pass into public ownership without giving the government direct control over those industries—a principle expressed in the slogan *nationaliser sans étatiser*. The second principle, closely linked to the first, is that of interest representation: all the groups with an interest in the enterprise should participate in its management. It will be noted that this principle corresponds to syndicalist doctrine. It meant a return to the formula of the Régie Coopérative, and it also was a step in harmony with certain evolutionary tendencies of private enter-

[5] The post-1944 statutes did not clarify the meaning of the concept of public enterprise (*établissement public*). The expression, which appears in some of the nationalization acts, seems to have been used unsystematically and, in any case, would not appear to be uniformly applicable, legally, to all the new public enterprises, some of which are not really public service industries.

prise, whose doctrine and, to a certain extent, whose practice tend to make the corporation a sort of community. The boards of directors of the new public enterprises were to consist of representatives of the state, the workers, and the consumers.

To say that these two principles were at the basis of all the major nationalization acts is not to say, of course, that they are not expressed in practice in a variety of forms. It is quite evident, as the experience of the mixed corporations had already demonstrated, that the state could not become a stockholder "like the others." The position of the state was even more unusual when it became the sole stockholder, because this situation reduced to nothing the sovereign corporate organ, the stockholders' meeting, whose authority had to be transferred to some other agency. Moreover, the practical consequences of the principle of interest representation on a tripartite basis could vary considerably depending upon the size of the representation given to the respective groups and the powers granted to the boards themselves.

The syndicalist tendency, which confers authority on a board of directors with a majority of members representing collective interests other than those of the state, has been doctrinally predominant and has been applied in the most important nationalization acts—those passed by the First Constituent Assembly in April and May of 1945 nationalizing the electricity, gas, and coal industries. Its influence, which is supported by an old tradition, is so great that few proposals for reform have openly rejected it, and some have adopted it. The experience of five years, however, has produced a reaction not only against abuses of this formula but against certain basic principles of the formula itself.

Another tendency can be called autonomist, which refuses to confer too much authority, control, and responsibility on either the government or representatives of various interests. This tendency has developed less clearly and often less consciously than have the others. It is nevertheless reflected in the nationalization of the banks and the insurance companies; it has been expressed in several bills; and it rests on a doctrine stemming from British and American practice.

But, finally, the statist (*étatiste*) tendency, which reserves the maximum of powers to the state and to its representatives, has not died. This tendency springs from the tradition of the office system and was applied in the first postwar nationalization acts, notably in the case of the Régie Renault. Some proponents of reform of the nationalized industries would like to move farther in this direction.

No effort will be made to give a complete description of each nationalization statute. Instead, a description follows of some typical statutes which express each of the tendencies enumerated above. Then the main changes, both legal and practical, which have been made since the statutes were passed will be discussed. Lastly, a section will be devoted to a general criticism of the nationalized industries and the proposals for reform will be examined.

THE SYNDICALIST FORMULA: GAS, ELECTRICITY, AND COAL

The three industries nationalized by the laws of April 8 and May 17, 1946, have several common characteristics, two of the most important being what may be called their federal and syndicalist features.

It appeared wise to the First Constituent Assembly to avoid both the disadvantages of bigness and the complaints directed at big public enterprises by creating decentralized organizations. In addition, the principle of tripartite management was at first applied in all its purity. Both the distribution of authority within the industry and the composition of the board of directors, therefore, reflected syndicalist doctrine. Very quickly, however, difficulties developed. Abuses, made possible by the vagueness of the tripartite formula, were committed by the Communist party in order to win exclusive control over the nationalized industries for political purposes. The government found it necessary to recover in fact the powers that it had abandoned in theory to groups which might not be operating in the general interest.

Decentralization

The nationalized coal, electricity, and gas industries have both national and regional offices. All of them enjoy the status of "national public corporations of an industrial and commercial character." They are all theoretically endowed with financial autonomy and technical and commercial independence.

Électricité de France and Gaz de France each have a national office and regional distribution offices.[6] In principle, the national office has the responsibility for over-all planning and supervises the production and transmission of energy, while distribution is left to the regional offices. These regional offices, however, have been organized slowly and, as yet, incompletely.

For the coal industry, the national office is Charbonnages de France, and the regional offices are the Houillères de Bassin, of which there are now nine. The Houillères are charged with the production and the sale of coal. Charbonnages directs, controls, and coordinates the activities of the Houillères. It prepares the production plan, proposes prices to the government, floats loans, and coordinates the borrowing done by the Houillères.

The authority of the central organs over the regional organs is ensured by a variety of methods. Representatives of the national offices are appointed to the regional offices of all three industries. The national offices play the same role in the appointment and removal of regional directors that the government plays with respect to the appointment and removal of national directors. The national offices, in short, carry out the major supervisory functions.

[6] Although governed by a single law, Électricité de France (EDF) and Gaz de France (GDF) were supposed to be independent of one another. This goal has been approached only slowly and partially. In fact, a convention of May 16, 1946, turned the administration of Gaz de France back to Électricité de France. It was not until January 1, 1949, that the separation of the two services was ordered. It is, however, still far from complete. Certain activities are carried out by common personnel and certain regional administrative offices are still jointly operated. Moreover, the two industries have the same treasury, and the deficit of the gas industry, which results from rates that are kept deliberately low for political reasons, is balanced by advances from Électricité de France.

It should be pointed out that this distribution of authority between two echelons of equally "autonomous" public agencies has not functioned without difficulty, especially in the coal industry. The reason for this is that the system of tripartite representation for all the boards of directors means that there are directors on both levels who have been nominated by the same organization and who have common interests. There may not be much difference in outlook between representatives of the consumers or the employees just because they sit on different boards with different responsibilities. As a matter of fact, there have been cases when the lower echelon has overruled the higher echelon because of a particular juxtaposition of directors named by the same groups.

Interest Representation

The tripartite composition of the managerial boards is an essential feature of syndicalist doctrine. It was applied strictly, at least outwardly, in the national board of directors of Électricité de France, Gaz de France, and Charbonnages de France until the reforms of May 11, 1953. Of the eighteen members of each board, six represented the state, six the consumers, and six the employees.

In the distribution services of Électricité de France and Gaz de France the general interest was represented by four delegates of the national office, while the employees had six representatives and the consumers eight. The boards of the Houillères de Bassin had nineteen members, six representing Charbonnages de France, six representing the consumers, and seven representing the employees.

Establishing mathematically equal representation for certain broad interests, however, is only the first and simplest step in the application of the principle of tripartite management. It is in the next steps that the really difficult problems arise, and if these problems are not solved, what outwardly appears to be a perfect application of tripartism may be something quite different.

Who, for example, is qualified to represent the employees? The nationalization acts for electricity and gas and for coal hardly answer this question with the precision that might be desired.

They do specifically state how many representatives the various kinds of employees—office workers, industrial workers, foremen, and so forth—should have. But they say only that the "most representative" unions are qualified to nominate the workers' representatives. This does not designate any one union, of course, but it opens the door to possibly arbitrary decisions. And nothing in the laws says that the representatives of the workers must be chosen from the workers in the enterprises themselves, which, in itself, poses a serious issue.

It is even more difficult to determine who should represent the consumers, as there are no consumers' organizations as such. Big industries are large consumers of electricity, gas, and coal, but they cannot be given too much representation without running the risk of creating a vertically integrated system for the benefit of the private industries. It is consonant with the tradition of the Régies Coopératives to allow delegates of local communities which are consumers to act as representatives of the consumers, but this system is workable only for the regional offices of the nationalized industries and not for the national offices. Under these circumstances, the law can either designate the categories of consumers to be represented or leave it to the government to name, at its discretion, the representatives of the consumers. The disadvantage of the former procedure is that it is arbitrary, while the disadvantage of the latter is that it permits the government to increase the number of its own representatives.

Even if the problem of determining which groups are to be represented can be solved, another important problem immediately arises. Who is to appoint and remove the representatives themselves? Pure syndicalist doctrine, as it is expressed in certain proposals for the general revision of the nationalization statutes, holds that the representatives of the various groups should be appointed by the groups themselves. The present laws provide for the appointment of the board members by the minister, after their nomination by the interested groups. It does not seem possible for the minister, in practice, to refuse to accept the nominations which are made.

The government representatives on the original boards of directors were jointly appointed by several ministers, who were frequently in disagreement. The decrees of May 11, 1953, reduced the number of government representatives on the major boards of directors to four and provided that these be appointed, one by the Minister of Finance, one by the Minister of Economic Affairs, one by the Minister of Industry, and the fourth jointly by these three ministers.

Each board of directors is presided over by a president, who is elected by the board from its own membership. The main executive of each office, however, is the general manager, who, according to the statutes, must be a "competent person." The general managers of the regional offices of the coal, electricity, and gas industries are appointed by the regional boards. The general managers of the national offices, however, are appointed by decree of the Council of Ministers, after nomination by the national boards. Theoretically, the government seems to have the right to remove the general managers of the national offices, but as a new appointment would require nomination by the boards, it would seem that the boards actually have the last word in the selection of the key managerial personnel.

Rise and Fall of Communist Domination

The composition of the first boards of directors for the gas, electricity, and coal industries revealed clearly the inherent difficulties of the nationalization laws and the large areas that they left open to political manipulation. The Minister of Industrial Production at that time was a Communist, Marcel Paul, and the leading union, the CGT, was Communist-controlled. The schism in the CGT, which produced the non-Communist union, the CGT-Force Ouvrière, had not yet taken place. As a result, the boards of directors quickly took on political coloration and tripartite representation vanished.

Paul took advantage of every opportunity—he named members of the CGT as representatives of the state and of the consumers (the CGT had always claimed that it was qualified to represent the consumers of coal, gas, and electricity)—and succeeded in giving predominance to one group, which directly contravened the spirit of tripartite management. Of the eighteen members of the first board of directors of Charbonnages de France, fourteen were union officials and twelve of these were leaders of the CGT. The president of the board was Victorin Duguet, the general secretary of the CGT Federation of Mine Workers. The presidents of the main Houillères were also members of the Communist party. A similar situation, although a less extreme one because the law was more precise in this case, developed at first in the electricity and gas industries.

A reaction quickly set in against this state of affairs, and various changes and adaptations were made, within the framework of existing laws. First of all, on August 5, 1946, a decree abrogated Marcel Paul's appointment of three leaders of CGT unions as representatives "of the major consuming industries and services." Between August 27, 1946, and April 11, 1947, the directors of the Houillères de Bassin were replaced.

When the Cabinet of Léon Blum was formed in December 1946, Robert Lacoste, a Socialist, replaced Marcel Paul as Minister of Industrial Production, and decrees affecting the organization of Charbonnages de France were issued on January 16 and June 17, 1947. These decrees clarified the way the representatives of the main consuming industries were to be named. The decree of June 12, 1947, said that "each member of the board must be independent of the interests he is not representing." The term of office of the directors was reduced from six years to three, with one-third of the directors to be renewed every year. Also, as in private corporations the directors now receive special fees for attendance at board meetings. The provisions of these decrees went into effect on January 1, 1948, and they produced some important changes in the membership and attitudes of the boards of directors of nationalized industries.

The political difficulties of interest representation, as well as the particular problems created by Communist pressures, are well illustrated by the experience of the Charbonnages de France. In the beginning the state was represented by six delegates; the consumers by three representatives of the "principal consuming industries and services" (nominated by the SNCF, Électricité de France, Gaz de France, and the employers' associations of the interested industries); and three representatives of residential consumers, two of whom are nominated by the most representative unions, the other being nominated by the Union Nationale des Associations Familiales; and the employees by six persons nominated by the most representative national organizations of the various categories of workers.

In the fall of 1948 there was a serious miners' strike, during which mine-safety measures were suspended. Three members of the board of Charbonnages de France, all members of the CGT, approved of the interruption of the safety measures. Two decrees issued on October 29 and November 10 removed these three directors from the board, on the ground that their attitude had been incompatible with their position as directors. One of them held his seat as a representative of the consumers and could be replaced by government action. The other two, however, were representatives of the workers, and they have not yet been replaced because no new nominations have been made by the CGT. The board of directors of Charbonnages de France, therefore, has operated since late 1948 with only four representatives of the workers and without a single member who is also a member of the CGT.

The syndicalist idea was unable to escape the consequences of its internal contradictions. It was adopted as a reaction against the system of offices, in an attempt to give a maximum of autonomy to the nationalized industries. But there was no reason to think that the general interest would emerge triumphant when those who were presumed to represent it were in a minority on the board of directors. On the contrary, especially when the Communists were in control, the nationalized industries threatened to operate against the general interest and as a constant drain on the public treasury.

Communist control of the coal industry is ended, and the state has moved into the dominant position because, of the fourteen active members of the board of directors of Charbonnages de France, eight are high civil servants (two of them representing Électricité de France and Gaz de France, on one hand, and the SNCF, on the other).

The most striking perversion of tripartite management is now, therefore, a thing of the past, but it has nevertheless left its mark upon the nationalized industries. In fact, it may have dealt the death blow to the syndicalist conception of how a nationalized industry should be managed, because it led to the multiplication of government controls.

These controls, combined with the measures which had been taken in order to rid the various boards of the Communists and which meant the assertion of the authority of the government, proved to be quite effective. But they also greatly changed the original syndicalist approach to nationalization. The state, through its agents, has taken over the most important powers of management. The old distinction between the office and the nationalized industry under tripartite management is hardly there any more.

The grave difficulties of managing nationalized industries under the interest representation formula finally led to the reform decrees of May 11, 1953. These basically altered the balance of power on the boards of Électricité de France, Gaz de France, Charbonnages de France, and Houillères de Bassin.

The statement of purpose of the reform decrees set forth the necessity of reducing the number of members of the boards of directors so as to permit them to "make rapid decisions on problems of management." Rather than to strip the boards of part of their powers and responsibilities, which might have been transferred to executive committees, the government decided to reduce their size in order to increase their efficiency.

Actually, the changes effected transcend this motive. They involve not merely a reduction in the size of the boards but a transformation of their constitutent elements.

In Électricité de France, Gaz de France, and Charbonnages de France, the boards are reduced from eighteen to twelve members. The four representatives of the state and the four employee representatives are still selected essentially in the same manner as were the former six representatives of these two categories. The important change is in the representation of consumers. The six consumer representatives are replaced by four individuals "chosen for their competence in industrial and financial affairs, two of whom shall represent consumers." These individuals are appointed by decree and without a preliminary process of nomination.

Organized labor is critical of the appointments made to the Charbonnages de France, asserting that the naming of an operator of inland waterway transport and of a private mine owner among the competent individuals destroys the balance of the board and plainly amounts to statism. On the basis of these criticisms all four of the wage earners' unions have actively opposed the reforms of May 11. The CGT nominated a representative whom the government found unacceptable. The CGT announced its intention of sending no representative at all to the new board. Force Ouvrière and the Confédération Générale des Cadres, whose representatives had been appointed, recalled them on June 8. On the other hand, the Union Nationale des Associations Familiales complains that its representative was appointed without prior consultation.

As far as the Houillères are concerned, their board of directors is reduced to ten members, of whom four represent employees, two the state, and two the Charbonnages de France. Again two individuals are to be appointed by virtue of their special competence. Trade union elements in particular regret the disappearance of representatives of local bodies (*conseils généraux*) and fear the eventual creation of a majority on the board which will support the state at the expense of employees. Protests on this score have again been lively.

It can no longer be said that the coal, gas, and electricity industries enjoy too much freedom. Rather it may be regretted that because of the breadth and multiplicity of control devices, responsibility is diluted while the ideal of businesslike management is as remote as ever.

THE AUTONOMIST FORMULA

Nationalized banks, insurance companies, and steamship and air lines are organized differently from other public enterprises for a variety of reasons. In the areas in which they operate only partial nationalization has taken place, and therefore they remain in competition with private enterprise. Even among nationalized banks and insurance companies, it is in the public interest to have competition. Finally, a shortage of top managerial personnel has justified the retention of the methods of private enterprise. In shipping and air transport, there is the additional reason that they received their present structure in 1948, at a time when the reaction had already set in against the doctrines of 1946, when the major nationalization acts were passed. Accordingly, the decisions made in 1948 are in effect a repudiation of the ideas which had been so popular only two years earlier.

Banking and Insurance

The nationalized banks and insurance companies may be placed in one category because they have two important characteristics in common: they remain in competition with private enterprise and they retain their individual identities as separate corporations. The nationalized banks and insurance companies continue to operate under their old names. The only difference is that the state has taken them over.

Of course, the "competitive" nature of the whole group of private and public enterprises in the banking and insurance fields has undergone some important modifications: two national councils (the Conseil National du Crédit and the Conseil National des Assurances) have authority over each area. Each national council is of tripartite composition. These councils have an important, although mainly a consultative role. In addition, the Commission de Contrôle des Banques, which is dominated by representatives of the state, has its own powers of control. It nevertheless remains true that, side by side with private organizations, the public enterprises must seek profits and remain as faithful as they can to capitalist practices.

Each of the former private enterprises, having retained its corporate form, has its own board of directors. For the banks, each board consists of four representatives of the industrial, commercial, or agricultural professions; four representatives of the big unions; two representatives of the Bank of France; and two banking experts. The boards of the insurance companies include three insurance experts; three representatives of the state; three representatives of the employees; and three representatives of the policy holders.

It is apparent, therefore, that the state is in a minority position, and that the boards contain a sizable number of "experts." The presence of the experts prevents, at least for insurance, domination by private interests. This can be considered one expression of the autonomist tendency.

The experts were recruited from the managerial groups of the old private banks and insurance companies in a way that ensured the selection of competent people—the same system that was used in England. Nevertheless, some critics have regarded the selection of experts as evidence of the unchanged character of banking and insurance after nationalization and as leading to the maintenance of "capitalist" attitudes. Undoubtedly it is in order to encourage continuance of the search for optimum operating conditions and maximum profits that competition has been maintained even among public enterprises and remains very active.

But the "private" approach is sharply limited in many cases. Although the Commission de Contrôle des Banques and the Conseil National des Assurances can be said to play the part of the stockholders' meeting, they do not have all the powers of stockholders: directors are appointed by the minister, for example, and so is the general manager of the insurance companies. An agent of the Commission de Contrôle, holding broad powers, sits with the board of directors of the banks. Loans cannot be floated by the insurance companies without the authorization of the government. Also, the organs of control over the entire public sector of the economy, the parliamentary committees and the Commission de Vérification des Comptes, have jurisdiction over the banks and insurance companies.

Despite these limitations, these state corporations enjoy a good deal of autonomy, because they operate in competitive areas. Their organization is a far cry from both the statist and the syndicalist models.

Shipping and Air Transport

A new step in the movement away from the prevailing fashions of April and May 1946, when syndicalist orthodoxy was at its peak of popularity, was taken by the law of February 28, 1948, on shipping.

The general supervisory agency, the Conseil Supérieur de la Marine Marchande, consists of representatives of the state, private shipping, and the employees, with the representatives of the state having a majority. It may make final decisions in certain cases, but the most important decisions must be made by the minister. A general program of organization, construction, and operations for the lines is drawn up by the minister, after consultation with the Conseil.

Both state-owned shipping companies are mixed corporations.[7] As mixed corporations, the two companies have stockholders' meetings. The boards consist of a president and a general manager, both appointed by decree, two representatives of the private stockholders, three representatives of the employees, and six other persons appointed by the government, three of whom are civil servants and three of whom are experts.

---

[7] The two nationalized companies are the Compagnie Générale Transatlantique (the French Line), in which the state holds 80 percent of the stock, and the Compagnie des Messageries Maritimes, which is the result of a merger between the former privately owned company of the same name with the Services Contractuels des Messageries, which was state property. The CGT continues to be a mixed corporation, while the CMM became one. This constitutes an innovation among the post-Liberation nationalization acts, which generally abandoned the formula of the mixed corporation.

The abandonment of tripartism is thus revealed in the composition of both the Conseil Supérieur and the boards of directors. Consumers are not represented because of the difficulty of identifying consumer interest. On the other hand, several experts, as for banking and insurance, are appointed by the state. The control mechanism indicates a desire to return to the customary procedures of private corporations. There are, however, a number of circumstances in which the prior approval of the minister must be obtained before action can be taken.

The organization of air transport presents many analogies with that of shipping, but it goes a step farther in repudiating pure syndicalist doctrine.

The government-owned air lines do not constitute a monopoly any more than government-owned shipping does. Private aviation companies exist, even though they are much less significant than private shipping companies. Also, while naval construction is in private hands, aircraft construction is mainly in the hands of the state.

The principal air line company is Air-France. It is the result of a merger of three former mixed corporations, Air-France, Air-Bleu, and Air-France Transatlantique, whose privately owned stock was transferred to the state in 1945. The new Air-France, unlike the Compagnie Générale Transatlantique, is an entirely new company, which acquired the property of other corporations, rather than an old company whose stock was transferred to the state.

Like the shipping companies, however, Air-France is a genuine corporation, and the law of June 16, 1948, went so far as to require the state to sell 30 percent of its shares. A maximum of 15 percent was to be sold to private individuals and the rest to local communities and other public enterprises.

Thus, the earlier tendency to abandon the mixed corporation was reversed in the hope of attracting a certain amount of private capital in a field in which the predominance of the public interest is not entirely clear.

The composition of the board of directors also demonstrates the retreat from the dogma of tripartite management. The board consists of four representatives of private stockholders, civil servants representing the state, four representatives of the employees, and four experts appointed by the minister.

Although this system still retains some vestige of consumer representation, the idea is practically abandoned and emphasis is placed on having trained managers represent the general interest.

It should be noted also that there is a somewhat unfortunate confirmation of the earlier tendency to regard the members of the board simply as instructed delegates of the groups which have nominated them. Article 5 of the statute states that the "representatives" must be replaced "when they cease during their term of office to represent the organization upon whose recommendation they have been appointed." On the other hand, it wisely requires that the representatives of the workers must have worked in the enterprise for two years.

THE STATIST FORMULA:
THE RÉGIE RENAULT

The Régie Renault was one of the first public enterprises to be created after the Liberation. While it has a status similar to that of a corporation, it is not a corporation. The authority of the state over its operations is much greater than it is over the other nationalized industries. This is quite remarkable, for if there is a company which faces the usual problems of business it is certainly the Régie Renault, whose activities cannot be called a public service and whose competitive character is beyond doubt. It is the largest automobile company in France, but it has, in firms like Peugeot, Citroen, and Simca, direct and active competitors.

The peculiar position of the Régie Renault and the predominance of the state are manifested in various ways. The board of directors of the Régie Renault is based on the tripartite formula. It includes, in addition to its chairman, fifteen members who are named by the Minister of Industrial Production for a six-year term, one-third of the membership being renewed every two years. The position of the government, however, is dominant: it appoints the chairman of the board and seven members who are to represent the consumers. Six representatives of the workers are chosen by the minister from the delegates elected by the workers to the central shop committee.

The shop committee has various functions involving social matters such as the direction of social work. In the economic sphere, it examines the general conduct of the business but has only a consultative role.

The general manager is appointed by decree. He is not a civil servant and theoretically has no guarantee of tenure, as the government may remove him by decree. The extent of his personal responsibility is not made clear by the law. He holds, however, extensive powers. The powers of the board of directors are broad also: it deliberates on all important matters concerning the company. But its role, in practice, is purely advisory. If there is a conflict between the board and the general manager—which is very unlikely—the conflict is resolved by the Minister of Industrial Production. It is, therefore, the executive branch of the government which has the last word.

In contrast with the system of offices, the administrative practices of the Régie Renault are completely different from those usually followed by public agencies. There is no budget, strictly speaking; there are only estimates, which have an indicative value but which are not limiting. These estimates, as well as projected loans, are approved by the appropriate minister.

The controls established by the decrees of October 25 and 30, 1935, over public enterprises and over associations do not affect the Régie Renault. Its accounts are not, like those of the coal industry, for example, subject to state auditing. The regular auditing is done by Commissaires aux Comptes, as it is for any ordinary corporation. These Commissaires, who are expert auditors, are appointed by order of the Minister of Finance.

The Régie Renault must follow the fiscal practices of ordinary corporations. If there are profits—there have been each year since it was created—the disposable balance, after deductions for depreciation and reserves, is distributed among the public treasury, social works, and the workers. As this distribution is not based on any single rule applicable at all times but is determined by annual ministerial orders, an antagonism that sometimes reaches violent proportions develops between the workers and the state.

When there is a loss, the state should not, theoretically, be responsible for making up the deficit. There is no legal reason why a declaration of bankruptcy cannot be made. In fact, the Régie, which is run like an excellent industrial enterprise, runs no more risk of failure than a private enterprise. The French government is always ready to extend aid either to public or private enterprises when important social considerations are involved.[8] The possibility of bankruptcy, therefore, is highly unlikely.

Theoretically subject to close state control, the Régie Renault is much more autonomous in actual operation than the law would lead one to think. The exceptional quality of the man who has managed it since 1944, P. Lefaucheaux, and the results that he has achieved seem to give him a very strong personal position in the management of the company. In circumstances like these, the consequences of a statute that gives dominant control to the state are, in practice, quite different from what they seem to be in theory.

The state has been able to reduce controls to a minimum, and they are much less rigid for the Régie Renault than they are for the public enterprises that are governed by the syndicalist formula. Therefore, to the extent that the present general manager of the company has firm control over it, the real operative system of the Régie Renault is very close to the autonomist ideal —paradoxically much more so than that of the public enterprises which are much less closely linked to the state in theory but which are nevertheless much more closely controlled by it in practice.

[8] With reference to private enterprise, the pre-World War II experience of assistance to the motor car manufacturer Citroen and the 1932 rescue of the Banque Nationale du Crédit (now Banque Nationale pour le Commerce et l'Industrie) might be mentioned.

THE CONTROL SYSTEM

It has already been remarked several times how the creation of new controls, especially after the 1948 strikes, reduced the autonomy of the public enterprises. Most of these controls apply to all the public enterprises, including the mixed corporations.

Controls can be exercised in advance of administrative action, or they can be set up to verify, after the event, the legitimacy of actions taken in the course of a given period of time, usually the fiscal year.

One important area in which advance controls are broadly applied is that of investment. Since 1949 the investment programs of Électricité de France, Gaz de France, Charbonnages de France, the Houillères de Bassin, and the SNCF have had to be authorized in advance by legislation. This authorization is included in the appropriation bill for economic and social investments which is presented by the government with the annual budget.

The annual investment programs thus authorized, as well as the methods by which they are to be financed, are related by the General Planning Commission (Commissariat Général du Plan) to the plan for each industry, including, of course, the nationalized industries.

There is also a Committee on Investment (Commission des Investissements) which was created by a decree of June 10, 1948. This committee consists of the Minister of Finance, the General Planning Commissioner, the representatives of various ministries, and high civil servants. It examines the investment programs of the nationalized industries and gives its advice on these programs, their timing, and the ways in which they are financed.

Control over the day-to-day operations of the nationalized industries can be exercised by investigating committees, which are authorized by a decree of November 12, 1947, and by several special committees. A Committee for Research on Contracts was created on September 16, 1948, and two days later Committees on Contracts were established. The latter are attached to the public enterprises and report to the Ministry of Industry and

Commerce. These committees, which consist of high civil servants, delegates of the employees, and representatives of business and other public enterprises, give their advice on prospective contracts and it is followed by the different industries. On several occasions the Commission de Vérification des Comptes has praised the effectiveness of these committees.

The most important operative controls, however, are those set up by the decrees of May 11, 1953. These very strongly reinforce the powers which the government can exercise in the management process, through the medium of the chairmen of the supervisory committees [9] and of government commissioners.

Whereas the supervisory committees act on behalf of the Ministers of Finance and of National Economy, the government commissioner is appointed by order of the Minister of Industry. His function is primarily technical and is exercised only in connection with decisions already taken.

At the Houillères de Bassin, Charbonnages de France, Gaz de France, and Électricité de France, the chairmen and commissioner operate as follows:

Within three days after a decision is made, the government commissioner may demand its postponement if it "seems to him to be contrary to the public interest." The decision becomes enforceable eight days after his intervention if the minister has not in the meantime required its modification.

The veto power exercised by the government commissioner is complemented by the veto power of the chairman of the supervisory committee. The latter, like the government commissioner, attends meetings of the board of directors in an advisory capacity and may also attend meetings of subordinate administrative groups. The chairman of the supervisory committee likewise has three days within which he may demand the postponement of "any decision which may sensibly affect the expenses or resources of the enterprise or whose financial soundness could be called in

---

[9] These supervisory committees had been established by a decree of August 12, 1950, but were not actually organized. The reforms of May 11 appear to have put some life into them.

question." The decision becomes enforceable twenty days after his intervention unless the Ministers of Finance, National Economy, and Industry jointly require its modification.

The double veto thus provided, as it may affect practically every measure considered by the board of directors, calls into being changes far more basic than those resulting from the altered composition of the boards.

Trade union opposition has also been directed against these changes in the supervisory structure even though not with the same vigor which marked opposition to changes in the composition of the boards of directors.

The most useful instrument of postoperative control is the Commission de Vérification des Comptes, which was created by the law of January 6, 1948. The most interesting feature of this commission is its judicial character. Its president, who is appointed by decrees, is a Président de Chambre of the Cour des Comptes. The commission is composed of several sections, each of which consists of three members of the Cour des Comptes, a representative of the Minister of Finance, and a representative of the Minister of Economic Affairs.

This commission examines the accounts of the public enterprises, including the mixed corporations in which the state has a controlling interest. It sends special reports to the appropriate ministers and also publishes a general report. It must not only certify the accuracy of the accounts but also make any observations about the management and recommend any changes it feels are necessary.

The three general reports of the commission which have been published have been circulated widely. Their objective character has given them great weight, even though their most important recommendations have not been followed.

While the Commission de Vérification des Comptes exercises its functions with regard to the entire field of nationalized industry, the decrees of May 11, 1953, establish separate supervisory committees, made up of high civil servants, for each nationalized enterprise. They are designed to be completely independent of private interests, of the interests of the enterprises under their control, and even of the government.

Their most important function is exercised in the form of an annual report presented to the Minister of Economic Affairs and of France. A committee of experts will study the report and is charged with the task of recommending possible action on it to the government.

Another measure of practical importance in the control of the accounts of the nationalized industries was the requirement, set on October 22, 1947, that these industries follow the general accounting system established by the Commission de Normalisation des Comptabilités and approved by the Minister of National Economy. This system has not yet been as widely used in the private sector as is desirable, but it at least permits the accounts of the nationalized industries to be presented in a uniform and coherent manner.

The Commission des Investissements is functioning also as an agency of postoperative control, since it does not confine itself to proposing investments for the coming year but also analyzes and discusses the effects of those made the preceding year. By the end of 1951 this committee had published three important reports.

This is an extensive list of controls. In trying to determine whether or not they have been effective, it should be noted that postoperative controls can be regarded in two ways. They can be viewed as a way of discovering whether certain past behavior deserves censure, or as a touchstone for the orientation of future policy. If the latter conception is adopted, then the controlling authority, the state, must be able to act and to correct the errors that have been uncovered. In short, the state must have decisive powers, but this is something that syndicalist orthodoxy refuses to concede. If such controls, especially those exercised by the Commission de Vérification des Comptes, have produced positive results in recent years, it is only because the syndicalist structure has been profoundly modified. The state, either through its representatives on the boards of directors or through its *contrôleurs,* has had the authority necessary to remedy, at least partially, the abuses which it discovered.

The syndicalist conception of the role of controls is indeed quite different: controls are an instrument of distributive justice. Because of their power to censure past misbehavior, they exist to guarantee that the general interest will be respected by boards of directors which consist largely of representatives of private interests and which have been made as free as possible from advance state controls.

The nationalization acts, therefore, colored as they are by the syndicalist outlook, place much emphasis on sanctions, and so do some of the bills proposing a general reform, like the Thorez bill. The experience of recent years, however, proves that these sanctions are not effective.

The legal responsibility of the directors is real enough in certain matters, but the extent of their personal liability is not so great as that of their counterparts in private corporations. The only real sanction for mismanagement is to remove the directors. The decrees tightening government control over the nationalized industries rely heavily on the threat of removal.

The government can remove a director for having made serious mistakes; the directors of an industry which is running at a deficit cannot continue in office without specific governmental approval. By virtue of the decree of January 16, 1947, the boards of Charbonnages de France and the Houillères de Bassin may be dissolved if, after having been warned by the relevant ministers, they fail in their obligations, "especially by not maintaining the rate of output required by the national economy."

These legal provisions, unfortunately, do not have as much practical significance as might be expected. The removal of an individual director implies that responsibility can be directly determined, but this can be done only when there are numerous controls over the day-to-day operation of the industry.

Furthermore, all removals must be followed by the nomination of new directors by the same groups that nominated the directors removed. The example of the three directors who were members of the CGT and who were removed from the board of Charbonnages de France proves that the nominating organization will ordinarily support its delegates. Removals, therefore, actually threaten to upset the balance of the boards and can be resorted to only in exceptional cases. It should be recalled that Communist control of the boards was mainly ended, not by removal, but by the annulment of irregular appointments and by the issuance of decrees changing the tenure of office of the directors.

In conclusion, the various new controls, in conjunction with those which already existed, have unquestionably produced favorable results. At least part of the improvement in the operation of the public sector since 1948 can be traced directly to them. But it should be noted, however, that the number and complexity of the control agencies (there are from ten to fifteen of them, depending on the enterprise involved) threaten to prevent the nationalized industries from operating on a normal business basis. The whole structure should be simplified. What is needed is a general reform of the organization of all nationalized industries.

The decrees of May 11, 1953, undoubtedly are a step in that direction. Unfortunately, however, they carry within themselves doctrines that are not only varied but more or less contradictory as well.

First, the composition of the boards, the role assigned to the chairmen of the supervisory committees, and the creation of a committee of experts may all be taken as evidence of a certain desire to approach the autonomist solution which characterized the Schneiter-Pflimlin proposals. Yet in several ways there have been marked departures from this solution, as can be seen, for instance, in the drastic reduction of consumer representation on the boards of Électricité de France, Gaz de France, and Charbonnages de France, or in the elimination of representatives of local bodies from the board of the Houillères de Bassin.

Second, the choice of individuals classified as particularly competent seems in practice to have been guided more by the desire to secure the representation of new categories of interests than by the goal of introducing onto the boards "magistrates" impartial toward all interests.

Third, and most important, the combination of greater weight given to the representation of government interests on the boards and of greater powers given to supervisory elements does, in effect, mean a step toward statism. The chairman of the supervisory committee and the government commissioner both possess the legal means, through the use of their veto powers, of depriving the board of directors of any initiative. This arrangement may lead toward a state of immobility, which is the very worst form of statism.

It should be added that the conflicts of the summer of 1953 may lead to a revision of some of the May decrees, or at least to their very gradual application. Thus there may still be a delay before reforms which had appeared to many people to contain new and interesting features are effectively realized.

≫≫≫≫≫≫≫≫≫≫≫≫≫≫≫≫≫≫≫≪≪≪≪≪≪≪≪≪≪≪≪≪≪≪≪≪≪

VIII

Problems of Nationalization

WHILE the discovery of a generally satisfactory form of organization for nationalized industries may be the central problem of nationalization—or at least the most publicized one, since the search for improved organization is a continuing one—it is by no means the only problem of nationalization. There are other problems, similar or identical to those that face any industry, public or private, such as establishing a rational price policy, discovering optimum output, or operating at highest efficiency. Others are exclusively connected with the process of nationalization itself and have no counterpart in the world of private business. One of the most important problems of the second variety is to determine whether the former owners of the nationalized industries are to be compensated for their property and, if so, by what methods.

COMPENSATION OF THE FORMER OWNERS

Although some of the recent French nationalization acts made no provisions for the compensation of the owners, but were acts of confiscation for punitive purposes, as in the case of the Renault auto works, the most important nationalization acts adopted the principle that a just indemnity should be paid to the former owners. Once this principle was accepted, the problem still remained of finding a way to determine what was a just indemnity in each instance.

The value of an industry could not be determined through the market value of its total assets as there was no normal market for most of the industries in the nationalized sector, nor could it be determined by evaluating the tangible and intangible assets, as each of these items acquires value only as a function of the other.

It was therefore necessary to resort to another criterion, which in the majority of cases was the value of the stock of the company; the direct appraisal of the property to be transferred was employed only in a few exceptional cases. But how could even the value of the stock in the industries to be nationalized be determined? The uneasy market of post-Liberation France hardly provided a reliable indication of real values.

Nevertheless, the value of bank stocks was defined as the average market price between September 1, 1944, and October 31, 1945. For the Bank of France, it was set at a point between the book value of the stock and its average market price between September 1, 1944, and August 31, 1945. An evaluating committee was to set the compensation price within these limits.

For gas, electricity, and coal, a different system was used. Recent market prices were used to set the value of the stock, but only because they represented a percentage increase over the average stock market prices of 1938 which the Constituent Assembly was willing to allow, and not because of any intrinsic significance. Two base prices were used for gas and electricity: the average price between September 1, 1944, and February 28, 1945, and the price on June 4, 1945. For coal, the base period was the first six months of 1944, although the prices thus determined were multiplied by different coefficients, depending upon the coal field involved, and other adjustments were made as well. For all three industries, committees of financial experts and high civil servants determined the indemnities due to each party entitled to compensation.

Once the amount of compensation was settled, there still remained the problem of how it was to be paid. Direct payment in currency was out of the question because of the magnitude of the transactions. The replacement of the old stock with new stock was also precluded, since there was no intention of creating mixed corporations on the model of the SNCF. Moreover, such a substitution would invite criticism of the new enterprises, which were primarily intended to preform public services, whether or not they made profits. Payment in the form of life annuities was suggested, but this would have approached confiscation.

The Communist and Socialist parties wanted to pay the former owners with ordinary bonds, and this was done in the case of the Bank of France, whose stockholders initially received bonds bearing 2 percent interest. The protests against this low rate caused it to be raised to 3 percent in 1946. The stockholders of the commercial banks and the insurance companies received profit-sharing bonds. For gas and electricity, fifty-year bonds were issued in the name of the Caisse Nationale de l'Énergie, bearing 3 percent interest plus a supplement of at least 1 percent of the total gross revenue. The procedure was the same for coal, except that in this case, the supplementary interest was to be equal to 0.25 percent of the total revenue.[1] Except in the case of the Bank of France, therefore, the former owners were given a chance to participate in any future growth of the nationalized industries. The appreciation possibilities of coal, gas, and electricity bonds, however, are limited by their amortization features. All the securities issued are negotiable.

The compensation methods were severely criticized for a number of reasons. First of all, the government was exchanging income obligations that were largely fixed for equity securities during a period of inflation. Secondly, delivery of the new securities was delayed long after the old stock had been transferred to the state. In fact, distribution of the bonds for the coal industry was not started until 1949, and the bonds for the electricity industry have not yet been completely delivered. Then, there was criticism of the base periods chosen for evaluating the stock, for despite the various coefficients and supplements, the base period of 1944–1945 remained decisive in the evaluation process. It has been pointed out that the compensation paid for the coal industry was about

[1] The measures increasing the compensation beyond a fixed rate of interest originated in bills proposed by the MRP. The MRP, which voted in favor of the nationalization acts, advocated nationalization with "just" compensation.

45 billion francs, which represents one-fourth of the value of the annual coal production in 1951. Would any private businessman, it was asked by the Federation of Stockholders, willingly sell his business for a price equivalent to its gross revenue for one quarter? [2]

It was finally pointed out, as additional proof of the substantial damage suffered by French stockholders, that foreign stockholders were exempted from the general terms of the nationalization laws. On the request of the Minister of Foreign Affairs, Article 13 of the law dealing with gas and electricity left it to the government to settle by decree the cases of foreign stockholders.

PRICE POLICY

The problem of establishing a price policy for the nationalized industries varies from sector to sector.

The problem confronting the industries of the competitive sector is essentially that of adopting price policies suitable for companies which seem to be operating in an area of competition but which actually are not. For it is not true, as might appear at first glance, that the prices of the automobiles produced by the Régie Renault can be set in exactly the same way that prices are set for the automobiles turned out by its private competitors.

In the first place, the competitive area in France has been controlled in various ways for a long time. Until 1951, for example, the prices of automobiles had to be approved by the government, a situation which led to complaints on the part of the private producers. They accused the government of basing automobile prices in general upon the requirements of the nationalized Régie Renault in particular and, furthermore, of setting unnecessarily high prices.

Secondly, and quite apart from the first consideration, the fraction of the total output of a given industry produced by the nationalized sector of the industry must be taken into account. The Régie Renault produces one-third of the total French automobile output, which leads, in any case, to the application of the theory

---

[2] Louis Baudin, *Vingt Ans de Capitalisme d'État* (Paris, 1951), p. 62.

of oligopoly rather than to that of perfect competition. Under these circumstances, it is impossible to regard the price policy of the Régie Renault strictly as a function of a perfectly competitive market.

It is in the noncompetitive areas, however, that the problems of establishing a price policy arise in all their complexity. It is extremely important that the big nationalized industries define their price policies clearly. And the adoption of a policy necessarily involves choosing among various alternatives: between giving the nationalized industry complete financial autonomy (and responsibility), on the one hand, and throwing the burden of any deficit upon the public treasury and hence upon the nation as a whole, on the other; between satisfying one group of consumers or another; between various methods of financing; and, in the final analysis, between various interpretations of the concept of public service.[3]

The Marginal Cost Controversy

Several contemporary economists have advanced the principle that the prices of public service industries should be set at marginal cost.[4] The concept of marginal cost rests on the distinction, assumed to be valid in the short run, between a firm's fixed costs and its variable costs. Marginal cost, which is the variable cost of each additional unit produced, is less than average cost while the average cost decreases and greater than average cost when the latter is increasing.

[3] Price policy has always intrigued the French. The first theoretical studies of the problem were made by French mathematical economists like Jules Dupuit, a civil engineer who published *La Mesure de l'Utilité des Travaux Publics* in 1844; Augustin Cournot; Léon Walras; and Charles Colson, whose *Traité d'Économie Politique* contains one of the most complete studies of railroad rates ever made. It is not surprising, therefore, that the writings of English and American economists on the subject have been received with interest in France.

[4] The important articles by James E. Meade, Harry Norris, and Harold Hotelling have been collected in *La Rémunération du Travail*, Annexe 3, "Le coût et les prix" (Paris, 1946), put out by the Institut de Science Économique Appliquée.

The prices of private firms tend to be fixed, under perfect competition, at marginal cost. If the private firm enjoys a monopoly, however, there can be a substantial difference between the price and marginal cost in both the phase of increasing average cost and the phase of decreasing average cost.

What should be the policy of a monopolistic nationalized industry? The theory advanced by James E. Meade and accepted with some modifications by other economists holds that the rate structure of such an industry should tend to correspond to marginal cost. The basis for this thesis is expressed by Meade in this way: "In order to achieve that use of the community's resources which is both the most efficient and the most in conformity with consumers' wishes, they should be distributed among the various uses in such a way that the value of the marginal product of a given factor is the same in every occupation." [5] If it were otherwise, the variable factor, assumed to be divisible, would be attracted "too much" to certain uses and not enough to others. Certain needs would be oversatisfied and others undersatisfied relative to the requirements for the optimum distribution of the variable factor. There would therefore be bad social usage. This argument leads to the conclusion that a public enterprise producing several products or providing various services must price each of them at its own marginal value. This is the only way in which a faulty distribution of the factors of production can be avoided.

Gabriel Dessus illustrates this proposition in the following way: Assume a rural community which exploits, for its fuel, both a forest on the side of a mountain and a coal mine. Under competitive conditions, the output of the last miner is exactly equal in value to that of the last lumberjack if the prices of wood and coal are fixed at marginal cost. If the town were to take over both the mine and the forest and set the prices of coal and wood at average cost, for example, the result might be that the price of coal would change only slightly while that of wood would decrease considerably. Under these conditions, the demand for wood would increase

[5] "Price and output policy of state enterprises," *Economic Journal*, December 1944, p. 321.

and some miners would quit their jobs to become lumberjacks, in order to exploit the forest higher up on the mountain. The inequality of marginal operations would then be reflected in a loss for the entire community in terms of optimum resource allocation.

The only rule which guarantees the optimum use of the factors of production consists in setting prices at marginal cost. But the application of this rule would have different effects in different situations. If the demand for the products of a public enterprise and the technical conditions in which it operates are such that it is in a phase of rising average costs, marginal cost will be greater than average cost and there will be profits, or at least no losses. The only problem which arises in these circumstances is how to distribute the profits among the employees, the state, and the reinvestment requirements of the enterprise.

On the other hand, if the conditions are such that the public enterprise is operating completely, or largely, in a phase of decreasing average costs, the marginal cost will be less than average cost, and pricing at marginal cost will result in a deficit. In these circumstances, several major questions arise.

First of all, it is essential to determine which costs may properly be charged against the industry itself, in order to ascertain whether there actually is a deficit and, if there is one, in order to measure its magnitude with precision. In this connection, the major problem is to decide which charges are to be included among the fixed costs of the industry. How should depreciation charges be computed, for example? Would it be appropriate to include development costs? Should the industry be expected to finance, out of its own revenue, either completely or partially, its development program?

Secondly, once the existence of a deficit has been demonstrated, the basic question of whether or not the industry should continue to operate has to be faced. Continuance would be impossible under competitive conditions, and a privately owned monopoly could afford to continue to operate only by setting its prices above marginal cost. A publicly owned monopoly, however, *can* continue to operate, even though pricing at marginal cost would inevitably result in a deficit. And it may even be in the interest of the collective well-being for operations to be continued, perhaps because a key industry is involved. In fact, some people think that the very criterion of a public service industry—and the main justification for its nationalization—is that it would run at a deficit if its prices were fixed at marginal cost.

Lastly, how should the deficit be covered? Should it be borne by the national budget, which means throwing the burden on the taxpayers? Or should the consumers be asked to pay, over and above the price corresponding to marginal cost, a surcharge, perhaps differentiated according to categories of consumers?

These are, in summary form, the problems facing the managers of the nationalized industries, and research has been underway for some time in the effort to solve them satisfactorily.

French Research on Price Policy [6]

Research on price policy is being carried on at Électricité de France by Gabriel Dessus, the head of the national business office, and by Marcel Boiteux, an engineer in the same office, and at the Société Nationale des Chemins de Fer Français by Roger Hutter, chief engineer of the business office, and by Maurice Allais, a professor at the École des Mines, who has taken issue with Hutter on several basic points.

The operating conditions of Électricité de France and the SNCF are similar in many respects. They are both public utilities, they are both monopolies, and neither the product nor the clientele of either industry is homogeneous.

On the other hand, there is a difference in the elasticity of demand for the products of the two industries. While the SNCF

[6] The principle of pricing at marginal cost has been criticized by several English economists, such as R. H. Coase, Harry Norris, and W. A. Lewis. The purpose here, however, is not to enter the marginal cost debate but only to show how this controversy is developing among several French economists who are employed by some of the nationalized industries and who are trying to establish for these industries the basic principles on which a rational price policy, already partially achieved, can be erected.

must take serious cognizance of the existence of private road transport, Électricité de France need fear the use of other forms of energy only in a limited number of cases. And the main substitute products—coal, gas, and oil—are themselves produced by nationalized or closely controlled industries.

The research carried out by Électricité de France reveals that the rates charged by the old private companies varied greatly. They were not based on a systematic and coherent policy but rather were based only on empirical evaluations. A thorough overhauling of the price structure seems to be necessary.

Boiteux accepts and uses as his starting point Vilfredo Pareto's axiom that "any decision which increases the satisfaction of at least one individual without diminishing that of any other is a measure in the general interest." Just as the maximization of profit serves as the criterion for the private entrepreneur, Pareto's principle should be the guide for the "managers of the public interest."

Pareto's optimum is achieved, theoretically, by setting prices at marginal cost. But the application of such a price policy runs at once into three kinds of difficulties.

First, what *is* the marginal cost of a public utility? The accepted economic definition of marginal cost (called differential cost by Électricité de France) is that it is equal, if there is only one product, to the cost of production of one more unit of the commodity produced and, if there are several products, to the cost of production of one more unit of one of the products, the output of the others remaining constant.

If the economic definition of marginal cost is simple enough, its exact calculation is nevertheless difficult. Unless production is carried out under conditions of constant costs, marginal cost does not depend only on technical conditions but also on the elasticity of demand and on the volume of demand that the industry will have decided to satisfy. Fluctuations in the value of the currency must be taken into account, and also the difficulties of comparing the cost of plants and equipment taken over at the time of nationalization and future development costs. Since we must take into account development factors, any static analysis is impossible. Once it is not possible to regard investment as constant, it is necessary to decide whether prices are to be based on the marginal cost for a certain amount of capital plant or the different marginal cost which would result if the capital plant were expanded.

The second problem which arises concerns the noneconomic factors which may control the policy makers. The public service industry, occupying a key position in a national economic complex for which the political authorities are responsible, cannot follow a price policy without considering the needs of the entire economy. In this connection, it is essential that the prices of a nationalized industry be stable. The development of one industry is part of a larger scheme designed to transform the entire economic structure; it involves a gamble on new plant, irrespective of any calculations about current marginal profitability. Under these circumstances, the price structure at any given moment may appear to be uneconomic. At the same time, however, it is impossible to neglect public opinion, which will tolerate operating deficits only if they are amply justified.

In addition, Électricité de France, as a public utility, must guarantee, in the long run, the production of all needed power. Gabriel Dessus insists on the importance, in establishing a price policy, of taking into account the cost of all new development required to fulfill this guarantee. As a result, alongside the notion of short-run marginal cost, something quite different and highly uncertain appears—long-run marginal cost, which may involve either expansion or contraction of the industry.

The third problem is to find a proper method of allocating prices to the various products of a single industry. Contrary to appearance, Électricité de France does not produce a single product—electricity—but a variety of products—electricity at different times of the year, different hours of the day, and different places in the country. The principle of marginal cost pricing, therefore, requires Électricité de France to isolate the price of each product.

Électricité de France, therefore, will have rates consisting of a fixed overhead charge corresponding to the cost of the necessary installation for the consumer and a variable charge for the electric current itself. The latter charge will vary according to the time of day, as consumption fluctuates between peak and off hours; according to the season of the year; according to whether the current is hydroelectric or generated by steam; and according to the area in which the current is distributed. On this basis, France would be divided into three main zones: one furnished with hydroelectric power at lower rates in the summer; another furnished with steam-generated power at more uniform rates; and a third also furnished with hydroelectric power but characterized by high transmission costs, in which rates would be somewhat higher than those of the other zones.

If all these principles are accepted—and they are logical within the framework of marginal cost pricing—the result will be a price structure based on long-run marginal cost, which is very different from pure short-run marginal cost pricing.

Such a price structure would not necessarily mean that Électricité de France would operate at a deficit. In fact, it would provide Électricité de France with a surplus that has been estimated at about 15 billion francs per year.

It is true, of course, that despite the efforts of the economists, the industry might still run at a deficit. This could happen if the state required it to finance internally an investment program beyond its capacity to support; or if the state, out of noneconomic considerations, like the desire to disperse industry or to favor certain groups of consumers, were to oppose pricing at long-run marginal cost because it judged the prices thus determined to be too high. It could also happen if there were competition between the particular industry involved and other nationalized or private industries. The general problem of how to cover a possible operating deficit, therefore, has to be faced.

The research carried out since 1945 by the SNCF parallels in many respects that carried out by Électricité de France. Unlike Électricité de France, however, the SNCF, because of growing competition from private road transport companies, is not, as a rule, using its facilities fully. Consequently, one important fact affects any discussion of the long-run marginal costs of the SNCF. Marginal cost based on expansion, which incorporates the price of new installations designed to satisfy excess demand, does not enter the picture; only marginal cost based on contraction is involved. This is similar to short-run marginal cost in that it includes no additions to plant, but its calculation is nevertheless difficult because the rate of contraction of operations must be determined.

If the contraction were to be very rapid, it might be assumed that it would leave intact those charges which, in the short run, are called fixed, such as amortization and salary and wage overhead. The long-run marginal cost would then be the equivalent of variable cost.

If, on the other hand, as is the case with the French railroads, there were to be a slow contraction of traffic, it might be assumed that both fixed plan and personnel costs would follow the traffic pattern. Then, certain amortization and personnel costs would be included in the long-run marginal cost.

The problem is further complicated by the necessity of taking into account the cost of certain technological improvements, like electrification, which will be made even if traffic is contracting. The long-run marginal cost based on contraction must, however, take into account the cost of modernization. But the SNCF being an industry with decreasing costs, that is, an industry whose marginal cost is less than its average cost, a rate structure based on marginal cost would result in a deficit.

If marginal cost pricing confers logical advantages in terms of optimum resource allocation, it must nevertheless be remembered that it is also not without certain practical disadvantages. Public opinion does not regard a chronic deficit with favor; on the contrary, it regards a balanced budget as the criterion of sound management, especially when public expenditure is already at a high level. A balanced budget may not be the best criterion of good management, but it is a convenient one, and in a parliamentary system the simplest criterion is often the best. Certainly, the opponents of nationalization could avail themselves of an easy argument simply by comparing the chronic deficits incurred under public ownership with the sizable profits earned earlier by the private owners, who set rates on the basis of what traffic would bear.

The attempt has been made to find a compromise solution between the requirements of economic logic and political necessity. The SNCF commissioned Boiteux to find a tariff structure which would ensure a balanced budget and at the same time satisfy as far as possible the desire to achieve an optimum allocation of resources. Boiteux, approaching the problem in the framework of Pareto's formula, resorted to the idea of compound social utility (*rendement social lié*)—that is, he added to the usual structural conditions of economic equilibrium, which are functions of consumer satisfaction, production, and free markets, the additional condition that the railroads, assumed to be a monopoly increasing in productivity, should have a balanced budget. The results of Boiteux's research have not yet been published, but some of their essential features are known.[7]

A surcharge to cover the potential deficit would be added to the marginal cost rates. This surcharge would be proportional to the economic value of the service, in conformity with the traditional differential principle, and to a coefficient of correlation between the market for the service and that for other services, in order to take into account the possibilities of substitution. In this way, it is possible partially to avoid the lack of precision that is inherent in an abandonment of the marginal cost formula.

This compromise solution has been vigorously attacked by Maurice Allais.[8] He argues that only rates set at marginal cost operate for the common good and that the marginal cost can vary depending upon the service involved. While recognizing that rates set at marginal cost would result in a cash deficit, he denies, by calculating marginal cost differently, that this deficit would be as large as the SNCF claims it would.

[7] See Boiteux's earlier study, "La tarification des demandes en pointe: Application de la théorie de la vente au coût marginal," *Revue Générale de l'Électricité,* August 1949, pp. 321–340.

[8] "Le problème de la coordination des transports et la théorie économique," *Revue d'Économie Politique,* March-April 1948.

Even supposing, however, that for extraneous reasons it were essential to eliminate the deficit, this could not be done by charging what the traffic could bear. It would be necessary to resort to some formula which would link the actual rates charged to marginal cost. A simple procedure would be to equate the rate for each service with the average cost if, as the author believes, in most cases where the average cost is higher than the marginal cost, it is proportional to marginal cost. Another method would be to apply to the marginal cost of each service the coefficient necessary to keep the rate higher than, but proportional to, the marginal cost.

The SNCF claims, however, that the precision thus envisaged in the establishment of isolated rates on the basis of marginal cost is impossible to achieve in practice. Marginal cost, which is always uncertain and arbitrary, is all the more so if it is used as the exclusive basis for the differentiated rates of multiple but interconnected railway lines.

The SNCF's tariff research has not been confined solely to theory. Only limited changes have been made in the rates for passenger service, but two important reforms have already been made in freight rates. The first, dating from December 1, 1948, and based on studies of marginal cost, produced an increase in the utilization of freight cars and effected economies which in 1949 were in the neighborhood of fifteen billion francs.

The second, dating from August 1, 1951, takes into consideration the fact that marginal costs vary a great deal depending upon the particular lines involved. It is more costly, for example, to transport goods between two rural towns than between two big cities. It also costs more to transport merchandise over mountainous than over level routes. Each railroad station will receive an index number, based upon its condition of access, the volume of goods it handles, and the nature of the terrain. The sum of the index numbers of the stations of departure and arrival for each route will provide the basis for setting the rate per kilometer. Thus, it will cost 2,497 francs to ship a ton of merchandise between Paris and Lille, while it will cost 2,790 francs to ship the same merchandise the same distance, but between Paris and Isbergue. The total effect of this system, although there will be an average increase of 5 percent in the rates, will be to decrease the rates 2.5 percent for traffic between two big cities and to increase them 13 percent for traffic between two secondary stations.

These measures have already been sharply criticized. The interests of the countryside have been invoked as well as the desirability of industrial decentralization. The complaints have been so effective that it has been necessary to exempt from the new price structure a whole series of important goods representing 60 percent of the traffic: wheat, flour, fertilizers, coal, minerals, and limestone.

These measures and the exemptions that were made to them are characteristic both of the need for a more economic price policy and of the resistance that such a price policy meets from a clientele that has too long regarded a public utility as a business whose policies are always to be attacked and from which special privileges are always to be sought.

Mention has been made several times of the effect of the increasingly acute competition of private road transport upon the price policy of the SNCF. The problems of establishing a price policy for the railroads and of resolving the question of the deficit cannot be completely solved without also solving the problem of road competition. This question is outside the realm of price policy, but some remarks can be made without wandering too far afield. Roger Hutter, in particular, has dealt with this question.

The theoretical solutions to the problem—and they are corollaries of the principle of marginal cost pricing—are simple enough. If it is in the general interest for prices to equal marginal cost, it follows that the choice made by the consumer between rail and road (the commercial choice) should be made solely in consideration of the different marginal costs of rail and road (the rational choice). This principle must apply in each specific case, and it assumes two completely isolated rates.

For the commercial choice to correspond to the rational choice, it is both necessary and sufficient that the difference in rates, in each case, correspond to the difference in marginal costs. If, therefore, in order to make up the deficit of the railroads, the imposition of a surcharge over and above the marginal cost price appears necessary, it is necessary that a similar surcharge be added to road transport prices. The coordination of rates would then rest on the principle of the equalization of surcharges on substitutable transportation systems.

But it is not enough to consider only short-run marginal cost in the debate between the rails and the roads any more than it is in the problem of railroad price policy generally. Long-run marginal cost and changes in the size of the capital plant must be taken into consideration.

If railroad rates are founded on marginal cost based on contraction, anticipating the abandonment of certain fixed expenses, trucking rates would have to be founded on marginal cost based on expansion, anticipating the supplementary fixed expenditures to be made necessary by the increase in traffic in the future.

In addition, it would be necessary for the extraeconomic considerations which may have controlled the decisions of the SNCF, forcing it in certain cases to set rates below marginal cost, to be either revised altogether or imposed equally on the road transport companies. Thus, in order to equalize the operating conditions of the two systems of transport, those obligations now imposed upon the SNCF, like that of accepting all traffic (which means supporting excess capacity in order to be able to handle peak loads), that of treating all customers equally (which prevents diversification in rates), and that of securing governmental approval for rates (which opens the way to "electoral" pricing and which restricts the possibilities of bargaining), would either have to be abolished or imposed upon the trucking companies.

INVESTMENT IN THE PUBLIC SECTOR

Since the Liberation, large-scale investments have been made in the French economy, especially in some of the nationalized industries. The size of the investment program and the results it has achieved have been an understandable source of pride for the spokesmen of the SNCF, Électricité de France, and the Compagnie Nationale du Rhône. The rapid restoration of the French railroads and the construction of great dams in the mountains or huge works like those of Donzère on the Rhône are certainly accomplishments without precedent in the recent history of France.

But the investment program has also precipitated some violent criticism of the nationalized sector, which is accused both of profiting from its privileged position by receiving the lion's share of the appropriations for investment at the expense of private enterprise and of using its funds uneconomically.

The following section will deal with the broad purposes of the investment program, the ways in which it is financed, its positive features, and its difficulties. The application of the investment program to specific nationalized industries will be discussed in Chapter IV, where the operation of nationalized industries is considered in some detail.

Purposes of the Investment Program

A decree of January 3, 1946, called for the preparation of a "preliminary general plan for the economic modernization and re-equipment of metropolitan France and the overseas territories." This plan was to aim at the development of production and foreign trade, an increase in productivity, a higher standard of living for the people, full employment of manpower, and, in particular, better living conditions.

In order to achieve these ends, it was necessary to provide not only for the reconstruction of the productive facilities destroyed by the war but also for the expansion and modernization of prewar facilities. And this meant not only making up a total of domestic disinvestment of 990 billion 1938 francs,[9] but translating this financial effort into concrete accomplishments, so that French production would catch up with that of other modern nations, behind which it had been lagging for some time. Thus, France

---

[9] Commissariat Général du Plan, *Données Statistiques sur la Situation de la France en Début de 1946 Rassemblées en Vue des Négociations de Washington* (Paris, 1946).

would again occupy a leading position in foreign markets and increase the national income.

On the eve of World War II, the average age of French machinery was four times greater than that of American machinery and three times greater than that of English machinery; new investments barely kept up with minimum replacement requirements; one-third of France's industrial capacity was unemployed; and the deficit of from 20 to 25 percent in France's balance of trade was supported only by income from foreign investments.

In 1939, for the same number of working hours, French industry produced one-third the output of American industry and one-half the output of English industry. Similar ratios existed for average per capita income. And, while there were new prospects of demographic improvement, the standard of living remained stagnant; per capita income in 1939 was the same as it had been in 1913, while everywhere else in the world it had increased.

To what extent was this situation the ultimate consequence of World War I, the depression of the 30's, and the burden of military expenses? To what extent was it due to the lack of initiative of private entrepreneurs or to a preference for Malthusian economics reinforced by commercial quotas and national and international cartels like the European steel cartel? It is difficult to answer these questions, but the advocates of nationalization emphasized the second explanation.

After 1945, when the burden of the new wartime destruction, the meagerness of the national income, the discouragement of private savings by monetary fluctuations, the necessity for solving with foreign aid the problem of the dollar shortage, all greatly aggravated the earlier problems, it appeared to everyone that the establishment of a general plan for a new organization of the national economy was necessary.

Prepared by a Planning Council (Conseil du Plan) consisting of the representatives of every branch of the national economy, the Plan for Modernization and Equipment (called the Monnet Plan after Jean Monnet, the General Planning Commissioner) was established in 1946 and designed for the four years from 1947 to

1950. Its goals were to achieve an annual rate of production in 1950 equal to 125 percent of that of 1929, a balance of international payments, and an average per capita income greater than that of before the war.

The essential feature of the plan was a system of investment priorities. Six basic industries were designated: those whose production shortages were most acutely felt after the war and those which, at the same time, furnish the key resources whose abundance and price exercise a determining influence on the development of the whole economy. It may be recalled that one of the criteria adopted for the systematic nationalization of industry was precisely that the industries should be basic or key industries. Only three of the industries designated as basic by the Monnet Plan—coal, electricity, and rail transport—have been nationalized; the other three—iron and steel, cement, and agricultural machinery—remain in private hands. Investment in the three main nationalized industries alone was to represent one-sixth of the total investment program.

Although the General Planning Commission has always adhered to the main features of the original plan, a certain amount of flexibility was bound to be necessary. The official explanation for deviations from the original aspects of the plan has been that they were compelled by changes in the international situation. For example, in October 1948, after the Marshall Plan went into operation, the duration of the Monnet Plan was made commensurate with that expected for the Marshall Plan; it was set to run from July 1, 1948, to June 30, 1952. The Monnet Plan proposed to make it possible for France to maintain its current standard of living after the end of Marshall Plan aid.

At the same time, the formation of the Organization for European Economic Cooperation and the "liberalization" of trade within the European framework were expected to stimulate production to the point where either dollar resources could be saved or exports could be stepped up to other European countries. Agriculture was then placed on the priority list, as well as the fertilizer and petroleum industries, while the development of the overseas territories was coordinated and emphasized. Conversely, the program for the re-equipment of the coal and electricity industries and the railroads was slowed down. The cement industry practically ceased to be considered as worthy of a special priority.

The new government directives [10] were made more specific at the end of 1949 in the first Monnet Report.[11] The industries which were expected to improve France's foreign trade position and in which new investments were to be made included chemicals, coke and gas, synthetic textiles, paper fibers, nonferrous metals, aviation, and shipping.

Another important factor should also be mentioned. The plan was never submitted to Parliament and never formally approved by it. As a result, Parliament makes its planning decisions annually, in the form of the vote on the budget. On several occasions Parliament has reduced the appropriations for investment for the benefit of other items of expenditure, thereby forcing a slowdown of the investment program.

It is difficult to compare the results achieved with the provisions of the original plan, as the latter was based on 1946 francs and the application of a corrective coefficient would be difficult. A report prepared by the Economic Council in January 1951 estimates the achievements at about 51 percent of the initial goals, an estimate that seems unduly low. On the other hand, the more modest projects outlined to the OEEC should have been, according to the same document, 96 percent completed at the end of 1950. What is directly pertinent to this study, however, is the fulfillment of the program devoted to the nationalized industries. By 1950 Charbonnages de France had surpassed the original construction and modernization programs by 29 percent. Électricité de France had completed only 57 percent of its planned program, and the SNCF only 60 percent. But the percentage of the pro-

[10] Cf. the *Réponse Française au Questionnaire de l'OEEC* (Paris, October 1948).

[11] Commissariat Général du Plan de Modernisation et d'Équipement, *Rapport du Commissaire Générale sur le Plan de Modernisation et d'Équipment de l'Union Française* (Paris, 1949).

gram completed in the other industries, except iron and steel, was even smaller, being less than 50 percent for agriculture and 35 percent for housing.

According to the initial plan for metropolitan France, which allocated 590 billion 1946 francs for reconstruction (exclusive of 610 billions for housing), nationalized industries were to receive only 87 billions. They were, on the other hand, to receive 292.5 billions out of a total of 1,150 billions for the modernization of equipment. Later revisions of the plan, in spite of the shift of emphasis to private industries, operated to the advantage of the nationalized industries. Between 1947 and 1950 the nationalized industries absorbed 150 billion current francs out of a total of 502 billions (518.4 if overseas France is included) for reconstruction, and 647.9 billions out of a total of 1,320.6 billions (1,530.6, including overseas France) for modernization. Thus, Électricité de France, despite delays in some of its projects, received 314.7 billion current francs between 1947 and 1950, placing it first in total investment; Charbonnages de France is third with 206.9 billions. (See Tables I and II for the over-all investment picture from 1947 to 1952.)

This privileged position is due not only to the fact that national industries are key industries, but also to two other factors. While the re-equipment of agriculture, for example, could be accomplished only to the extent that the farmers asked for the new agricultural machinery and fertilizers—something that market prices for basic agricultural products did not always encourage them to do—decisions affecting the nationalized industries were based on other considerations. The program for electrification, for example, was based on forecasts of future growth in demand.

Many people think that Électricité de France and the SNCF have been overambitious, that the dam-building program was postulated on the autarchic economy, and that the construction of certain marshaling yards was based on overestimates of the probabilities of expansion of traffic. It is, of course, impossible to make a final judgment on such assertions. But the huge development programs of the nationalized industries would undoubtedly

TABLE I. FRENCH INVESTMENTS AND RECONSTRUCTION EXPENDITURES BETWEEN 1947 AND 1952 (in billions of current francs)

	Investments						Total		Reconstruction 1947–1952
	1947	1948	1949	1950	1951	1952	Current francs	1952 francs	
Metropolitan France									
Nationalized industries									
Coal	22.8	49.3	65.4	66.0	69.5	91.9	364.9	539.1	3.8
Electricity	33.3	80.6	105.8	112.4	115.7	121.3	569.1	847.7	5.2
Gas	—	5.4	11.5	13.3	16.4	20.2	66.8	88.8	2.1
Railroads	10.5	28.4	22.2	21.0	15.8	14.8	112.7	184.8	214.0
Airlines	4.0	4.9	4.7	5.4	6.6	6.3	31.9	50.8	—
Total	70.6	168.6	209.6	218.1	224.0	254.5	1,145.4	1,711.2	225.1
Private enterprises and mixed corporations									
Rhone power authority	4.0	11.0	18.4	16.7	18.9	18.7	87.7	128.6	—
Iron and steel	7.5	17.4	35.2	52.8	60.2	78.5	251.6	341.0	—
Fuel	8.0	15.0	27.0	31.0	40.0	43.0	164.0	233.4	40.0
Other industries	29.3	43.7	64.7	79.0	94.4	94.7	405.8	588.0	—
Agriculture (including food, fertilizers, and machinery)	47.0	60.8	93.7	107.7	153.8	168.6	631.6	918.3	140.0
Inland waterways	0.5	1.2	4.9	3.3	2.4	2.3	14.6	20.8	12.1
Merchant marine	—	—	—	1.0	4.0	5.0	10.0	6.3	244.7
Total	96.3	149.1	243.9	291.5	373.7	410.8	1,565.3	2,296.4	416.8
Total for metropolitan France	166.9	317.7	453.5	509.6	597.7	665.3	2,710.7	3,947.6	641.9
Overseas France									
Total	10.0	38.0	122.3	160.4	202.6	268.0	801.3	1,053.0	23.0
Grand Total	176.9	355.7	575.8	670.0	800.3	933.3	3,512.0	5,000.6	664.9

Source: Commissariat Général du Plan, *Rapport sur la Réalisation du Plan de Modernisation et d'Équipement de l'Union Française* (Paris, 1952), pp. 78, 79, 80.

not have been carried out without access to special sources of financing. While private saving—reduced by the smallness of the national income and discouraged by monetary instability—virtually disappeared, nationalized industries were able to draw on public funds and to resort to special financing methods. It is this disparity in means rather than the inequality of planned goals which has been so bitterly criticized by private enterprise.

TABLE II. PERCENTAGE DISTRIBUTION OF INVESTMENTS BY MAJOR SECTORS *

	1947	1948	1949	1950	1951	1952	Total
Nationalized industries	39.7	47.4	36.4	32.5	28.0	26.9	34.1
Private enterprises and mixed corporations	54.5	41.9	42.4	43.4	46.7	43.8	44.7
Overseas France	5.8	10.7	21.2	24.1	25.3	29.3	21.2
Total	100	100	100	100	100	100	100

* Source: See Table I.

Sources of Invested Funds

Investments can be classified according to the sources used to finance them. One source of investment is public funds.[12] If public funds are not the only source of investment, Table III demonstrates that they are the major source. During the four years from 1947 to 1950, public funds accounted for 63 percent of the total investments, the percentage increasing from 54 in 1947 to 68.5 in 1950. During the same four-year period, private financing and bank credits decreased from 14.7 to 2.9 percent and from 18.5 to 6.6 percent, respectively. On the other hand, self-financing increased from 12.8 to 22 percent of the total. By 1952, however, public funds accounted only for 40 percent of total investments, while self-financing increased further and had reached 34 percent. In OEEC countries not more than 30 percent of the total investment comes from public funds,[13] a sharp contrast to the 45 per-

[12] French budgets appropriate investment funds under several chapters. We are considering here only "social and economic" investments, which in the 1950 budget accounted for 449 billion francs out of a total of 868 billions.

[13] "Troisième rapport de la Commission des Investissements," in Ministère des Finances, *Statistiques et Études Financières, Supplément Statistique,* No. 9 (Paris, 1951), p. 14.

TABLE III. SOURCES OF INVESTMENT FUNDS BETWEEN 1947 AND 1952 (in billions of 1952 francs)

	Own resources		Public funds			Total
	Self-financing	Long-term private borrowing	Monnet Plan*	Budget and Treasury advances	Bank credits and sundries	
Metropolitan France						
Nationalized industries						
Coal	96.8	39.3	339.0	—	64.0	539.1
Electricity	123.0	103.0	552.5	3.6	65.6	847.7
Gas	48.1	—	37.7	—	3.0	88.8
Railroads	12.0	8.0	156.8	—	8.0	184.8
Airlines	6.4	—	16.5	24.9	3.0	50.8
Total	286.3	150.3	1,102.5	28.5	143.6	1,711.2
Private enterprises and mixed corporations						
Rhone power authority	9.6	19.5	52.5	—	47.0	128.6
Iron and steel	105.7	24.3	116.0	—	95.0	341.0
Fuel	163.0	25.0	2.0	15.7	27.7	233.4
Other industries	243.1	140.3	8.5	—	196.1	588.0
Agriculture (including food, fertilizers and machinery)	405.3	10.0	188.0	89.0	226.0	918.3
Inland waterways	4.9	—	—	1.0	14.9	20.8
Merchant marine	—	—	6.3	—	—	6.3
Total	931.6	219.1	373.3	105.7	606.7	2,236.4
Total for metropolitan France	1,217.9	369.4	1,475.8	134.2	750.3	3,947.6
Overseas France						
Total	366.8	20.6	386.0	251.4	28.2	1,053.0
Grand Total	1,584.7	390.0	1,861.8	385.6	778.5	5,000.6

Source: See Table I.
* By Monnet Plan funds are meant the funds provided by the Plan for modernization of equipment. The Plan itself obtained about 45 percent of the total of 1,862 billions of 1952 francs from United States counterpart funds and another 45 percent from the Treasury.

cent figure for France in the period 1947–1952. Public financing of investment, therefore, plays a particularly important role in France.[14]

The main source of public funds is the Fonds de Modernisation et d'Equipement (FME). For the six years from 1947 to 1952, it furnished 1,476 billion francs out of total investments of 3,948 billion francs in metropolitan France.

The resources of the FME, which has functioned since 1948, have been the counterpart funds of the Marshall Plan, (about 45 percent of the total), the revenue from the special tax of 1947, and Treasury drafts on budgetary appropriations. The repayment of earlier loans granted by the state provided a small amount.[15]

The percentage of total investment furnished by public funds is much greater for the nationalized industries than for the private sector. In 1949, for example, the former received 40 percent of the public funds, and if the nonindustrial public services are added, it received 51 percent, while private industry and agriculture received only 28 percent.[16] In the entire period from 1947 to 1952, if new investments only are considered, nationalized industries obtained 68 percent of their resources for investment from public funds and other enterprises only 21 percent.

But this is not the only advantage that the nationalized industries enjoy, according to the opponents of nationalization. They have not often resorted to bank credits, but they have occupied a favorable position on the financial market due to their size and to their position vis-à-vis the state. Moreover, they have benefited from certain procedures of doubtful legality, like the action of the Caisse Nationale de l'Energie in floating a loan with the interest rate linked to electricity rates.

The nationalized industries have not plowed back earnings to the same extent as a private enterprise, which uses the process as the major source of investment, but reinvestment of earnings has

---

[14] See Table III for over-all data.

[15] The loans made by the FME are repayable and bear interest. Nationalized industries have been granted certain reductions in interest rates on loans that they have received from sources other than the state.

[16] "Troisième rapport de la Commission des Investissements," p. 8.

not been negligible in the nationalized sector and it plays an important role in the development program of Électricité de France. Self-investment, however, raises a basic problem. Is a price policy which provides enough revenue for reinvestment appropriate for a public service industry? Theoretically, the answer is that such a policy is not appropriate at all: self-investment, from the point of view of the general interest, is the worst procedure for a nationalized industry. In practice, however, given an anemic financial market and the defects of the French tax system, it seems that developments in the nationalized sector will be toward increasing self-investment.

PERSONNEL

One of the most common charges leveled at all the nationalized industries is that they are overstaffed. As labor costs represent the bulk of the operating expenses of the coal industry and the railroads, the tendency is to blame the personnel situation for all the financial difficulties of these industries. The charges, even though not fully substantiated, have been repeated often enough to have been effective, especially as they satisfy the traditional liberal stereotype concerning state-owned enterprise.

One of the purposes of organizing the major industries that were nationalized after the Liberation in a way that would compel them to act like private enterprises was precisely to avoid criticism of this kind. The syndicalist organizational form, however, was most unsuitable in this respect. The system of tripartite management, with the legal and the actual role that it conferred on the unions in the management of the nationalized industries, could only serve to bolster the position of the workers. The desire to give wage earners the feeling that a great change had taken place and that the industries were theirs, in the hope of increasing production, led to the inauguration of policies favorable to the workers.

The political manipulation of the nationalized industries by the Communist party accentuated this tendency. The Communist ministers willingly granted favorable terms to the workers in the coal and electricity industries because they were increasing their popularity by doing so.

Syndicalist organization and Communist manipulation are not the only reasons why the personnel policies of the industries lent themselves to criticism. The personnel policy of the SNCF, which is not organized on syndicalist lines and which was not dominated by the Communist party, has been criticized at least as violently as those of the industries nationalized since 1945. The reason is that the powerful railroad workers' unions, which had won favorable terms in the days of private ownership and which used the strike weapon in an industry vital to the national economy, were able to win further benefits under public ownership. The SNCF has not been criticized as much as the other nationalized industries for individual employment abuses, waste, or absenteeism. The authority of the management has been well maintained. But the critics object to the collective privileges which the railroad workers have acquired.[17]

Number and Distribution of Employees

In the coal fields now run by Charbonnages de France there were 292,000 pit and surface workers in 1930; 209,000 of these were pit workers, and total output was 55.1 million tons. In 1946 there were 319,000 workers, 211,000 of whom were pit workers, producing 46.7 million tons. In 1952 there were 169,000 pit workers out of a total labor force of 245,000, producing 53.6 mil-

[17] The position of the SNCF is particularly interesting, since the state, whose representatives dominate the management, is in a position to protect its interests. Yet in the test of strength launched by the unions in 1947 and 1948, the state was no less defeated than were the boards of directors of Charbonnages de France or Électricité de France.

In view of all this, it is difficult to understand the paradoxical position of a liberal like Senator Marcel Pellenc, who proposes to abolish the present organization of the SNCF and turn the management over to the state unless one recalls how much the political orientation of Parliament has changed since 1948. But it may properly be asked if it is reasonable to make fundamental decisions on the basis of momentary and transient attitudes, and if, outside the syndicalist and the statist formulas, the best way to give the nationalized industries effective bargaining power is not granting real autonomy to the management of nationalized industries.

lion tons. As the legal work week was the same at all three periods, in spite of a 15 percent reduction in the labor force production in 1951 was somewhat higher than in 1930. And the reduction of personnel was accomplished almost painlessly, by not replacing repatriated German prisoners of war who had been working in the mines.

On May 1, 1946, before nationalization, the companies that now constitute Électricité de France and Gaz de France employed 108,-000 workers. On January 1, 1950, there were 110,200, unquestionably an increase but one which cannot be considered excessive in view of the fact that production increased 28 percent during the same interval.

In 1929 the private railroad companies had 502,400 employees working 2,384 hours annually; in 1938 the SNCF had 514,700 employees working 1,951 hours annually; in 1950 it had 451,000 employees working 2,232 hours annually. The number of units of traffic per labor hour varied from 60 to 50 to 67 in the same years. It does not seem possible, in view of these figures, to accuse the SNCF of overstaffing. While the number of workers per kilometer of road is greater in France (11.35 in 1949) than in the United States (3.63 in 1948), it compares favorably to that of countries of similarly dense traffic, like Great Britain (19.80).

An examination of the relevant statistics for the major nationalized industries, therefore, shows no obvious evidence of waste. It has not been demonstrated, however, that the operation of marginal facilities like poor coalpits and short railway lines has not been continued in order to avoid firing workers. Nor has it been demonstrated, given the vast scope of the investment program, that the increase in production could not be even greater. Furthermore, as the second report of the Commission de Vérification des Comptes points out, there has been some inflation in office and managerial personnel.[18]

18 The technicians and specialists of the Houillères, who numbered 13,502 at the end of 1946, grew to 16,336 in December 1950. The personnel of the national and regional adminitrative offices of the SNCF climbed from 27,000 to 29,400 between 1938 and 1950.

A related problem is that of absenteeism, the source of great difficulties in 1947 and 1948. Much progress has been made since then, however. "Illness, injury, and excused and unexcused absence," which accounted for 23.7 percent of potential working hours in the coal industry in 1947, accounted for only 12.4 percent in the third quarter of 1950. The restoration of safety measures and of discipline contributed to this improvement.

Terms of Employment

The terms of employment of the coal miners have been carefully defined for a long time, and they were codified in a decree issued on June 14, 1946. This decree classified jobs; prescribed methods of payment; established rules for promotion, safety and hygiene requirements, and a regular retirement system; and granted a certain amount of free coal to the miners. It also created, on different levels of organization, joint worker-management committees to handle problems of discipline and to act as conciliation agencies.

The status of the personnel of the gas and electricity industries has attracted more attention because of its unusual features. The terms of employment of these workers had been largely left unsystematized before the government intervened, and the new organization established by the government displays the features that one might expect to find in a decree bearing the signatures of two Communist ministers and issued on June 22, 1946, shortly after a general election, when the Cabinet was responsible only for handling ordinary day-to-day business. It provided for a particularly large number of salary classifications—something which encourages promotions—and for numerous bonuses, and it also established a most favorable retirement system.

Joint worker-manager committees were also established which only theoretically consisted of an equal number of representatives of labor and management. The Commission Supérieure Nationale which had eighteen members—nine to represent the companies —was manipulated by methods which have already been described in connection with the boards of directors of the coal industry.

One representative of "management" was in fact the delegate of the representatives of labor on the boards of directors of the two industries.

The controlling position of the workers was especially significant because the joint committees held extensive powers of decision in personnel matters, depriving the boards of directors of one of their normal functions. The Commission Supérieure Nationale was empowered to establish general rules for recruitment, promotion, and discipline; to assign the jobs within each salary classification; and to decide on expense accounts, bonuses, and free gas and electricity for the workers.

The abuses which these two decrees invited—especially the one affecting the gas and electricity for the workers—made revision essential. On September 18, 1949, a decree was issued which made it possible for the management of the coal mines to dismiss workers without having to consult the joint committees in advance. The same decree and another one issued the same day tightened control over and stiffened the penalties for absenteeism. Since then the Commission de Vérification des Comptes has asked that the joint committees be continued only in a consultative capacity.

The position of the employees of Électricité de France and Gaz de France was changed by a decree issued on May 4, 1950, which amended the original 1946 decree. The composition of the joint committees was changed in order to prevent the representatives of the workers from dominating them. The foremen and other quasi-managerial employees who count as workers when the joint committees are formed were given more delegates. The joint committees were also relieved of their authority over questions of promotion and discipline, which was transferred to the management. The committees now have only an advisory role.

The position of the railroad workers, defined by two decrees issued on June 1, 1950, does not threaten to undermine the authority of the management, as had been the case earlier in the gas and electricity industries. Nevertheless, a wide range of salary classification was established, as well as provisions for numerous bonuses, and these gave rise to criticism.

These great nationalized industries—rail transport, coal, and gas and electricity—occupy a peculiar place in the national economy from the point of view of labor relations, especially since collective bargaining was restored to private enterprise in January 1950. The workers of these industries have acquired a degree of security and stability analogous to that of civil servants; their retirement program is even more generous than that for civil servants. But at the same time the hierarchy of wages, the promotion system, and the bonuses give them advantages over civil servants of the same general rank, and they defend these advantages on the ground that the workers in private industry claim them also. Such a situation must inevitably lead to greater demands from other wage earners as well as from the whole body of civil servants.

Wages and Social Benefits

The wages of the different grades of workers, which were initially fixed in 1946, have been maintained at parity with the cost of living. They have paced, rather than followed, the trend of other wages, the unions in the nationalized industries having been particularly demanding and effective.

Comparisons between the wages of workers in the nationalized industries and the salaries of civil servants, taking account only of the basic wages or salaries and excluding bonuses and special privileges, are particularly revealing. In September 1948 a railroad worker of the highest grade earned 62 percent more than his counterpart in the Ministry of Public Works. Less striking but nevertheless similar contrasts appear in the lower grades. For example, in 1949 a clerk at Électricité de France earned a base salary 50 percent greater than that of a clerk holding a similar job in a prefect's office.[19] The contrast between the salaries of professors and the salaries of employees of the SNCF was one of the reasons for the 1952 strike in the universities.

[19] Marcel Pellenc, *Le Bilan de Six Ans d'Erreurs* (Paris, 1950), p. 8.

The hierarchy of wages is elaborate: there are nineteen classifications for the SNCF, as well as supplementary categories running from A to M for the higher classifications. (There are only eight classifications in the civil service.) The Commission de Vérification des Comptes points out that the lower classifications, and especially the base one, are purely theoretical. This multiplicity has encouraged a general upward trend, since it is more difficult to deny promotions when the gap between one classification and the next is a very small one.

The Commission de Vérification des Comptes has also pointed out the existence of a great number of bonuses. These bonuses have produced a whole vocabulary of satire: people often speak of the "landscape bonus" for the engineers of the Houillères de Bassin and the "cat bonus" of the barrier guards of the SNCF. Nothing, however, could be more real than the importance of these bonuses. An employee of Électricité de France usually receives a year-end bonus which doubles his salary for December. If he marries, he receives a bonus of two months' pay. If his wife has a child, in addition to the regular social security benefits, he receives a bonus equal to one month's salary if it is his first child, two and one-half months' if it is his second, and three months' if it is his third.[20]

The workers in the nationalized industries receive other benefits in addition to cash bonuses. The workers in the coal industry receive a large amount of free coal; those in the power industry receive free electricity. Railway workers and their families receive passes. The SNCF runs company stores which are very advantageous for the employees. And the Houillères de Bassin provide free housing for the miners, which represents a considerable item in view of the size of their building program. Moreover, free housing is provided for retired miners as well as active ones.

The social security system theoretically provides the same benefits for workers in nationalized industries as it does for everyone else, but the social security offices for the railroads and for the coal, gas, and electricity industries—the industries where conditions of

20 *Ibid.*

employment are systematically defined by government decree—are autonomous agencies. A number of scandals have developed because of this, one in particular at the Houillères du Nord in 1952.

Pensions are more generous in the nationalized industries than they are ordinarily [21] and, what is more serious, they are granted too early to certain kinds of workers. Railroad workers, for example, retire at 50 or 55 years of age, depending on their jobs. As a result of this retirement program, the SNCF was paying pensions to 324,600 retired workers in December 1949, while it had 470,000 active employees. And the situation is becoming worse because of the generally advanced ages of the present workers, a situation which has come about because contraction of personnel has been accomplished largely by stopping the recruitment of young workers.

The exact cost of the SNCF's retirement program is difficult to determine because the pension fund is contributed to by both the SNCF and the employees, and it is difficult to isolate the separate items in what is a confused system of accounts. The contributions made by the SNCF are growing, however; in 1950 they were forty-four times what they had been in 1938. A general picture of the SNCF's labor costs can be gathered from 1950 figures. Total operating expenses reached 370 billion francs. Of this sum, wages absorbed 134 billions; pensions, 42; and other social charges, 33.[22]

Conclusions on Personnel

It should be clear from this survey of the personnel situation of the leading nationalized industries, which is a focal point for polemics over nationalization, that hasty generalizations must be avoided, that a proper perspective should be maintained, and that arbitrary figures should not be employed as conclusive proof of one position or another.

There can be no question that the personnel policies of the nationalized industries were at first characterized by serious abuses,

---

[21] The system of vacations with pay is better too. And periods of military service are included in the years counted toward retirement.

[22] Cf. SNCF, *Rapport à l'Assemblée Générale des Actionnaires* (Paris, 1950).

which can be explained by the general absence of authority in France after the Liberation, the need for production at any price, and the unusually great strength of the unions in the nationalized industries. Certain abuses were made possible by the managerial organization of the new nationalized industries and encouraged by the desire to establish working conditions that would compensate for any disappointment the workers might feel after the original illusions about nationalization had vanished. The situation was aggravated by the manipulation of the new organizations by the Communist party.

It did not take long for a double reaction to set in. One, of a general nature, consisted of the effort to rid the industries of the influence of the Communists and to improve their operation by the establishment of a number of control mechanisms. The other consisted of a variety of specific measures, which have been mentioned above, designed to cope with individual problems. This burst of activity for the reform of the nationalized industries dates primarily from the opening of the Parliament elected late in 1946 and was given added impetus by the failure of the 1948 strikes. Moreover, this activity produced results, for which much credit must be given specifically to the Commission de Vérification des Comptes, whose reports have been an important factor in the improvement process. The nationalized industries have efficiently coped with the problem of overstaffing, the terms of employment which caused the most serious difficulties have been remedied, and an effective control system has been established. Most important of all—in fact, the prerequisite of all the rest—has been the restoration of the authority of management.

Not every defect in the nationalized industries has been corrected, as we have seen. The nationalized industries will necessarily bear for a long time the scars which marked them at birth. But certain obstacles to the economic operation of the industries, such as the multiplicity of bonuses, the special privileges the employees enjoy in obtaining the goods or services of the industries for which they work, and the low retirement ages, should be and can be removed gradually.

This is not to say that all the advantages which the workers of the railroad, coal, gas, and electricity industries gained when their working conditions were defined by governmental action should be rescinded. This is neither possible nor desirable. It is not possible because the resistance to fundamental changes in their working conditions is too great. It is not desirable because progress is not achieved by a purely reactionary policy. One aspect of the position of the workers in the nationalized industries which is constantly denounced, for example, is that they have acquired privileges similar to those of civil servants while they retain all the advantages of industrial workers in private enterprise. But the terms of employment in the civil service in France are obsolete, and the trend must be to improve the position of the civil servants, not to worsen that of the employees of the nationalized industries.

In the future, therefore, the interests of the management and the economic operation of the industries will have to be defended, as has been the case since 1947, by modifying or adding to existing personnel regulations, not by abolishing them and establishing a new set. In this way, reductions in personnel and its more efficient use can be brought about, and this, combined with improvements in plant and equipment, will increase productivity.

A final note of caution must be introduced, however. As regrettable as some defects in the personnel policies of the nationalized industries may be, the most objective observers, including the Commission de Vérification des Comptes and the *rapporteur* of the Economic Council for the recent government bill concerning the SNCF, do not consider them to be the main causes of the difficulties facing the nationalized industries.[23] Other factors, especially the price policy of the industries, have played a more important role. Expectations of improvement derived from further betterment of personnel policies, therefore, should not be set too high.

23 Commission de Vérification des Comptes, *Deuxième Rapport d'Ensemble, Annexe Administrative, Journal Officiel,* January 26, 1951; *Avis et Rapports du Conseil Économique,* No. 8, *Journal Officiel,* December 13, 1951.

IX

The Operation
of Nationalized Industries

F RANCE's experience with large-scale nationalization of industry has been short, and it is therefore too soon to draw any final conclusions about the effectiveness of nationalization as a form of economic organization in France. Nevertheless, it is not too soon to draw up an account of the operations of some of the more important industries that have been transferred to public ownership since the end of World War II and to try to derive conclusions from available facts.

COAL

The performance of the coal industry has varied considerably since it was nationalized, partly as a result of unfavorable conditions that were beyond the control of the industry itself. In 1947 and 1948, for example, there was a shortage of coal because the war-damaged mines had not yet been rebuilt. The political manipulation of the industry by the Communists—at cross purpose with the efforts of the Communist ministers to increase production while they were in power—is another reason why production was retarded. And the politically motivated strikes of 1947 and 1948 had a serious effect on coal production.

The strikes of 1948, however, represented an important turning point. The decrees issued in that year and the changes made in the membership of the boards of directors reflected a desire, which was to become increasingly strong, to put an end to Communist control of the mines. In addition, the creation of the Commission de Vérification des Comptes and the new controls over contracts and investments seem to have been effective. The coal shortage ended and was even followed in 1950 by the danger of overproduction, which led to the closing of certain pits, unemployment, and a stretching out of investment programs. After July 1950 production increased again, and the investment program was accelerated in order to lay a firm basis for the eventual implementation of the Schuman Plan. The year 1951 was a record one for Charbonnages de France. In view of this, much of the criticism of the nationalized coal industry is unwarranted, a verdict that is supported by the latest reports of Charbonnages de France and by the second report of the Commission de Vérification des Comptes.

Personnel

During the period from 1947 to 1949 persons as little suspect of systematic hostility to the coal industry as Étienne Audibert, who is now president of Charbonnages de France, joined the Commission de Vérification des Comptes in denouncing some of the deficiencies of the industry. The lack of authority of the politically controlled boards of directors and of the managerial personnel generally was reflected in overstaffing, especially of surface workers; very low production; excessive absenteeism; and various kinds of waste. All this, however, has now largely been remedied.

The personnel situation of the coal industry must be regarded with a certain amount of historical perspective. After World War I there was an even greater increase in the number of workers than after World War II. The 316,000 workers (219,000 in the pits, 97,000 on the surface) of 1929 were reduced to 260,000 (169,-000 in the pits, 91,000 on the surface) in 1938.

After nationalization, from a maximum labor force of 322,000 in March 1947 the total number of workers dropped to 248,000 (167,000 pit workers) by the middle of 1950. (See Table IV.) This reduction was accompanied by a reduction in the proportion of surface workers to the total labor force. This proportion was 31.8

percent in 1938; it had risen to 33.9 percent at the end of 1947; and it fell to 32.8 percent at the end of 1950.

TABLE IV. LABOR FORCE IN THE COAL INDUSTRY

Year	Pit workers	Pit and surface workers
1930	209,000	292,000
Average 1946–1948	214,000	319,000
1949	193,000	284,000
1950	178,000	264,000
1951	167,000	248,000
1952	169,000	245,000

Source: Charbonnages de France, *Résultats et Perspectives,* supplement to the *Rapport de Gestion* (Paris, October 1951), p. 3; Institut National des Statistiques et des Études Économiques, *Bulletin Mensuel de Statistique,* January 1953.

Production increased in spite of the reduction in the work force. The maximum prewar daily output per man was surpassed in 1951. (See Table V.) This increase in productivity is obviously due largely to improved machinery. But it is also due to factors in which the human element is of great importance.

TABLE V. PRODUCTION AND PRODUCTIVITY OF THE FRENCH COAL INDUSTRY

	1929	1938	1946	1947	1948	1949	1950	1951	1952
Production (in millions of tons)									
Charbonnages de France		46.8	47.5	45.4	43.6	51.5	51.2	53.6	55.8
All French mines	55	47.6	49.3	47.3	45.1	53	52.5	55.3	57.3
Daily output per man (in kilograms at the pit)	986	1,229	935	959	970	1,095	1,203	1,310	1,362

Source: Charbonnages de France, *Rapport de Gestion* (Paris, 1947), and Commissariat Général du Plan de Modernisation et d'Équipement, *Quatre Ans d'Exécution du Plan de Modernisation et d'Équipement de l'Union Française: Réalisations 1947–1950 et Programme 1951* (Paris, 1951), p. 80; Institut National des Statistiques et des Études Économiques, *Bulletin Mensuel de Statistique,* January 1953.

An index of the improvement in individual interest and effort can be found in the statistics on absenteeism. Between 1947 and 1950 absences declined from 27.69 to 20.42 percent of the total number of work days. Absences because of illness dropped from 5.13 to 4.93 percent; absences because of injuries dropped from 6.19 to 3.92 percent; excused and unexcused absences dropped from 4.96 to 3.97 percent, and, most important of all, absences because of strikes dropped from 5.93 to 0.12 percent.[1]

Investment and Development

Table I (p. 140) showed the large role that the coal industry played in the investment program of the Monnet Plan. Between 1946 and 1952, 365 billions of current francs were invested in the coal industry. Production was raised from 47 million tons in 1938 to 56 millions in 1952.

The relative importance of the various sources of funds for investment has varied considerably. In 1950, of the 62.6 billion francs actually spent for construction and equipment, 12.7 billions came from earnings, 5.2 billions from bank credits, and 44.7 billions from loans from the Fonds de Modernisation et d'Équipement.

Since 1950 reinvestment of earnings has been regarded as the appropriate way to finance modernization projects, such as equipping existing mines with new machinery. Reinvestment, which did not cover 4 percent of investments in 1948, covered 20 percent of them in 1950—a trend which continues. It is estimated that in 1950 it represented 270 francs per ton of coal, against a net sale price of 3,483 francs per ton.[2]

The emphasis placed on borrowing through ordinary commercial channels and on borrowing from the FME has been shifting. In 1950 loans from the FME accounted for 72 percent of the total.

[1] Charbonnages de France, *Rapport de Gestion,* Exercice 1950, p. 21.

[2] Conseil de la République, *Rapport Annuel au Nom de la Sous-commission du Conseil de la République Chargée de Suivre la Gestion des Entreprises Nationalisées,* No. 824 (Paris, 1950), p. 28.

In 1951, of a total investment of approximately 58 billion francs, the FME furnished only 28 millions, or 48 percent, while a bond issue raised about 20 billions and plowed-back earnings accounted for about 10 billions. For the period 1947–1952, FME funds have provided 63 percent of total investments, own resources 25 percent, and bank credits 12 percent (see Table III, p. 142).

Such fluctuations in emphasis on the various sources of funds for the development of the industry are not without disadvantages. Earnings cannot be depended upon to produce the large sums of 1950, which were undoubtedly due to the lag in wages behind prices. In addition, reinvestment of earnings might be said to impose a direct and heavy tax on the national economy.

Recourse to the banks is limited, and although recourse to the open market, which was exploited considerably in 1951, is sound in theory, it puts nationalized industries in competition with both the state and private enterprise. And while the nationalized industries have employed seductive techniques, like floating loans bearing not a fixed rate of interest but one linked to some variable index, like real output or gross revenue, these techniques are justified only to the extent that inflationary pressures can be controlled.

The development program of the coal industry covers a wide range of projects. In 1950, 4.5 percent of the funds were devoted to housing for the miners; 22.5 percent went for long-term projects designed to restore and increase capacity; 28 percent went for the modernization of important complementary industries, like steam-generated electricity, coke, and the processing of coal derivatives; and 13.3 percent went into projects designed to maintain the level of production.

Some of the most important projects completed have been in the Lorraine basin, a very productive field. These include the construction of power plants, which have doubled generating capacity since 1946, and especially the development of complementary industries. The French metallurgical industry lacks coke; hence an attempt was made to produce coke from Lorraine coal. Ratification of the Schuman Plan by the French Parliament has accelerated this program. It seemed indispensable for the iron and steel industry of the northeast to be able to produce, locally and under the best possible conditions, a large proportion of the fuel it needs. The government is therefore continuing and even accelerating the investment program for the coal industry, as well as for transportation and iron and steel.

Against the obvious advantages of the large investment program for coal, certain disadvantages should be mentioned. In the first place, a long-term development program has been started which bears no relationship to immediate profitability but which is considered important for the French economy in what may be a remote future. The inevitable result must be a certain amount of instability and uncertainty about ultimate goals.

In the second place, by virtue of its privileged position, the coal industry cannot resort as freely as a private enterprise to the customary sources of capital. Necessary capital will come mainly from public funds. But this means annual appropriations, which are regrettably undependable. Program delays are not always determined by the economic or technical reasons which are announced publicly but by purely budgetary considerations.

This problem is particularly acute in view of the present competition between expenditures for armaments and expenditures for investment. Many people feel it would be futile to arm if to do so would mean dashing the hopes for greater well-being which the Monnet Plan raised and driving a large part of the population into the camp hostile to the "Western way of life." The only way to avoid costly interruptions of projects already underway—of which there were several in 1950—and to ensure the accomplishment of the objectives of the Monnet Plan, would seem to be for Parliament to vote guaranteed long-term investment appropriations.

Production Results

All the goals of the Monnet Plan for coal have not been reached. But the results achieved merit attention. There has been, first of all, an almost continuous increase in production (see Table V).

Thanks to this increase, French production, which in 1938 covered only 69 percent of consumption, covered 77.5 percent of it in 1951 (87 percent if the output of the Saar is included). If the target of 60 million tons annually were met, imports from elsewhere than the Saar would be needed only as supplementary stocks to cover peak needs. Coal costs are largely a function of labor costs. Costs per ton, therefore, should decline with an increase in productivity, other things being equal.

What is the competitive position of the French coal industry on the European market, in particular among the Schuman Plan countries? Hourly wage costs, including social benefits, are comparable in France and Germany. The major difference between the two countries is in productivity. (See Table VI.) It seems, therefore, that German competition can be met by the average French coal mines only by further improvement in productivity, especially if the Ruhr should someday attain, as appears probable, an output of 2,000 kilograms per man. The French specialists believe that further progress is possible.

TABLE VI. PRODUCTIVITY AT THE PIT IN THE FRENCH, GERMAN, AND
BELGIAN COAL INDUSTRIES *

	Output per man per 8-hour shift		Cost of labor per ton of coal (in French francs)
	In kilograms	% of 1938	
Germany	1,455	76	1,160
Belgium	1,074	99.	2,300
France	1,074	103.5	1,750

* Germany: second quarter of 1951; Belgium and France: first quarter of 1951.

Productive conditions in France are not, of course, uniform. In the Lorraine basin, which compares favorably with the best European coal beds, output per man is 65 percent greater than in the Nord-Pas-de-Calais. The investment program has thus concentrated chiefly on developing Lorraine production, which has doubled since 1938. Unfortunately, the mines of Nord-Pas-de-Calais still account for 53 percent of the total output, against 20 percent for Lorraine, and it has been necessary to modernize facilities in this area also. However, certain pits in the Nord-Pas-de-Calais, as well as in the Loire, Auvergne, and Cévennes areas, have already been closed, and it seems that this procedure will have to be continued.

Financial Results

The financial results depend principally upon the price of coal. In 1948 the price was set at a level twenty-one times as high as that of 1938, while the level of wholesale industrial prices was but eighteen times as high. Since that time the situation has been reversed. In April 1951 the level of coal prices was twenty-four times, that of industrial prices thirty-five times, that of 1938.

The price of coal, therefore, was then lower than it would have been under private ownership. But the price of coal was regarded as an instrument to produce certain effects upon the general economy.

Charbonnages de France and the Houillères de Bassin have not received any subsidies since 1948, and they do not benefit from any tax relief. They pay interest on their loans from the Fonds de Modernisation et d'Équipement; this amounted to over 6 billion francs in 1950. They must also pay the interest on and the amortization costs of the bonds issued to the former owners; on May 1, 1951, this amounted to 7.9 billion francs. Lastly, as has already been noted, they must be able to finance new construction partially out of earnings.

It would appear desirable for them to be able to set aside about 10 percent of their receipts for depreciation. This was not possible under the market conditions of 1950, and a deficit of more than 2.5 billion francs was reported that year, which means inadequate provision for depreciation. The gap between the adjustment of wages in October 1950 and the adjustment of prices in March 1951 seriously affected the financial position of Charbonnages de France.

Because of three successive wage increases during 1951, further price increases were authorized during the same period, raising the selling price per ton by approximately 750 francs. Altogether, the operating accounts for 1951 showed a net profit of 955 million francs, to be applied to the deficits of the previous years. This favorable situation was endangered by the price cut decreed by the Pinay government on May 16, 1952. The cut amounted to about 200 francs per ton, which will result in an over-all decrease in receipts of 5 billion francs.

Conclusions

A number of conclusions emerge from this brief review of the operation of the nationalized coal industry. First, most of the complaints about the initial Communist control of management, the disorder which existed, and the abuses which were committed because of it, no longer apply. Second, concrete and positive results have been achieved, like the 35 percent improvement in productivity between 1947–1948 and 1951. Lastly, the major criticism is that the policies of Charbonnages de France are tightly controlled by the state. The system of setting prices, the system of compensation between profitable and unprofitable Houillères, the method of financing investment, and the pace of development are all economically irrational from the point of view of the industry. They are based on economic, social, or purely budgetary considerations which often have no relation to the requirements of sound management. But this criticism, which applies equally to the policies imposed by the state on certain private industries like iron and steel, does not impugn the ability of the present management of Charbonnages de France.

POWER: ÉLECTRICITÉ DE FRANCE

In 1950 Électricité de France furnished 64 percent of French electricity production, including 78 percent of the hydroelectric output, and distributed 78 percent of this production. In addition to those of Électricité de France, there are power stations belonging to other public enterprises, such as the Compagnie Nationale du Rhône, Charbonnages de France, and the SNCF, and a few relatively unimportant private plants belonging mainly to the iron and steel industry.

Investment and Development

The annual rate of increase in power production in France had reached 8 percent from 1914 to 1929; it fell to 4 percent during the depression period from 1929 to 1939; during the war it fell even further. In consideration of the normal 7 percent growth of an expanding economy and the past lag, the 1946 Monnet Plan expected production to be increased from 23.5 billion kilowatt hours (of which 13 would be hydroelectric) in 1946 to 37 in 1950 (of which 20.5 would be hydroelectric). The electricity output in 1950 actually reached 33.2 billion kilowatt hours (of which 16.2 was hydroelectric).

In the meantime the original plan had been scaled down. On the one hand, after the period of shortage which ended in 1949, it was feared that consumption would not absorb the increased output. On the other, a reaction set in against the heavy emphasis which the earlier proposals had placed on developing hydroelectric production as an instrument of economic self-sufficiency, and the emphasis was shifted to steam plants, which have a number of economic advantages. Their output is constant, and they can consume the low-quality output and by-products of the coal mines and cokeries. Moreover, steam plants are cheaper to build than hydroelectric ones. The goal for 1953 was raised only to 43 billion kilowatt-hours, and production had reached 41 billions by 1952, thus narrowing the gap between plan and fulfillment.

The result of the revised plan was the suspension of certain development projects under way, a costly and regrettable policy. In order to justify these interruptions in the various projects, some people were forced to appeal to the arbitrary character of any plan and to the uneconomic nature of certain large-scale construction projects.

But the ambitiousness of the Monnet Plan was fully justified. In 1947–1948 a balance between consumption and production was achieved only because consumption was restricted, power was being imported at an annual rate of one billion kilowatt hours, and hydroelectric conditions were unusually favorable. Supply and demand were balanced in 1950 without restricting consumption, but the balance was precarious. If a new investment program had not been undertaken in 1951, electricity would still be "a limiting factor on French production. In particular, industries like electrometallurgy and electrochemistry will probably continue to operate at a lower level of output than a balanced economy requires." [3]

Great progress has already been made. The consumption of electricity rose 58 percent between 1938 and 1950 and 23 percent between 1947 and 1950—an increase of 8 percent a year for these last four years—which made it possible to reduce imports of coal and coke.

The magnitude of the projects already carried out is well known. Some of the projects are works of art and reflect exceptional skill. The dams on the Rhône at Génissiat (five power units of 65,000 kilowatts each) or at Donzère (six power units of 50,000 kilowatts each) are mass structures of great beauty.

There is more to the development program than the construction of new generators. It was necessary, in connecting the hydroelectric and the steam plants, to rationalize the transmission system of the whole country. Before nationalization, power was produced by 86 steam and 300 hydroelectric plants belonging, respectively, to 54 and 100 private companies. Transmission was in the hands of 86 companies, while there were 1,150 companies holding franchises to distribute the current in the towns. All these different units had to be coordinated and integrated into a coherent system. It was also necessary to construct new transmission lines: between 1947 and 1950 3,200 kilometers of new lines were put into service, out of a total of 14,500 existing at the end of 1950.

The entire development program for electricity completed or in progress between 1947 and 1954 represented, at 1952 prices, an

[3] Commissariat Général du Plan de Modernisation et d'Équipement, *Rapport du Commissaire Général sur le Plan de Modernisation et d'Équipement, de l'Union Française* (Paris, 1949), pp. 62–63.

outlay of 1,475 billion francs. A little less than 60 percent of this amount was for Électricité de France.

The financing of the program for Électricité de France was at first done through medium-term bank credits. Beginning in January 1948 with the creation of the Fonds de Modernisation et d'Équipement, this unorthodox practice ended and the FME financed expansion operations with thirty-year loans. Recourse exclusively to the FME proved to be adequate in 1948. In 1949 and 1950, however, two bond issues (with a variable rate of interest) were placed which brought in 12.6 and 14.1 billion francs, respectively.

It has already been pointed out that, for budgetary reasons and because of the end of Marshall Plan aid, the present tendency is to reduce the size of the state's contribution to the investment program. In 1951 loans from the FME covered only 62 percent of the development outlay of Électricité de France, 30 percent (30 billion francs) was obtained on the financial market, and 10 percent through reinvestment of earnings (10 billion francs). For the period 1947 to 1952, FME funds have provided 65 percent of the total investment funds, own resources (including long-term market borrowings) 28 percent, and bank credits 7 percent. What has proved to be a general tendency in the nationalized industries will not apply too readily to Électricité de France unless there is a great change in its rate structure. Recourse to the financial market may appear to be desirable, provided, at least, that inflationary pressures are contained. But reinvestment of earnings can be considered only as a last resort, both because it runs contrary to the very notion of a public service industry and the price policy that such an industry should follow and because it prevents an optimum distribution of the resources for investment.

Financial Results

A comparison of the accounts of Électricité de France from 1947 to 1950 is difficult because a new accounting system was adopted in 1949. It seems, however, that the fiscal years 1946–1947 (starting June 1, 1946) and 1949 ran deficits of 7.4 and 5.5 billion francs respectively, with amortization costs taken into account. On the other hand, there was a surplus of 5.4 billions in 1948. The most plausible explanation for the 1949 deficit seems to be the poor water conditions of that year. In 1950 there was a surplus of 5 billion francs. If the profits and losses of the earlier years and the amortization costs of the compensation to the former owners are charged to the 1950 balance, the year 1950 shows a credit balance of 3.1 billion francs.

A bare statement of the financial returns of Électricité de France hardly provides an adequate basis for judging it. It must be remembered that Électricité de France has made large advances to Gaz de France. The common treasury which the two companies still maintain has enabled the deficit of the latter to be covered by the surplus of the former. The advances made by Électricité de France to Gaz de France climbed steeply until 1949, when they amounted to 30.5 billion francs, rose slightly to 33.5 billions in 1950, and decreased in 1951. In addition, the charges on Électricité de France's earlier loans, especially those from the FME, are continually growing; in 1951 they totaled 7 billion francs.

Personnel costs in 1951 accounted for only 47.2 billion francs out of total operating expenses of 280.6 billions. However justified some of the criticisms of the personnel policy of Électricité de France may be, therefore, it is clear that they should not be exaggerated. The situation has unquestionably been improved. And the tightening of controls over contracts has eliminated another source of waste.

The main reason for the financial instability of Électricité de France and for its difficulties in increasing reinvestment from earning lies in the disparity between its rates and its wages and other costs. The importance of the studies being pursued by Électricité de France in order to establish a rational rate structure, with seasonal and hourly variations, based on long-run marginal cost, has already been pointed out. It has not yet been possible to apply new rates based on these studies because the nationalization law itself prevents it. The law simply substituted Électricité de France for the old private companies in the contracts which had been made by the latter. It has been possible, therefore, to make rate adjustments only under special circumstances, like the renegotiation of an expired contract or a mutual agreement between the parties to change the terms of an existing contract.

Another difficulty is that some customers of Électricité de France enjoy special privileges. Special contracts have been made with the electrometallurgical and electrochemical industries, which continue to enjoy lower rates just as they did earlier. Since December 1947, moreover, some industries in these fields have been partially exempted from general rate increases. Électricité de France estimates that this exemption caused it to lose 1.2 billion francs in 1949.

Even more serious are the government's infractions of the very contracts inherited by Électricité de France from the private companies. Before the last war, power indices based on such items as the cost of coal and wages had been prepared to serve as a basis for power rates. The price of power, like the price of many other basic products, must be approved by the government, but the approval orders constantly kept power rates below what the prewar index indicated they should have been. As a result, the coefficients of increase in electricity rates between 1938 and 1950 are abnormally low. For industrial consumers the coefficients varied from 11.3 to 12.6 depending on the region; for residential consumers they varied from 7.9 (for rural lighting) to 18.3 (for the third period of the urban-winter rate). The average coefficient for the industry was 12. For the same period the coefficient of increase in the average price of coal was 22.2; that of wholesale industrial prices 24.9; and that of retail prices at Paris 19.5. At the end of 1950 electricity rates were more than 25 percent lower than they should have been on the basis of the prewar index. Électricité de France estimates that the direct application of the index system would have brought in 100 billion francs of additional revenue between 1946 and 1950, 36 billions in the single year 1950.

Confronted with this situation and counting heavily on earnings as a method of financing the investment program, the government decided in 1951 to reapply the index system gradually. The implementation of future investment programs depends to a large extent upon the speed with which this gradual return to the old system can be made effective.

An increase in electricity rates which had been scheduled to go into effect before April 1, 1952, was canceled by the Pinay government. The result was a loss of approximately 15 billion francs in revenue and a sharp blow to the investment program. Furthermore, a decree of May 17, 1952, canceled budgetary authorization for 6.5 billion francs and suspended budgetary authorization for 14 billion francs which had been allocated to electricity investments.

The 1951 annual report of Électricité de France, published in 1952, records these cancellations and suspensions of funds. Only to the extent that these decisions may be revoked will it be possible to consider new construction. If they are not revoked, work stoppages may be unavoidable. The report favors an increase in rates (which stand in a ratio of 15.6 to the 1938 level, a ratio considerably lower than that set by the general price level). The recommended increase would not only provide the necessary funds for the investment program, but would also reduce the wasteful use of electric power by some consumers.

COMMERCIAL BANKS AND INSURANCE COMPANIES

It is remarkable that in spite of the law of December 2, 1945, which nationalized the four large commercial banks, the public has taken such little notice of the fact that all major banks are not government banks. The attacks of the economic liberals on the intervention of the state in the field of banking have been very careful to distinguish between the general control over credit and the position of the Conseil National du Crédit and of the Bank of France, on one hand, and the position of the commercial banks, on the other. The criticism against the former has sometimes been violent. The criticism against the position of the commercial banks, however, has been limited to complaints that so little has been changed that "it was not worth the trouble of changing their ownership."

In effect, the banks' boards of directors chose to leave the former managers in their administrative positions. The main reason for this attitude toward the old managers lies in the essentially conservative provisions of the nationalization law. Contrary to what was done in the case of Électricité de France, for example, no large new agency was created to replace the existing companies. An *esprit de corps* continued to exist in each bank, and so did a spirit of competition with the other banks. The maintenance of the individual identities of the banks seemed to be indispensable in a field which relies heavily on building up good will on a personal basis with a large clientele and which was to continue to compete with the remaining private institutions.

The results of this policy have been good. Gross receipts were maintained, and for the fiscal year 1949 a dividend of 267 million francs over and above the legally required compensation of 338 million francs was paid on the stock issued to the former owners, while the state received a dividend of 267 million francs also.

As a rule, banks have continued to pay a higher dividend than they are compelled to on the stocks issued to former owners. For example, in 1952 the board of directors of the Société Générale proposed the following division of net profits totaling 410.5 million francs: 100.75 million francs to be paid to former stockholders to meet the minimum legal obligation, 107.65 million francs to be paid to these former stockholders as a supplementary payment, and 116.25 million francs to be paid to the state, the remaining sum to be carried forward. Likewise the board of Crédit Lyonnais distributed an additional sum of 148.9 million francs among former stockholders to supplement the legal minimum of 129 million francs. The state received 160.75 million francs.

The critics of nationalization, however, have not been silent. They have emphasized the failure of the efforts made by the Conseil National du Crédit to rationalize the banking system. Far from decreasing, the total number of branch banks and agencies of the nationalized banks has grown slightly, and there is always, even in the smallest cities, an office of the Crédit Lyonnais next door to one of the Société Générale.

The representatives of the banks claim that the economies that would be realized if some branches were closed would be small and would lead to inconvenience for the public and to a reduction of competition between banks. It is difficult to know to what extent the corporate interests of the employees influence this attitude.

Some progress has been made, thanks to the creation, under the auspices of the Bank of France and a Comité d'Études Techniques et de Normalisation Bancaire, of a few central, joint agencies. The most valuable one is the Centrale des Risques, which gathers information on the credit standing of all customers. These agencies work for the private banking sector as well as for the nationalized one.

The position of the insurance companies is similar to that of the banks. In this field, also, there is still a large privately owned sector, which underwrote, in 1948, 68.5 percent of the property insurance and 36 percent of the life insurance in the French Union. The identities of the old companies have been retained—likewise, to an even greater extent than in the case of the banks, the old managerial groups and the old traditions.

The old companies which were nationalized therefore continue to compete with one another. Some people have attributed the 5 percent increase in the number of employees between 1946 and 1949 either to this refusal to rationalize operations or to nationalization itself.

In addition, the insurance companies have met with difficulties springing both from the social security system and monetary inflation. But these difficulties are common to both the nationalized and private companies.

To sum up, it can be said that the banks and insurance companies are criticized more in Socialist circles for their conservatism than they are criticized by liberals for being nationalized. The experiment that they have undertaken of maintaining a rivalry between nationalized but competing companies is in conformity with certain doctrines which call for the maintenance of competition, even if it is artificial, in order to make some economic forecasting possible. The autonomy of the companies has been protected thanks to the continuance in leading positions of "independent persons," who were the managers of the former companies.[4]

THE RÉGIE RENAULT

The success of the Régie Renault, which is uncontested by the opponents of nationalization, is frequently pointed to by the advocates of nationalization. The Régie Renault, as has been pointed out, is an autonomously managed company, competing with private industry, under the direction of a highly respected executive.

The output of vehicles in 1938 was 55,000 (41,000 automobiles); in 1950 it was 142,000 (86,000 automobiles). The 4 CV passenger car has been successful throughout the world, and a new and more powerful model, the Frégate, came out in 1951. Thirteen thousand commercial vehicles were produced in 1938, compared with 48,000 in 1950. A new tractor has been put into production, and 8,600 were turned out in 1950. Renault, therefore, produced 40 percent of the 358,000 vehicles manufactured by all French companies in 1950; this position has since been maintained.

Rational organization of production has brought about an increase in productivity. The number of hours of labor required to produce one unit dropped from 653 in December 1947 to 543 in January 1951. This improvement just about compensated for the increase in salaries which took place during the same period. Profits, which amounted to 762 million francs in 1948 (2.5 percent of gross sales) and to 696 millions in 1949 (1.46 percent of sales), declined to 84 millions in 1950 (0.11 percent of sales), to reach a new high in 1951 of 896 million francs (9.4 percent of sales).

Total receipts would have been greater if the prices of automo-

[4] On the liberal attitude toward the banks and insurance companies, see Mireaux, "Banques, assurances, commerce," in Louis Baudin, *Vingt Ans de Capitalisme d'État* (Paris, 1951), pp. 147–176.

biles were free. As late as 1951 delays in delivery were as long as two years. This situation, which encourages speculation in second-hand cars, could have been avoided if the government had let prices reach their own economic level.

In addition, a large portion of French automobile production is exported to foreign countries and to the French Union, while assembly plants have been installed in various countries. The favorable international situation is threatened, however, by the high prices of French goods made out of steel: French sheet steel is 30 percent more expensive than German sheet steel bcause of the policy of the Comptoir Français de la Sidérurgie (French Steel Cartel). Only firm application of the Schuman Plan can remedy this situation.

Two types of criticism have been directed at the Régie Renault. One concerns its policy of participating in other enterprises, which has been characterized as "imperialism." The affiliated companies, of which there are fifteen, are either sales companies in various countries, companies manufacturing certain accessories, or steel companies. The latter, in particular the Société des Aciers Fins (SAFE), represents a typical example of integration for the purpose of escaping the dominance of the Comptoir Français de la Sidérurgie. It is, therefore, sharply attacked by the representatives of the Comptoir. The general manager of the Régie, considering all the affiliated companies and especially the steel companies indispensable, vigorously opposed some recent proposals to liquidate them in order to increase investment in automobile production proper.[5]

The second criticism, advanced by the Commission de Vérification des Comptes, concerns the distribution of profits. "Without any legal basis," a ministerial order of May 17, 1949, in conformity with the proposals of the Régie, authorized the distribution, out of the 1948 profits, of 300 million francs to the employees and 300 millions to the state. The balance sheet for 1951 shows a net profit of 896 million francs. The general manager proposed that of these

[5] Régie Renault, *Rapport de Gestion* (Paris, 1950).

profits 800 million francs be distributed, half to employees and half to the state.

This act reflects the strongly entrenched power of the workers of the Régie. Nationalization should have resulted, according to them, in a sort of cooperative management for the benefit of the workers. The idea has been pressed so far that in 1951 the workers demanded that the Régie be exempted from taxation so that the share of the profits going to the workers could be increased. It seems to be a matter of urgency for the government to take steps to specify the conditions under which the workers should participate in the profits, which is desirable, in order to avoid arbitrary demands on their part in the future.

X

The Future

THE history of the nationalized industries, the most important of which have been in existence only since 1946, is a record of major changes. These changes have seldom been the result of amendments in the original nationalization laws. They have come about, on the one hand, as a result of the application of new decrees and administrative measures and, on the other hand, as a consequence of sharp changes in the political and economic climate of the country—changes which greatly affected the way in which the existing statutes were applied. The changes have, therefore, not been the product of legislation but rather the product of practice.

TRENDS IN NATIONALIZED INDUSTRIES

Nationalization of industry took place in France for reasons which are, in a sense, objective. But it is also true that nationalization in France took place mainly in near-revolutionary circumstances; this is as true of the period after 1936 as it is of the period following the Liberation. At these times, an almost mystical tendency dominated most of the nation and impelled it to make broad structural changes, to use the language of those years. These circumstances explain the wide scope of the measures that were taken, especially after 1944, as well as their confused nature. They also explain some of the methods that were employed.

Nationalization, even if it were to be applied to the entire economy, is regarded by pure collectivist doctrine as a means of improving the collective well-being only *in the long run*. This sort of modest expectation was all the more necessary in a complicated political situation which, even after 1944, never found the advocates of complete collectivization in absolute control of the state. It was to be expected, therefore, that the "bourgeois state," having possession of new instruments of control, would use them in a conservative manner.

Under these circumstances, in order to satisfy the revolutionary mysticism which existed it was necessary, on the one hand, to produce certain immediate advantages and, on the other hand, to do this by not placing under direct and strict state control the new economic instruments acquired by the nation. As early as the post-1936 period, this was the underlying significance of certain aspects of the composition of the boards of directors of the Bank of France and the SNCF. The nationalization acts of the post-Liberation period reveal even more clearly these basic considerations.

The syndicalist formula, with its tripartite system of management, contributed to this dual objective. Like the mixed corporation which had prevailed after 1936, it provided on paper for a system of management having a maximum amount of independence from the government. But more so than in the case of the mixed corporation, it permitted the workers to participate in the management. The fixing by law of the status of the employees and the establishment of shop committees, along with the comments of the press and the declarations of prominent political figures, contributed toward strengthening the idea that nationalization was for the workers. It should be understood that, in a period when the authority of the managerial groups was generally weak, many people counted on this idea to encourage the increase in production which was so necessary.

Such an initial situation could have led to the creation of real producers' cooperatives, fulfilling the slogan "the mines to the miners," if the new boards of directors and the cabinet ministers had been seeking purely economic ends. The ends themselves would have been debatable and the effectiveness of the method doubtful. But there would have been, in any case, a different experience from the one which actually occurred.

The Communist party, participating in power and installed in the key economic ministries, intended to use the tripartite formula and the independence that it conferred on the nationalized industries as a method of creating, outside of the "bourgeois state" and, ultimately, against it, a number of strongholds in key positions of the economy over which it would have control. The first boards of directors that were appointed were, as has been pointed out, tripartite only in the most formal sense. Profiting from the strength of the CGT, especially in the industries involved, the Communist party at one time acquired the absolute control it was seeking.

The evolution of the parliamentary majority in the direction of increasing hostility to the Communists' policies, the departure in 1947 of the Communist ministers from the government, and the failure of the political strikes of 1947 and 1948 altered this situation. The difficult task of reorganization was undertaken. It was possible to rid the nationalized industries of Communist control without making any basic changes in the original nationalization statutes. By 1951 it could be said that the process had been successfully completed.

But the political manipulation of the nationalized industries by the Communist party had only aggravated and made more visible certain vices inherent in any system of management having its own interests and lacking authority and responsibility. In addition to the political problem, the government was confronted with financial difficulties stemming from the autonomy of the nationalized industries.

The shortcomings in their operation were evident mainly from two points of view: the economic and the financial. From the economic point of view, in a period of scarcity, any decrease in productivity was a serious matter. But it was chiefly the financial consequences of the operation of nationalized industries which attracted attention, especially after they had been brought to light by the parliamentary subcommittees and the Commission de Vérification des Comptes.

The state was finally linked to the nationalized industries in two ways. First, it furnished, with American aid, most of the funds that were needed for their modernization and development. The alarm was the greater in this connection because the private sector of the economy could complain of being relatively neglected in the distribution of resources for investment, which it claimed the government was wasting. Secondly, the government supported, either legally as in the SNCF or merely practically, through subsidies, as in the coal industry, or through Treasury advances, the operating deficits of the industries.

In order to protect the national budget from the consequences of policies adopted by theoretically autonomous agencies, the government took a number of measures: from 1947 on it issued more restrictive decrees, regulations, and orders than the original nationalization laws had envisaged and it created a rigorous and multiple control system.

It is important to note that most of the controls applied not only to the new nationalized industries but to every enterprise in which the state had a financial interest. The mixed corporations, the SNCF in particular, which were managed by boards of directors composed of civil servants, were also affected because of their lack of responsibility, because of the strength of the unions, and also, it is worth repeating, because of the price policy which the state imposed upon them and which exposed them to attacks on financial grounds similar to those made against Électricité de France or Charbonnages de France.

The result of the new general policy was to standardize to a great extent the organization of the nationalized industries. On the one hand, the "public enterprises of a commercial and industrial character" organized on the basis of syndicalist doctrine lost much of their autonomy. Representatives of the workers and consumers continued, usefully, to sit on the boards of directors; the working conditions fixed by law were helpful in promoting social peace and progress; but the authority of the representatives of the state, the Contrôleurs d'État and the ministers tended to recreate the earlier system of the "offices."

On the other hand, it should be recalled that the mixed corporations in which the state holds a controlling interest are often only theoretically "mixed." The state's share of the capital is often preponderant, and the rules established in 1935 guarantee the state a dominant role in the management. The workers are represented in the management and their working conditions are often fixed by law, but the multiplicity of new controls tends to make the mixed corporations, like the completely state-owned industries, similar to the old offices.

The authority of the state is not confined to its power in the management of the industries and in the control system which exists. To the extent that the major nationalized industries represent key sections of the economy, they are levers of control over the economy. Because of this, a policy of modernization and development has been imposed upon them at a pace defined not by them but by the government. Whatever errors may have been committed in the implementation of this policy cannot, therefore, be attributed principally to the nationalized industries themselves. Nor can the industries be blamed because there has been waste and loss in production due to a periodic scaling down of their activities as a result of fluctuations in the size of the annual budgets passed by Parliament.

Nevertheless, there has been a genuine investment policy. It cannot be said that there has been a genuine price policy. The extent to which the noneconomic character of the prices imposed by the government hinders the nationalized industries has been indicated above. It is essential to the proper functioning of the nationalized industries that the government as such and the management of the industries be aware of their separate responsibilities and that there be as thorough advance study as possible of the financial consequences of any government policy.

PROPOSALS FOR STRUCTURAL REFORM

Since 1945, when the Council of State (followed the next year by the Comité de la Réforme Administrative) declared that because of the variety of statutes dealing with the nationalized industries it was necessary to systematize and standardize them, many attempts have been made to draft a suitable general law. These attempts have been inspired by different doctrines, which in most cases merely reflect the doctrines of the various political parties.

There has not yet been any parliamentary discussion of the various private members' or government bills which have been introduced, although on several occasions, particularly in 1948, such discussion was declared to be a matter of great urgency. The official explanation for this delay is that it is useful to let the experiment of nationalization run for a fairly long period before introducing changes. The great number of matters which are considered to be more urgent and Parliament's dislike of changing laws that are stoutly defended are two other possible explanations for the delay in revising the nationalization laws.

At the last general election in June 1951, several parties, the MRP in particular, announced that they would press for the passage of a new general law on the nationalized industries. It should be noted, however, that by virtue of the law of August 17, 1948, the government retains the right to institute reforms, by decree, in certain aspects of the operation of the industries and that it has not, to the author's knowledge, made any use of this authority. It should be recalled also that as of December 1951 the government had introduced a bill for the reform of the SNCF, but it did not appear to be considering the possibility of developing this particular reform program into a more general one affecting all the nationalized industries.

The matter of systematizing the nationalized industries first came under serious discussion in 1947, when several reform programs were offered. The syndicalist formula, although supported by only a minority of the Oudinot committee, was embodied in a bill introduced by Maurice Thorez of the Communist party—a bill which was supported in 1947 by a large majority in the Economic Council, where the bill was reported on by Pierre Le Brun of the CGT. The bill was approved in this advisory chamber by 57 votes against 5, with 9 abstentions. The Communist party supported the syndicalist thesis and continues to support it.

The Thorez bill makes no distinction between different types of public enterprise; it calls for tripartite boards of directors, with the workers, the consumers, and the state equally represented, the various representatives to be removable by the organizations which nominate them; it would reduce to a minimum the controls over day-to-day operations; it would grant basic authority over the industries to the boards of directors; and it would make the penalties imposable by the organs of a posteriori control more severe.

Opposed to this thesis is a statist formula which, after having been adopted by the majority of the Oudinot committee, was taken up by a Socialist minister, Robert Lacoste. The chief characteristics of this formula are that it grants basic authority over each industry to the president and general manager appointed by the government, and it establishes tight controls over current operations.

A bill signed by Jacques Bardoux, an Independent, and by several members of the Rassemblement des Gauches Républicaines (RGR) would transform the nationalized industries into mixed corporations by providing for the introduction of private capital.

The last proposal of 1947, a bill signed by Pierre Schneiter and Pierre Pflimlin of the MRP, was for an autonomist solution to the problem. The nationalized industries would be divided into two sectors, one monopolistic and the other competitive. The boards of directors would be quadripartite in composition; "competent executives," expected to ensure that the boards would be independent of private interests, would be nominated by a Conseil Supérieur. Controls over current operations of the monopolies would be reduced to a minimum; the minister could intervene only in certain exceptional financial operations which would require his authorization. The principal control over current operations would be exercised by the Conseil Supérieur. Controls would be reduced practically to nothing in the competitive sector, which would not be able to appeal to the government for any support or privileges and which could be placed in bankruptcy.

The major role in the monopolistic sector would be played by the Conseil Supérieur, to consist of independent persons appointed for a long term of office. Its major tasks would be to guarantee the independence of the boards of directors from the cabinet ministers (political manipulation from above having been as obnoxious as that from below in the experience of the offices and the mixed corporations); to control impartially the activities of the boards of directors; and to enlighten Parliament on the financial consequences of its and the government's measures in any way affecting the operation of the nationalized industries.

The government bill introduced in 1948 by the Queuille Cabinet adopted several of the proposals made by the Schneiter-Pflimlin bill: the division of the industries into two categories, the large amount of autonomy given to the industries in the competitive category, and the quadripartite composition of the boards of directors. Nevertheless, the bill of the Queuille government is more statist than the MRP bill. The board of directors only "assists" the president and general manager, who is appointed by the government. There is no provision for an agency similar to the Conseil Supérieur proposed by the MRP to guarantee a certain amount of independence to the management.

The government bill was referred to the Committee on Economic Affairs of the National Assembly, and in 1949 the committee reported unfavorably on its major provisions. In the name of the committee, its *rapporteur*, Maurice Guérin of the MRP, presented a bill which borrowed from the Schneiter-Pflimlin bill the idea of a Conseil Supérieur. In the committee's bill, however, this Conseil was given only a few control functions and not the broad powers initially designed to protect the board of directors from government interference. The new bill also borrowed some syndicalist ideas in that it would have transferred the basic authority from the president and general manager to a tripartite board of directors and would have reduced the advance controls.[1]

In more recent years, the growing influence of conservative

---

[1] Contrary to the Schneiter-Pflimlin bill, the Pellenc bill, and the Armengaud bill, which apply to the mixed corporations in which the state has a majority interest as well as to the completely public-owned industries, the other bills do not apply to the mixed corporations.

economic doctrines has been reflected in two types of bills which seem to be contradictory but which actually are not. One type represents a movement in favor of reducing the role of the state in the nationalized industries in the competitive area. There have been several proposals to turn over the smaller nationalized industries to private owners. The Armengaud bill,[2] which would reorganize the subsidiaries of the nationalized industries, reflects the criticism of the practice by those industries of acquiring interests in other companies. And the formula of the mixed corporation, which enjoyed widespread popularity from 1936 to 1939 and then seemed to be abandoned, is now regaining popularity as a method of organizing the government-owned companies in the competitive area.

This formula has the advantage of providing a convenient way to replace state financing with private financing. It also makes it possible to confer the broadest freedom of management and the most complete responsibility on the companies in the competitive area. These are the general purposes of the bill introduced in 1950 by Senator Armengaud—a bill which would maintain complete public ownership of all nationalized industries of a monopolistic nature.[3]

The second type of bill, in particular the Pellenc bill, which was introduced in 1950, would transform some of the mixed corporations, even the monopolistic SNCF, into public service agencies depending upon annual budgets annexed to the general state budget.

PROPOSALS FOR OPERATIONAL REFORM

The major criticisms of the operation of the nationalized industries have been mentioned at various points in this study. These criticisms have given rise to proposals designed to affect

[2] Senator Armengaud belongs to the MRP, but he represents a conservative economic tendency which seems to be in the minority in that party.

[3] The RPF announced that it would propose transforming the nationalized industries into "corporations." The details of this proposal are not known to the author, but they are probably similar to those of the Armengaud bill.

virtually every aspect of the industries' activities: basic policy as
to management and its usual concerns such as employment and
contracting and financial operations; the investment program;
and price policy as it is related to the obligations of public service
industries.

In the area of basic management policies, there has been criticism of overstaffing, a charge that seems to be justified even though
present employment figures compare favorably with those of the
first years of nationalization; of the way in which the industries
have awarded contracts; and of indiscriminate participation by the
nationalized industries in other companies. All these criticisms
have been followed by numerous controls over current operations.
This remedy, however, combines the disadvantages of statism (for
purely businesslike management becomes impossible) with those
of complete autonomy (because the division of responsibility between the controller and the controlled creates difficulties).

One possible solution would be to establish direct state control
over the industries, as Senator Pellenc proposes to establish for the
SNCF, but this has the serious disadvantage of subjecting the operation of the industries to the whims and mercies of politics.
Another solution would be to grant the industries a great deal of
autonomy on the condition that their managerial organs represent
the general interest exclusively, that the directors and other executives be chosen on the basis of competence, that the managers be
given real authority, and that they be held responsible for their
actions.

With respect to investment policy, the present tendency among
the reformers is to emphasize financing by borrowing and by internal investment, rather than by relying on the budget, which as
a general rule (after the termination of American aid) would mean
financing through taxation.

Resorting to borrowing corresponds, of course, to the orthodox
solution. It is desirable and perhaps can be successful on the
double condition that new methods of borrowing be permitted
and that inflationary pressures be reduced. However, in view of

the scope of the plans for modernization and development and of the tightness of the financial market, this procedure may not be adequate.

Reinvestment of earnings and taxation have similar repercussions on the national economy. The choice between them is the same as that between direct and indirect taxation. Internal investment, however, offers special temptations to distribute the national costs of development uneconomically. In the present situation, recourse to the budget and to taxation seems to be inevitable.

Whatever method the government chooses to use in financing the investment program, it must be able to supervise the use of the funds that it provides. But if the state intervenes, the responsibility for errors in investment policy falls on it. The relationship between the rate of development of the nationalized industries, the annual hazards surrounding the passage of the budget, and the fluctuations of parliamentary majorities is most complicated and perilous. Of course, the existence of the General Planning Commission, with its prestige and its influence, contributed toward protecting the development program over a number of years. But Parliament, which did not vote on the Monnet Plan, is not bound by it, and has already on several occasions and for purely budgetary reasons refused to maintain the desirable pace of investment. Here again the solution might be to confer on the investment program more immunity from the vicissitudes of politics.

In connection with price policy as it is related to the obligations of public services, one of the larger paradoxes of recent years is Parliament's criticism of some of the nationalized industries, like the SNCF, for running at a deficit, while the "political prices" that Parliament itself forced upon them was the major cause of the deficits. The rate structures which Parliament required to be maintained were contrary to optimum economic operation and did not permit a sound distribution of goods and services throughout the nation. Moreover, the obligations imposed on the nationalized industries by Parliament in the name of public service were poorly considered, inequitable, and often uneconomic.

It is remarkable that under these circumstances most of the nationalization laws required the nationalized industries to balance their budgets. The studies of price policy referred to above refuse to regard this requirement as a principle that it is imperative to follow.

It seems to be indispensable for Parliament not to oppose the adoption of an economic price policy and, to the extent that such a price policy appears to lead to deficit operation, Parliament should agree to accept the supplementary surcharges which should be applied. It is also necessary that the costs attributable to the peculiar nature of the nationalized industries as public services be shared equitably. If a deficit appears to be inevitable, it must be correctly estimated and provision should be made for the public appropriations necessary to cover it.

All these rules, which were prescribed not only by the conventions with the SNCF but by those made with the private companies which preceded it, have remained virtually a dead letter for thirty years. Parliament, while refusing to adapt rates and charges to the needs of the industries, has also refused to recognize clearly the financial consequences of its behavior.

Here again a possible solution seems to be the establishment of a quasi-judicial agency, independent of the government and charged with forecasting and announcing the economic and financial consequences of political decisions, and therefore capable of presenting Parliament with clear-cut alternatives. In other words, the autonomist solution seems appropriate.

GENUINE AUTONOMY AS A SOLUTION [4]

The errors committed in the nationalized sector do not stem only from the nationalized industries themselves but also from the

---

[4] On various occasions for a period of five years the author has been expressing his views on the way in which an over-all reorganization of the nationalized industries should be effected. He participated actively in the preparation of the Schneiter-Pflimlin bill. He spoke at the Economic Council against the Thorez bill and in favor of the autonomist solution (*Bulletin du Conseil Économique*, Nos. 19, 20, 21, November 6, 7, 1947). He presented this thesis in an article in *Politique*, October 1947, and in L. Julliot de la Morandière and

intervention of the government. More specifically, they stem from errors in the relationship between the nationalized industries and the organs of political power. These errors will not be corrected by substituting statist management for syndicalist management; one kind of defect would only be replaced by another. The only solution is to adopt the autonomist formula—to guarantee the autonomy of the state-owned economic enterprises within the limits established by Parliament, which must remain sovereign. This solution is especially necessary because the imperatives and the vicissitudes of politics in any kind of a political system, and especially in the French parliamentary democracy, do not correspond to the requirements for the economic operation of industry generally and of the French nationalized industries in particular.

The English nationalization laws avoided both the syndicalist solution and the statist solution. It is true that for the nationalized coal industry there are councils consisting of representatives of the workers and the consumers, but they are strictly consultative bodies. The entire burden of management rests on competent individuals who are given the greatest amount of independence. The British system can be compared with that adopted for the Tennessee Valley Authority, whose board of directors, appointed by the President with the consent of the Senate, enjoys the greatest freedom of action.

Even in France there are several examples of management under the direction of independent individuals or groups of individuals who have a responsibility to carry out a job within a defined framework but who have, within this framework, broad powers of decision. There is the example of the Régie Renault, which enjoys a great deal of autonomy in practice and whose operations have been, as a rule, successful. There are the further examples of the banks and the insurance companies; of the General Planning

Maurice Byé, *Les Nationalisations en France et à l'Étranger* (Paris, 1948), Vol. I; in a lecture given at the first Semaine Sociologique and published as "Vers un quatrième pouvoir?" in *Industrialisation et Technocratie* (Paris, 1949); in two articles on the "Conseil économique" in *Politique,* July 1948, and *Mélanges Magnol* (Paris, 1948); and in a lecture at the Semaine Sociale of Lille published as *Le Pouvoir Économique* (Paris, 1949).

Commission, which plays a vital role; of the Commission de Vérification des Comptes, a judicial body which has been responsible for many important improvements in the operation of the nationalized industries. Although this commission is without authority to enforce its recommendations, it has been able, because of its prestige as an agency independent of political considerations and because of the publicity given to its reports, to persuade the political authorities to translate its recommendations into practical steps. And there is no reason why mention should not be made of the role on the international scene, which will devolve upon the High Authority of the European Coal and Steel Community.

It is the opinion of the author that a dominant role in the management of the nationalized industries should be given to competent individuals who will be nominated by a nonpolitical body, who will be independent of both political and private interests, and who will not be hindered by numerous advance controls, which should be maintained over only a few matters of major importance. The postoperative controls should be confided largely to nonpolitical agencies.

It is equally important to avoid confusing politics and economics in the area of investment policy. The fulfillment of plans that are considered indispensable to the economic development of the nation must not be jeopardized each year when the budget is before Parliament. The Economic Council and Parliament have already agreed that the investment programs for iron and steel, transporation, and coal, which are regarded as necessary if the French economy is to occupy the place that it must in the European Coal and Steel Community, should be embodied in a law authorizing financial commitments over a period of years.

The plans which will follow the first Monnet Plan should be adopted by Parliament, with commitments authorized for a period of several years, and appropriations to cover all necessary investments. Then the General Planning Commission would legally hold the position of an independent economic authority with the function of overseeing the investment program, particularly its timing and rate of speed. The irregularity of the program has been one of the major problems of the present Monnet Plan.

Lastly, there should be a complete revision of the price policies of the nationalized industries and a thorough study to determine which costs these industries should be required to bear. An agency similar to the Commission de Vérification des Comptes should be empowered to report annually on the budgets and on the financial prospects of the industries, so that Parliament will be presented with clear choices.

Innovations like these will require important changes in the political mores of the nation and even in the mental habits of the nation's leaders. But when the country made the transition from an individualistic economy to a special system involving state control over the key areas of the economy, it wanted a revolution. The revolution has been achieved and it is apparently irrevocable. The nation must accept all its consequences.

Part III by Ernesto Rossi

NATIONALIZATION IN ITALY

XI

Beginnings of the Institute of Industrial Reconstruction

HISTORICAL SUMMARY

Any study of the nationalized industries of Italy must begin with a brief historical inquiry into the role played by banking institutions at the end of the nineteenth century in the development of the country's economic life, for many of the later events are due to the initial tie-up between banks and industry.

Both the Banca Commerciale Italiana and the Credito Italiano, for a long time the two leading Italian commercial banks, were founded at the end of the nineteenth century, with the backing of German financial interests, to permit the participation of German capital in Italian industry and trade.[1] Owing to the auspices under which they were started, the two banks adopted some of the typical policies of German banking, that is, they undertook both normal commercial operations as well as long-term industrial investments. Therefore, certain precedents were established which were to be followed later when other banks were organized with purely Italian capital.

It must be emphasized that this type of banking policy, which brought together under one roof both commercial short-term lend-

[1] The Banca Commerciale Italiana was organized in October 1894 with capital funds of 20 million lire subscribed by German, Austrian, and Swiss banks. The Credito Italiano was organized in 1895, when the old Banca di Genova was taken over by new interests, largely of German origin.

191

ing and long-range investment operations (and in this was quite
different from prevailing banking practices in Anglo-Saxon countries) was one of the main factors in the industrial development of
Italy. For in this manner the deposits of hundreds of thousands of
small savers, who had not yet formed the habit of investing their
money in risky industrial undertakings, were used as a pool on
which the banks could draw to foster Italy's quickened economic
expansion at the turn of the century. On the other hand, this policy has also contributed to the long series of major disturbances
which have brought confusion and crisis to Italy's productive and
financial structure.

The banks appointed representatives to the boards of directors
of the industrial enterprises in which they had invested their
depositors' funds. As dominant stockholders, the banks sometimes
yielded to the temptation of managing their industrial brood
with an eye to financial profits rather than with any concern for
economic efficiency and long-range profitability.

All too often the banks left the economic sphere to invade the
political arena. By intervening in party and governmental life,
banks sought to extend their influence and to secure the granting
of subsidies, of tax exemptions, of tariff protection, and of government contracts and in this way either to increase their industrial profits or to share with the taxpayer the losses of their costly
speculative adventures.

Concerning the period under review, which is roughly that
between the beginning of the century and the start of the Fascist
regime in 1922, Luigi Einaudi has written:

In the steel, shipbuilding, and shipping industries, the close relationship
between banking and industrial interests became part of a system which
had already made the survival of those industries dependent on tariff
protection and government contracts. Since profits were easier and safer
if guaranteed by shipping subsidies or by sales to government agencies
or by the elimination of foreign competition, banks were induced to
favor those industries which could prosper because of these artificial
arrangements, rather than the industries which had to fight in a free
market in order to obtain their customers. . . . We find the financial ad-

venturers exploiting the political worries of the government. And when the problem became that of forcing the state to take over losses running into the billions of lire, the same people proclaimed themselves partners of the government. . . . It became a habit with them to manipulate the press: new papers would be started and existing ones purchased, in an effort to create, next to a class of persons subservient to their plans, a press ready to indoctrinate the public on the advantages of the tariff and of fiscal and banking policies useful to their interests.[2]

Later the new class of businessmen which rose to power and wealth during World War I tried, in a strange reversal of roles, to conquer the banks, which until then had been industry's masters:

In the last years of World War I some of the industrialists most deeply in debt to the banks thought it would be a good idea to gain control over the banks themselves so as to have their managers at their discretion. Between Ansaldo and the Banca Italiana di Sconto, between FIAT and the Credito Italiano, epic battles were fought, aiming to establish the big industrial clients of the banking system as the masters of the funds of hundreds of thousands of small depositors.[3]

The small size of the capital funds involved encouraged these attempts, which, however, usually failed, but not without creating violent commotion in the stock markets and severe losses to those who were caught in these reckless speculative plays. As the present governor of the Bank of Italy, Donato Menichella, has written:

Italy never had a financial class interested in banking activities as such, ready to invest its money in banking enterprises and to manage a bank only with the purpose of making it a profitable, dividend-paying enterprise. What Italy possessed in abundance were industrialists who from time to time suddenly developed an urgent desire to become stock holders of big banks. But a uniformly painful experience has shown that such people were not really interested in securing mere dividends from the shares they acquired, or in providing the banks with their, or their friends', normal commercial business. What they wanted was to gain

[2] *La Condotta Economica e gli Effetti Sociali della Guerra Italiana* (New Haven: Yale University Press, 1933), pp. 18, 277, 288.

[3] *Ibid.*, p. 271.

control over the funds of the army of small depositors, to be used to the advantage of their own industrial undertakings, to provide them with fresh capital funds or to recover their outlays in the purchase of those very same banking shares (thus reducing their investment to a fictitious bookkeeping move).[4]

In times of economic prosperity and expansion and of booming stock exchanges, long-term industrial investments yielded Italian banks profits much higher than those normally obtainable from ordinary commercial operations. But in times of economic depression, of declining stock market values, and of the freezing of long-term investments, those same banks found themselves in severe difficulties and at times unable even to meet normal depositors' withdrawals. Then the government would be asked to step in to avoid losses to depositors by taking over the frozen banking assets on behalf of some state agency. The government, confronted by the wide repercussions of possible bank failures, would usually surrender. The basic idea was simplicity itself. When profits were fat, they went to small private financial groups, as the proper rewards of the capitalistic system; when losses where heavy, they were distributed among the taxpayers, as an expression of community spirit.

This curious notion of the private enterprise system received its first large-scale test during World War I. The Banca Italiana di Sconto, founded in 1914, played a particularly important role in this connection. The bank itself was a typical war baby. It financed on a large scale wartime enterprises, chiefly heavy industries, naval yards, and cotton mills. As the war ended, the termination of military contracts and the collapse in maritime freight rates and in the prices of raw materials brought about a serious crisis in these industries. Some of the largest firms, among them the Ansaldo works of Genoa, went bankrupt in 1921, bringing down with them the Banca Italiana di Sconto, which had

[4] From an unpublished report prepared by Governor Menichella on July 2, 1944, for the Finance Sub-Commission of the Allied Commission in Rome, entitled: "Le Origini dell'IRI e la Sua Azione nei Confronti della Situazione Bancaria."

financed them. The crisis was a major one, for it affected some
of the leading industrial and financial corporations of the country.

After a number of partial measures had proved ineffective to
stem the tide, the government was forced to act as a result of
the pressures of the interested parties. It therefore set up, in
March 1922, under the direct jurisdiction of the Bank of Italy
(Italy's central bank of issue), the so-called "Autonomous Bureau
for Industrial Advances" (renamed in 1926 "Liquidation Institute"). This was to be the first of several government agencies
that, after a period of eleven years, led in 1933 to the establishment of the Institute of Industrial Reconstruction (IRI). The
Bureau was authorized to pay to the creditors of the Banca
Italiana di Sconto up to 1 billion lire, if liquidation of the banks'
assets proved inadequate to meet the claims recognized by bankruptcy proceedings.

It will be noted that these decisions were taken before the
advent to power of the Fascist regime. But the start of the dictatorship caused no change in the policy of assistance to private business in distress. At the beginning of 1923 the Banco di Roma,
generally classified as a "Vatican" bank, began to show signs of un-
steadiness. The Fascist government at once intervened to prevent
its collapse and with a decree of March 22, 1923, removed the
1-billion-lire ceiling of the Autonomous Bureau. Thus able to
increase the amounts of money it could dispense, the bureau proceeded on a greatly expanded scale to carry out its role of rescuer
of banking and industrial enterprises that had fallen on evil times.

Between 1922 and 1933 government interventions of this type
continued to be fairly frequent. As pointed out by Governor
Menichella in the report quoted above, such interventions "were
never disclosed and they were only vaguely known to a very
limited number of interested persons. In any case their details
were never made public." Mussolini, who was busy in those years
announcing to the world the great economic success of the Fascist
regime in all sectors of economic life, clearly had no interest in
advertising a long series of costly government interventions, and
through his complete control of the press, something never

achieved by his predecessors, he succeeded in preventing any public discussion of the matter.

The total cost of this policy has never been made public. In 1947 the Economic Commission of the Constituent Assembly estimated the loss suffered by the state at about 5 billion pre-1929 lire, a sum which might be roughly translated into 1 billion dollars at the current valuation.[5]

THE GREAT DEPRESSION AND IRI

The beginning of the great depression in the United States had, of course, severe repercussions in Italy, where a domestic crisis had been in progress for some time, owning in part to the "prestige" financial and monetary policies of fascism. Among the chief features of the policy had been borrowings in the United States and a revaluation of the currency at an untenably high level. (Between August 1926 and May 1927 the international exchange rate of the lira had been forced up by about 40 percent.) The crisis hit sharply the three major banking institutions in Italy, the very pillars of the entire credit and industrial system of the country, the Banca Commerciale Italiana, the Credito Italiano, and the Banco di Roma.

As the crisis deepened in 1930 and the stock exchanges collapsed, the boards of managers of the three banks, instead of following a cautious policy of disposing of some of their industrial holdings and of writing off what were still relatively small losses, continued along their previous lines and even entered into further commitments in order to sustain market values. This was due to an optimistic view of the future, based on the expectation—shared, it is true, by many political and industrial leaders through-

[5] In the report of the Economic Commission of the Constituent Asembly (*Industria* [Rome, 1947], II, 152) we find for the first time a listing of government interventions in those years. Among the firms aided were practically all the smaller financial institutions, many of the regional Catholic banks, and a number of land companies and of wartime industries. Sometimes the recipient of government aid would be forced to go into receivership, and the remaining assets were turned over to the state. More often the subsidies were given without any expectation of reimbursement.

out the world—of an imminent return to "normalcy." When times were once more normal, the banks would still be found in control of all their major investments, and life would continue as happy as before.

But when large-scale withdrawals of demand deposits got under way, the banking system found itself with an increasing proportion of frozen assets, so that the available liquid assets were no longer adequate to meet the normal credit requirements of industry and trade, not to mention the abnormal pressure of depositors. Following well-established precedents, the three banks appealed to the Bank of Italy. At first, help was forthcoming through large-scale discounting of commercial papers. It was continued through discounting of notes released by the bank-controlled industries themselves, and finally through outright advances which the Bank of Italy made to industrial "holding" companies that the three banks had set up in the meantime as part of a plan to begin a disengaging operation, whereby industrial and ordinary banking commitments were to be separated.

The government, concerned about the excessive involvement of the Bank of Italy in such dubious activities and by the widespread inability of even sound industrial undertakings to satisfy their normal credit needs, set up at the end of 1931 the Istituto Mobiliare Italiano (IMI). The IMI's capital fund of 500 million lire (equivalent to about 70 million 1951 dollars) was underwritten by a number of public bodies. IMI was authorized to issue bonds and to make medium-term industrial loans. These measures proved inadequate, for IMI never had at its disposal adequate funds either to take over the industrial assets that had already been transferred to the Bank of Italy or to meet the pressing problems that were confronting it.

The final stage in the evolution was reached when, on January 23, 1933, the Institute for Industrial Reconstruction (IRI) was founded. The government assigned two tasks to IRI. In the first place, it was to grant long-term loans to industry. In the second place, it was to proceed to the liquidation of all the assets and liabilities that had accumulated in public hands up to that time as a result of past interventions. In this connection IRI was authorized to cut through the confused relationships existing between the industrial world and the banking system, on the one hand, and between the banking system and the central bank of issue, on the other. The goal was to create a new framework that would lead to a general reorganization of the banking system itself and to a sharp separation between commercial banking and investment banking. To fulfill its two tasks, IRI was organized around two main divisions with separate capital funds and budgets: the Financial Division and the Liquidation Division.[6]

The decisions of January 1933 were taken as the following situation came to light:

1. The Big Three, that is, the three banks most affected by the crisis, had as their chief liabilities about 14 billion lire in deposits and 5 billion lire in advances from the Bank of Italy (in all, 2.6 billion 1951 dollars). As against these liabilities, no less than 12 billion of their assets (1.6 billion 1951 dollars) were tightly frozen in industrial investments.

2. In spite of previous government grants amounting to 3.5 billion lire to cover the Bank's earlier losses between 1922 and 1933, the Bank of Italy had 7.5 billion lire (equal to about 1 billion 1951 dollars) committed in the various salvage operations then under way. This was a truly abnormal amount, corresponding to 56 percent of its entire circulation and 88 percent of all its discounts and advances.

3. The government therefore felt bound to relieve the pressure on the Bank of Italy, as well as to restore a substantial measure of liquidity to the Big Three. The solution chosen was that of taking over all the Big Three industrial investments, against cash

---

[6] When the worst of the crisis was over, a decree of March 12, 1936, transferred the Financial Division of IRI (which until then had made loans to industry amounting to 1.2 billion lire, or about 150 million 1951 dollars) to IMI, which then became the only public agency authorized to make loans to industry and had its loaning powers widened. On the other hand, the Liquidation Division of IRI took over the Liquidation Institute of the Bank of Italy. Thus a much larger share of the industrial assets acquired by the Italian government was housed under one roof.

or the promise of cash. But in so doing, and this is the most un-expected chapter in a complicated story, the government took over the banks themselves.

4. The Big Three had, in the course of years, acquired prac-tically all their own capital stock (sometimes to prevent unfriendly industrial groups from gaining control) and had placed it in the hands of holding companies under their control and financed, of course, with depositors' funds. These holding companies were now taken over by the Liquidation Division of IRI along with the industrial assets proper. In this way IRI acquired 94 percent of the stock of the Banca Commerciale Italiana, 78 percent of that of Credito Italiano, and 94 percent of that of the Banco di Roma. This was startling proof of the extent to which bank managers had succeeded in contravening the prohibition of buying their own stock. In practice, bank managers could no longer be con-trolled by outside stockholders, as they had replaced outside capital with the depositors' own money.

As Governor Menichella in 1944 summed up the resulting state of affairs:

It only remained to draw the logical consequence from the existing situa-tion and recognize that the government had become the owner of the banks as well as the owner of the industrial assets owned by the banks. It had become the duty of the state to manage this patrimony in the best possible way and either keep it or dispose of it, in whole or in part, sooner or later, according to its convenience.[7]

For the most part IRI undertook to keep its vast assets. In some instances, however, they were sold whenever a purchaser could be found. As general economic conditions improved after 1933, some sales were made at prices substantially above cost. IRI was also authorized to issue bonds in order to obtain the funds necessary for the carrying out of the large-scale industrial operations it had assumed.

By 1936 the initial phase of the most "unplanned" nationali-zation of industry in the Western world, was concluded, as fas-cism entered its phase of aggressive expansion overseas.

[7] Menichella in unpublished 1944 report, cited above.

In 1937 IRI was given a new, and more permanent, legal structure. Not only was IRI to continue to manage the assets it then owned, but it was also authorized to make new investments in "industrial enterprises having as principal aim the solution of national defense problems, or the attainment of national economic self-sufficiency, or the industrial and agricultural exploitation of Ethiopia." IRI had become a principal economic arm of the Fascist regime. From a mere device used to rescue the banking system, it was transformed into an instrument for the furtherance of the industrial policy of the Fascist state. "Nationalization" had taken place in 1933 under the pressure of events, and with little thought given to the problems of the future. It was to be continued as a deliberate policy in ever-widening fields. After 1937 the policy of liquidating the assets of IRI gradually came to a stop.[8] IRI slowly proceeded to invest in the industrial areas that were being developed by the Fascist policies of self-sufficiency (in cellulose, synthetic rubber, chemicals), as well as to expand the capacity of those industries that were specifically devoted to war production. Only the disastrous events of World War II were to put a stop to these plans of the Fascist dictatorship.

[8] Total sales of IRI assets from 1933 to 1951 amounted to 792 million 1951 dollars. Of these, 512 million were sold before 1938.

XII

The Postwar Structure of IRI

THE LEGAL STRUCTURE

As ITALY shifted from fascism to democracy, IRI underwent some important changes between 1946 and 1948.

The statement of IRI's general purposes was modified to eliminate any mention of the Fascist corporative state, of economic self-sufficiency, or, naturally enough, of the development of Ethiopia. The Cabinet was identified as the controlling policy-making body, to which was entrusted the task of establishing IRI's policies in the public interest. The board of directors' freedom of action was expanded with regard to the purchase and sale of assets. The board's authority to issue bonds was equally extended, but the granting of government guarantees to new bond issues was subjected to the fulfillment of more specific requirements. The number of the members of the board of directors was increased from nine to thirteen. The general manager of IRI was no longer to be appointed by the president of IRI but, upon his recommendation, by the Prime Minister.

Under the Fascist system neither Parliament nor the Cabinet, but only the Minister of Finance was to receive IRI's annual balance sheet and report. The new rules required that those documents be presented before the end of April each year to the Minister of the Treasury for communication to the Cabinet and to Parliament.

On the other hand, IRI was permitted to retain a legal structure which allows it to operate as an ordinary joint stock corporation. IRI can purchase and sell and can manage its assets without regard to the administrative norms that apply to all government departments and outside the controls of the general accounting office. It is liable to the same taxes paid by private corporations. It can hire and fire its personnel outside civil service regulations. In effect, IRI operates as a private investment trust might operate, by owning stock in industrial undertakings in which private shareholders also may own stock. IRI may be by far the largest stockholder, but, legally, its rights are the same as those that would normally accrue to any private stockholder.

The administrative officers of IRI are the president, the vice-president, the board of directors, and the executive committee.

The president and the vice-president are appointed by a decree of the President of the Republic, upon recommendation of the Prime Minister, who, in turn, has sought the advice of the Cabinet. They are appointed for three years and can be reappointed.

The board of directors, meeting at least once a month, is made up of thirteen directors, as follows: the president, the vice-president, the director of the general accounting office, seven divisional chiefs of interested government departments, designated by the departments themselves, and three financial and industrial experts appointed by the Prime Minister. The board of directors has sole authority concerning all transactions affecting the assets of IRI.

The executive committee of five is made up of the president, the vice-president, and the three experts. This means that the eight civil servants are excluded.

IRI has now grouped its major assets (excepting the banks) into five subholding companies: (1) Finsider (iron and steel); (2) Finmeccanica (engineering, including shipyards); (3) Finmare (shipping); (4) Finelettrica (electric public utilities); (5) STET (telephones).

IRI operates with capital funds provided by the government, which today amount to 120 billion lire (equal to about 200 million 1951 dollars), in addition to whatever funds may from time to time be procured on the market. Since 1948 profits are to be distributed as follows: 15 percent for industrial training fellow-ships; 20 percent to a reserve fund; 65 percent to the Treasury. These provisions remain theoretical, however, since IRI has so far registered only losses.

THE ECONOMIC STRUCTURE

IRI came out of World War II in a badly battered condition. As Professor Saraceno points out,

War damages of IRI plants have been far heavier than those suffered by any other industrial group, and this because of IRI's particularly important assets in shipping and shipbuilding, nearly all of which were destroyed during the war; in iron and steel and engineering, which of course were primary targets of air bombardment, sabotage, and other forms of war destruction.[1]

With the end of the war in 1945, reconstruction and recon-version of the industrial plants of IRI might very well have been preceded by some careful planning of the outlines of future policy. The problems to be clarified included the fixing of the goals to be reached by publicly managed industry; the establish-ment of a boundary line between private and public industrial activities; the liquidation by the state of those assets clearly be-longing to the private sector; the reorganization under uniform management of all economic activities of the state which were then managed in confused fashion not only by IRI but also by many other government departments; the selection of the organi-zational forms best suited to the efficient economic management of what was to be retained by the state; and finally the selection of an efficient and competent body of managers.

It proved, however, to be impossible to do anything in any of these areas, and large amounts of money were consequently wasted in the absence of any comprehensive plan. It should be added, however, that postwar Italian governments have been con-fronted by such urgent international and domestic difficulties that many observers are not surprised by the absence of any co-

[1] Cf. P. Saraceno, "L'IRI nell'economia industriale italiana," in *Rivista Bancaria*, No. 4, 1951.

herent IRI plan. Italy's necessary reliance on foreign trade and aid introduced an element of uncertainty, since the volume, the markets, and the distribution of both trade and aid have varied unpredictably from year to year in the turmoil of the postwar period.

Nor have stubborn internal issues confronted IRI with smaller difficulties. The fall of fascism brought to power a political class not adequately prepared for administration in a democratic society. Coalition governments including the Communists were necessary until June 1947, and since then Communism has retained a preponderant influence on large strata of the population and a dominant one among trade unions. Faced by these problems, republican governments until recently have proceeded on a day-to-day basis and have devoted most of their energies to the solution of such immediate problems as foodstuff distribution and unemployment control, rather than to the planning of long-range reorganization and recovery programs. Nor should it be forgotten that it has been impossible to do away with the inefficiency, lack of discipline, and corruption that twenty years of Fascist rule have introduced in the Italian bureaucracy.

It is therefore not at all surprising that in effect IRI should have been leaderless for several years after the conclusion of the war. In the four years from 1945 to 1949, IRI had five presidents. As a result of the lack of an authoritative and efficient central management, IRI developed centrifugal tendencies, and the narrow and egoistic interests of the managers and workers of single establishments often took the upper hand.

This was particularly true in the most gravely sick of all IRI-owned industries, the engineering industry, the managers of which, in order to recover the privileged position which fascism had allotted them and in order to be freed from the worry of reconversion to peacetime uses, sought to rebuild their destroyed plants without taking into account the requirements of peacetime markets or of modern technology. As an extreme example can be mentioned the unwarranted rebuilding of shipyards up to their prewar capacity, a capacity which had been inflated by

Mussolini when he was confidently expecting the downfall of British maritime power.

The fragmentation of objectives and the setting up of autonomous empires within IRI sometimes led to curious developments, such as agreements with private industry for the joint exploitation of consumers, the adoption of legal subterfuges to escape price regulations imposed by the government, cutthroat competition among IRI industries in foreign markets, or the secrecy with which each IRI manager surrounded his own plants and manufacturing programs, with resulting duplication and excess capacity.

When IRI took a hand in the over-all management, it often subsidized the losses and uneconomic policies of its least efficient members with the profits of the efficient ones, thus blurring the concrete details of IRI's situation and making impossible any careful appraisal of IRI's problems and the merits and demerits of the various managers.

TABLE VII. IRI's LABOR FORCE

(as of January 1, 1954)

Industries	IRI	IRI as % of national total
Engineering	77,000	13.3
Iron and steel	52,500	48.6
Shipping	12,600	48.6
Public utilities and broadcasting	18,540	38.0
Telephones	13,000	70.0
Banks	26,000	30.0
Total	199,640	22.8

To obtain an idea of the relative importance of IRI-owned industries in the various fields in which IRI operates, a first test may be that of comparing the number of persons employed by IRI and by private industry in the most important areas in which IRI is active. As the figures in Table VII indicate, IRI has a dominant position everywhere except in engineering. Indeed, this influence is sometimes even greater than the percentage figure would indicate, as in banking, where IRI's ownership of the three largest commercial banks guarantees to IRI a decisive voice in the credit field.

IRI's enterprises outside the fields listed in Table VII had a labor force of 14,500, which, added to the rest, brings IRI's total labor force to 214,000. IRI is thus by far the largest employer in Italy, since the two next largest industrial groups are the FIAT motor works with 63,000 and the Montecatini chemical corporation with 50,000 workers.

In weighing IRI's relative position in the Italian economy, we shall next look at the productive capacity or the extent of the available resources of IRI-owned industries and banks. In engineering, IRI accounts for the following percentages of Italy's total productive capacity:

Shipyards	80%
Railroad and transportation equipment	40%
Electrical and electronic equipment	30%
Machine tools	20%
Tractors	20%

In iron and steel, IRI's productive capacity in 1953 and planned capacity for 1954 are given in Table VIII. In shipping, IRI owns about 20 percent of the merchant fleet, including, however, most of the passenger liners. IRI accounts for 28 percent of the electric power output and 60 percent of the telephones, and it owns the Italian Broadcasting Corporation, which has a radio and television monopoly. In banking, IRI controls about 25 percent of all bank deposits, including saving accounts.

These are impressive figures, but they do not tell the whole story of public ownership of industry in Italy. IRI is by far the largest and the most significant of the public bodies controlling Italy's economic life. But there are large economic assets outside IRI. Italian railroads were nationalized at the beginning of the century and are run by an independent public corporation. All long-distance telephone lines and telegraph lines are government-owned and are separately managed, even though an obvious case can be made for their management by IRI. The state has a tobacco monopoly. The Public Domain owns and manages all coal mines as well as another steel plant (Cogne), which accounts for 25 percent of Italy's production of pig iron (the remaining 75 percent is produced by IRI plants, so that the government has a pig-iron monopoly) and for an additional 5 percent of steel production.

TABLE VIII. IRI's PRODUCTIVE CAPACITY IN IRON AND STEEL
(1953, actual—1954, planned)

	March 31, 1953		December 31, 1954	
	Thousands of long tons	% of national capacity	Thousands of long tons	% of national capacity
Pig iron	1,050	72	1,300	76
Steel	1,900	44	2,500	50
Sheets	320	47	920	72
Pipe	410	81	450	83

The government owns the General Italian Petroleum Corporation (AGIP), which controls 60 percent of natural gas production and the refining of about 25 percent of imported crude oil. Through its control of another chemical company (ANIC), the government shares with Standard Oil of New Jersey the refining of another 25 percent of imported crude oil. The Public Domain has virtual control also over all domestic and international air lines. It also controls the production of quicksilver; it has substantial interests in the film industry, in hotels, and in other smaller activities that are too numerous to mention. Finally, a number of very important engineering enterprises have been laboring under increasing difficulties in recent years, and they appear to be on the verge of being taken over by the state as a consequence of the usual social and political considerations which render the government hesitant to adopt more drastic policies of outright liquidation.

Adding to IRI's labor force the workers and employees of these other industries, exclusive, however, of the postal, telegraph, and railroad operations, which by now have become traditional government activities, a total is reached of over 300,000 persons engaged in industrial and other economic activities on behalf of the Italian state.

XIII

The Scope of IRI's Power

IRON AND STEEL

IRI's effective control of the Italian iron and steel industry goes a long way toward establishing its economic power.

Until recently the steel industry has had a troubled history. The productivity per worker was one-third that of the United States, while the prices of finished products were from two to three times higher than the prices of similar foreign products. The industry was scattered among eighty-five mills, of which only six had a productive capacity of more than 200,000 tons of steel a year. As a result of these disabilities Italian per capita consumption of steel has been very low in comparison with that of other industrial countries. As a matter of fact, Italy's relative position worsened between 1938 and 1952, as during that time its per capita consumption of steel declined from one-fifth to one-sixth of that of the United States. According to the Stanford University report,[1] two or three modern and fully integrated steel mills would be capable of meeting all current Italian requirements.

The war struck a particularly heavy blow to the iron and steel industry. By 1945 production of pig iron had practically stopped, while production of steel, in IRI-owned plants, had decreased by 60 percent. Furthermore, the Germans had removed in its entirety the new integrated steel plant, by far the largest in Italy,

[1] For a history of the report, see the Bibliographical Note, pp. 255-256.

which had been completed by IRI in the vicinity of Genoa. But while the reconstruction task was particularly difficult, it also offered a real challenge to government planners as it afforded an opportunity to modernize the Italian steel industry in order to enable it to compete in international markets. That challenge has been met to a greater extent in the steel industry than in other areas where similar issues might have been faced.

With the help of Marshall Plan funds, IRI's iron and steel sub-holding company, Finsider, has been engaged in a vast program of reconstruction and modernization of its mills. By 1955 a total of 250 million dollars will have been invested in what, it is hoped, will be the first modern steel industry ever possessed by Italy. By then Finsider's productive capacity should be at least that given in Table VIII.

Finsider's production is divided among four major subsidiaries: SIAC, Ilva, Dalmine, and Terni.

SIAC (100 percent government-owned) is operating the largest and most modern integrated steel plant in Italy at Cornigliano, outside Genoa, with a total capacity of 600,000 long tons of steel. The plant is built at the seaside with modern facilities for the unloading of iron ore. It will be producing ingots as well as finished products on a continuous rolling mill. Ilva (78.9 percent government-owned) is one of the oldest of Italy's steel producers, with important electric power interests. It will operate two major new mills, one on the island of Elba, the other at Bagnoli, outside Naples, with a total capacity of 860,000 tons. Dalmine (52.1 percent government-owned) is one of Europe's most modern and important producers of pipe. Together with other establishments, it has a total capacity of about 550,000 tons. The main plants are located in the small industrial city of Dalmine, not far from Milan, and are historically notable for being the first industrial factory seized by the workers after World War I, at the urging of Mussolini. Terni (50.1 percent government-owned) will be the smallest of IRI's steel mills, with a production capacity of 100,000 tons of pig iron a year. But Terni, which is located in central Italy, has also an important stake in electric power and in the electrochemical industry.

In spite of these notable efforts, which are now approaching their final phase, it is clear that Italy's steel industry is in a particularly delicate transitional phase. Just as the expectations of the benefits that Italy can derive from the fulfillment of the goals of the European Coal and Steel Community are great, so are the fears that a too sudden application of the common market may catch the Italian industry as yet unprepared. For this reason Section 27 of the Convention containing the Transitional Provisions of the Community undertakes to recognize Italy's special position as follows:

In view of the special position of the Italian coking plants the High Authority is empowered to authorize the Italian Government, to the extent necessary, to maintain customs duties on coke coming from the other member States during the transition period defined in Section 1 of the present Convention; during the first year of this period, these duties may not exceed those resulting from Presidential Decree No. 442 of July 7, 1950. This ceiling shall be reduced by 10% the second year, 25% the third year, 45% the fourth year, and 70% the fifth year, and these customs duties shall be eliminated entirely by the end of the transition period.

It will be the responsibility of IRI to see to it that the legitimate protection extended to Italian industry by the above provision is not used to justify the continuation of those practices which have been the cause of past difficulties.

ENGINEERING

Pride of place, among the varied assets of IRI, should go to the engineering industry. For it employs the largest number of workers and offers the most difficult problems, technically and politically.

A few figures will show the importance of IRI's engineering interests. At the beginning of 1952 they accounted for 42 percent of IRI's employees and included 34 percent of the largest engineering enterprises of the country. To the 80,000 engineering workers directly employed by IRI one may add perhaps 70,000 more employed by IRI's engineering subcontractors. Furthermore, IRI's holdings in this field are concentrated for the most part in a few large urban centers, of which Genoa is the most representative. As a result, serious social and political problems are brought into existence which exercise a decisive influence on economic issues.

Finally, it is in this field that large-scale losses have been sustained by IRI. Confronted by factories that were obsolescent, or geared only to war production, or had a capacity greatly in excess of any conceivable peacetime level of production (especially in the case of shipyards), IRI suffered severe losses throughout the postwar period, totaling in the seven years from 1945 to 1951 more than 86 billion 1951 lire (about 133 million dollars). In addition, working capital funds had to be replenished and certain efforts undertaken either to repair war damage or to provide a beginning of modernization and conversion to peacetime usage. From 1945 to 1951 these outlays amounted to almost 100 billion 1951 lire (about 150 million dollars).

In all, the financial requirements of the engineering sector alone were equal to about 39 percent of the total financial requirements of IRI. But while IRI could meet part of its financial needs in the nonengineering sectors by recourse to private capital, this was impossible for the engineering industries. Their bankrupt conditions were so obvious that the public could not be induced to channel its savings in that direction, even with a state guarantee. Thus, while the private capital provided 71 percent of all the funds needed by IRI in the nonengineering areas, they provided only 6 percent of the funds needed in engineering.

It is, therefore, appropriate to concentrate our attention on this area, for it is clearly the one that presents the most serious challenge to government ownership.

From the very beginning Italian engineering industries have had to contend with the severe handicap of the high cost of their raw materials. In a protected market, their only source of supply was domestic iron and steel, and, as we have seen, domestic prices have in the past been much higher than foreign ones. Since the end of the nineteenth century the iron and steel industry had succeeded in forcing these uneconomic prices upon domestic consumers. More than forty years ago Luigi Einaudi pointed out how freight charges for imported raw materials constituted an intolerably high percentage of the prices of finished products.[2]

The protection of the domestic iron and steel industry against foreign competition led in turn to equally high protection of the engineering industries that were compelled to use high-cost domestic steel. The result was that the industry, on the one hand, reduced its chances of expansion on the domestic market and, on the other hand, virtually eliminated itself from competitive selling on foreign markets. Thus it was that the Italian engineering industry, which could have fulfilled the peculiar needs of the Italian economy, such as large-scale use of skilled manpower and relatively small capital investment for each labor unit, was sacrificed to the iron and steel industry, which had to import its raw materials at excessive cost, could employ only relatively few workers, and required a heavy investment. And this paradoxical, costly, and damaging situation was allowed to develop in a country in which capital formation was limited and population pressure high.

Born under the destructive protective wings of an extravagant tariff system, Italy's engineering industry lacked normal inducements to technical and organizational improvements to reduce production costs and to increase foreign sales. For this reason, a substantial part of the industry has led in the past, and is still leading today, a parasitic life. This is true also of that part of the industry which has not fallen under government ownership. A good example is afforded by Italy's largest private automobile firm, FIAT, which controls about 80 percent of Italy's automobile and truck production. FIAT prices are substantially above comparable foreign prices, and even now, despite the liberalization

[2] "Polemizzando con i siderurgici," *La Riforma Sociale,* 1912, p. 869.

policies followed by Italy within the framework of the European Payment Union, FIAT is protected not only by a high tariff wall but also by quotas and other restriction devices.

While a good many of the assets taken over by IRI in the course of the 1931 crisis represented substantially sound stocks of industries that were facing serious but presumably temporary difficulties owing to the general economic crisis, the engineering firms were to a large extent war babies organized to meet temporary military needs or represented activities started under fundamentally uneconomic conditions and premises, which could not be remedied without drastic measures.

The seriousness of the problem was hidden when in 1935 the engineering industry, including of course the IRI-owned sector, entered a period of full utilization of its capacity because of the Ethiopian war and the increasingly heavy Fascist emphasis on policies of self-sufficiency and armaments. In a report prepared by IRI in 1948, these comments are found:

Between 1935 and 1943 employment in the industry increased by 100 percent. However, the number of skilled workers and technicians, who are the backbone of the engineering industry, failed to increase in the same ratio. Plants were expanded too quickly and located in answer to political and military pressures and in disregard of the conditions which were most appropriate for their future development. The present structure of the engineering industry possesses serious weaknesses and shortcomings as a result of past Fascist economic policy.

By 1938 the government was the principal customer of the industry, and military goods accounted for no less than 58 percent of the output of IRI's engineering plants.

After the armistice of September 8, 1943, the engineering industry, whose plants were for the most part in northern Italy, provided an admirable shelter for many young men who were seeking to escape military service under Nazi controls or forced labor in German concentration camps. Employment in war factories was for a time accepted as a sufficient excuse to avoid both calamities. But in spite of the patriotic and praiseworthy motivation, the fact remains that employment continued to increase in factories which, as a result of allied bombing or Nazi depredations, had practically stopped production. Nor was the trend broken in 1945, for in the immediate postwar period, as a result of the demagogic policies of mass political parties exploiting the general confusion in order to find gainful employment for their followers, more workers found their entrance into industrial plants, particularly in those that were known to have free access to the resources of the public treasury.

As a result of these inflationary trends in personnel, IRI shipyards had 37,000 workers on their payrolls in 1949, as against 27,000 in 1938, and this in spite of the fact that the volume of production had been sharply reduced in the meantime. The other IRI engineering plants gave employment to 43,000 workers in 1949 as against 41,000 in 1938, when 60 percent of the workers were employed in military production. Even today, in spite of some labor cutbacks, the problem of payrolls greatly in excess of needs remains a most serious one for IRI.

These developments had certain inevitable consequences. The workers were for the most part unskilled. Meetings to prepare strikes and wage demands were continuous and factory discipline broke down. As the CISIM report stresses:

While many plants gradually succeeded in reducing excess man-power, the policies adopted to that end were such that, generally speaking, the best of the workers and the more competent technicians have left for new jobs which would afford them better opportunities to use their professional skills. As a result, the average quality of the workers who remained was lowered. Furthermore, management, after years of work in an impossibly difficult atmosphere, amidst strikes and continuous agitation, could not be expected to follow with care problems of production efficiency and to put forth any serious effort aiming to support new initiatives.[3]

Finally, we have to take into account the fact that the output of IRI's engineering industries is for the most part in the field

[3] CISIM, *Rilievi e proposte sulla industria meccanica Italiana* (Rome, 1952), pp. 66–67.

of cyclical capital goods, such as ships, railroad equipment, heavy machinery. It therefore suffers greatly from variations in the business cycle and the policies of governments.

IRI's shipyards are a perfect illustration of the difficulties faced by public ownership. They account for 80 percent of Italy's productive capacity. They accounted as well for 80 percent of IRI's postwar losses in the engineering field (not to mention the subsidies paid by the government in order to cover the differential between domestic and foreign production costs). From 1950 to 1953 European shipyards have, as a whole, operated at nearly full capacity, but Italian shipyards have operated at 35 percent of capacity, when according to the Stanford report their break-even point is 65 percent. The fact of the matter is that shipbuilding costs in Italy are from 45 to 75 percent higher than shipbuilding costs in Great Britain.

Three main reasons explain the damaging situation:

1. A productive capacity far in excess of needs. Even before World War II, when navy contracts accounted for about half of the total output, capacity was only half used. Present capacity at 300,000 deadweight tons a year, is about equal to 1938 capacity. Since there are no navy contracts, present capacity is three times greater than the normal requirements of the Italian merchant fleet, and present manpower is 100 percent in excess of real needs.

2. Largely obsolescent plants and technical organization. Most shipyards were started as a result of urgent military need and in total disregard of the costs involved. The assumption was that the government would underwrite all expenses. The best example of inefficiency is given by the great Ansaldo shipyards near Genoa. Wedged in between urban areas and the sea, cut in half by main railroad tracks, plagued with scattered construction and finishing docks, and suffering from many other serious disabilities, the Ansaldo shipyards cannot build at reasonable costs. Staggering financial losses have yet to be met, while at the same time shipyard workers form one of the main centers of Communist power

in northern Italy, kept together by the battle for survival and a sense of impending doom.

3. The excessive cost of all the items that go into the building of a ship. The cost of steel plates, which make up 30 percent of the cost of a ship, is about 150 percent above British costs. This is why so much importance must be attached to the reconstruction program for the steel industry undertaken by IRI with American aid. For if and when it is possible to bring Italian steel costs close to international costs, one of the major handicaps under which the Italian engineering industry, and the shipbuilding industry in particular, has been suffering, will have been removed.

Even so, a complete reorganization of the shipbuilding industry would still require a decrease in productive capacity. According to the Stanford report, at least six of the fifteen major Italian shipyards should be closed. This is of course a very difficult task since, in the present economic and political condition of the country, no government has the strength needed to close down industrial plants giving employment to tens of thousands of workers. Only within the framework of an expanding economy could such a decision become politically possible.

It might be possible to maintain that, in a country such as Italy, there are peculiar reasons which justify the retention by the government of branches of the engineering industry such as shipbuilding and heavy equipment manufacture. These are production areas either of a cyclical nature or in which government decisions have great weight. Therefore, it might be said that, once the government has acquired control over these industries, it is not practical for the government to surrender them to private control.

But certainly these arguments do not always apply to continued government ownership of plants engaged in the production of consumer goods or smaller tools, such as trucks, motorcycles, textile machinery, precision tools, optical instruments, refrigerators, and pumping machinery. Both IRI and the national economy would stand to gain from a return to private initiative of such enterprises. Buyers might not be easy to find, but the main obstacle comes today from the resistance of bureaucratic centers, which benefit, in terms of power and personal advantages, from the perpetuation of the present unsatisfactory and complex state of affairs.

It should be added that next to the unwillingness of the Roman bureaucracy to give up acquired power, no matter how indefensible and how costly to the state, the lack of an over-all government industrial policy is a chief source of current troubles. Thus, to cite two fairly recent examples, in 1949 and again in 1951 IRI extended the boundaries of its engineering operations under quite peculiar circumstances.

In 1949 a new railroad and aviation equipment plant, capable of employing 3,000 workers, was built near Naples. As the CISIM report points out, the new factory was started at a time when no one had any idea as to the requirements of the Italian market in the aviation field, when similar existing plants were totally idle, when the needs of the country's railroads for rolling stock were already almost entirely met. No long-term plan dealing with the future needs of national and the international markets was prepared. Not surprisingly therefore, the new plant has added to the existing liabilities of IRI, while increasing an already sharp competition for a limited and uncertain volume of government contracts. In 1951, without public notice of any kind and without any debate in Parliament, IRI took over two more engineering plants in the Naples area, with a payroll of 1,600 workers. Both plants were totally bankrupt.

Thus not only is the Italian government saddled with the very difficult inheritance of fascism, but by its lack of policy and as a result of the free hand it has given to irresponsible bureaucratic elements, it continues to make a difficult situation worse.

Even these engineering commitments of IRI are not the end of the story as far as the *total* public liabilities in this field are concerned. In 1947 the government felt compelled to aid a group of private engineering firms which were then facing very serious difficulties, because of overextended war-production capacity which could not be converted economically to peacetime uses. Included in this group were some of the better-known Italian firms such as Breda, Caproni, and Ducati. For the most part centered about Milan, they gave employment to more than 20,000 workers.

The government did not feel that IRI should assume responsibility for this new batch of casualties. A separate government corporation, FIM, was created with an initial endowment fund of 40 billion lire (about 70 million 1951 dollars). Its avowed task was that of proceeding to an orderly liquidation of those enterprises, and they were the majority, whose existence could no longer be justified. Inevitably the liquidation process was almost entirely unsuccessful as the workers, strongly led by the Communist party and the General Confederation of Labor, succeeded in blocking every effort to carry out any rational policy. As the "liquidation" proceedings dragged on, the deadline for the winding up of FIM's affairs was postponed to June 30, 1953. It has since been postponed further. New funds have brought the total of public commitments to 56 billion lire (about 90 million 1951 dollars), and the end is not yet in sight. For new engineering firms, as they reach the end of the road, are being "rescued" by FIM. In 1951 two of the oldest and largest of Piedmont's industries, Nebiolo and Savigliano, ended up under its protective wings, thus adding thousands of workers and billions of losses to the public burden.

Indeed, a new game seems to be developing whenever a private engineering firm goes bankrupt and has to be (the premise is no longer discussed) taken over by the state: Where, among the many public agencies, shall the new public ward be housed? The most recent example arose during the Pignone crisis. Pignone, a machine tool firm near Florence owned by Snia Viscosa (a noncontrolled affiliate of the British rayon firm of Courtaulds) was to be closed down, as profitable operation proved no longer possible. Immediately a public outcry against this "unsocial" act arose. The Communist party, the Christian Democratic mayor of Florence, the Church, all joined hands in asking the government to intervene. Members of religious orders went about distributing soup to the workers. The only question was: Who should take over Pignone? Apparently, in an unprecedented show of firmness, both IRI and FIM refused the new charge. The discovery was then made that among the machine tools manufactured by Pignone were some that could be used for oil drilling. Thereupon, with the Alice-in-Wonderland economic logic of the bureaucrat, AGIP, the rather healthy government oil and gas enterprise, was called upon to buy a controlling interest in Pignone from Snia Viscosa.

The following results were achieved at one stroke: (a) A private business firm once more was allowed to unload its losses upon the community. (b) A relatively sound public enterprise was forced to take over a heavy liability, which cannot fail to weaken it. (c) The over-all picture has been further confused, while no rational plan for the modernization of industrial firms which find themselves in difficulties has yet been formulated.

SHIPPING

Before World War II Finmare, IRI's shipping subholding company, owned about 85 percent of the tonnage used in regularly scheduled maritime services. The companies owned by Finmare included, among others, the Italian Line with its great ocean liners *Rex* and *Conte di Savoia,* and Lloyd Triestino with its extensive routes throughout the East and the Far East. Adriatica and Tirrenia completed the worldwide network.

During the war more than 90 percent of this tonnage was sunk. Having started the war with 205 ships (plus twenty-three under construction; total tonnage 1,484,000 gross tons), Finmare found itself at the end of the war with only seventeen seaworthy ships (120,000 gross tons). A reconstruction program was immediately inaugurated: damaged boats were repaired, sunken ones were salvaged wherever possible, and work was completed on unfinished boats. Liberty ships were acquired from the United States, and new construction of medium-sized ocean liners, to re-establish in some measure prewar scheduled services, was planned. By the

end of 1954, eighty-seven ships (623,000 gross tons) were in operation. Thus, roughly half the ground lost as a result of the war
had been recovered. The distribution of ships and tonnage was as
follows (by company and geographic areas):

	Number of ships	*Gross tons*
Italian Line		
(North and South America)	19	296,000
Lloyd Triestino		
(Africa, Asia, and Australia)	26	201,000
Adriatica		
(Eastern Mediterranean)	17	57,000
Tirrenia		
(Western Mediterranean and		
northern Europe)	25	69,000
	87	623,000

Almost all cargo boats were sunk during the war, but the tonnage is now 40 percent of the prewar high of 500,000 gross tons.

The recovery in revenues has been greater in passenger than in
freight services: freight revenues are now only one-third, while
passenger revenues are now two-thirds of the prewar levels. About
one-third of the required funds needed to meet reconstruction
costs was obtained through public borrowing, while only 5 percent was secured from the government as indemnity for war losses.
The remainder was provided either through amortization funds
or IRI or Finmare financing.

A main issue of public policy concerns the subsidies paid by the
Treasury. These subsidies are of two kinds. The first and by far
the smallest is an outright subsidy related to the total volume of
traffic and tonnage employed. The second and most important is
a subsidy that is supposed to bring Finmare's returns on invested
capital up to a minimum of 4 percent. In 1950 and in 1951, with
average annual revenues of 43.5 billion lire, the Treasury had
to pay subsidies which amounted to more than 20 percent of the
total revenues. It is clear that with a floor of earnings thus guaranteed, the possibility exists of careless control of costs.

PUBLIC UTILITIES AND COMMUNICATIONS

IRI's public utilities were placed in 1952 under the control of yet another of IRI's subholding companies, Finelettrica. Most of the power is produced by two companies, one (SIP) in northern Italy, the other (SME) the largest public utility of southern Italy. As in several other instances IRI ownership is only partial; a little less than half in SIP and 31.4 percent in SME.

The output of IRI's public utilities reached about 8 billion kwh in 1953, or about 28 percent of the total Italian production of power. With municipal plants accounting for another 7 percent and the state railroads for 3 percent, about 38 percent of Italy's output of electric power is thus controlled by public agencies. By 1952 installed power reached a total of approximately 2.3 million kilowatts, almost 50 percent above the prewar level of 1.6 million kilowatts.

The demand for complete nationalization is strongest in the electrical power companies, for here is a typically monopolistic industry, exploiting for the most part public waters and producing services of vital importance to the community. It is true that the government already regulates electric rates so as to prevent the exploiting of consumers or the granting of favored conditions to privileged industrial groups. But as long as the present political situation prevails, no government will succeed in exercising an effective control because of the low efficiency of the bureaucracy and the influence of the business-controlled public utilities. The latter will continue to subsidize political parties and newspapers in order to influence political decisions and public opinion and will continue to seek the granting of water franchises without fulfilling their obligation to make use of them promptly. The rates charged by private companies to their largest industrial customers and the gross revenues from power sales are only vaguely known. Under such conditions, the administrative bodies charged with the determination of power rates lack many of the essential data, in spite of their sustained efforts to get at the heart of the matter.

Furthermore, localized planning prevents rational water management; it prevents the integration of the complementary water systems of the Alps and the Apennines; it renders more costly the integration of steam and hydroelectric power production; it slows down the construction of a national power grid.

For all these reasons, there is a widespread feeling that the uneven balance of power cannot be redressed without full nationalization. Presumably the threat of nationalization (coupled with the anticipated expiration of some power franchises from 1977 onward) is making increasingly difficult the private financing of the power industry to the extent required to meet the economic needs of the country. The present state of affairs combines, therefore, the worst features of both public and private ownership. Finelettrica, which IRI succeeded in organizing in 1952 in spite of industry opposition, could readily become the instrument through which total nationalization might be carried out.

Prior to 1925 the Italian telephone system was state-owned. In 1925, in what is usually called the laissez-faire phase of the Fascist regime, the telephone system was turned over to private business on the basis of franchises that were to run for thirty years. At the end of the franchise period the government would recover ownership of the telephone network on stated conditions. Five regional companies were set up, and to them all local telephone services and regional long-distance services were turned over, the state retaining the national trunk, long-distance system. The five private companies were (the names are followed by the area they service): STIPEL (Piedmont and Lombardy); TELVE (Venetia); TIMO (Emilia and the Adriatic coast line); TETI (Liguria, Tuscany, Latium, and Sardinia); SET (southern Italy and Sicily).

By 1933 a controlling stock interest in the first three of the five companies listed above (accounting for about 60 percent of the country's telephones) had become part of the industrial portfolio of the Banca Commerciale. It was obtained along with other banking and industrial assets taken over by IRI. In this particular instance, control by private business interests had lasted for the brief space of eight years, from 1925 to 1933. Following its usual practices, IRI placed the three telephone companies under the control of a telephone subholding company, STET.

As of today, therefore, the Italian telephone network is split into three parts. The first, directly and fully government-owned, is the sector to which national long-distance lines belong. In the second, made up of IRI's holdings in STET, private interests are still represented to an important extent (for IRI, as a result of the conversion of convertible debentures issued by STET to private investors, owns only 85 percent of the capital of STET). The third is made up of the two remaining private telephone companies (in which, however, IRI has acquired a small interest).

The diversity of legal status of the telephone industry has led to no small operating difficulties, and it would seem appropriate to state that the conclusions which seem to justify full nationalization of the power industry, apply also to the telephone industry. The competition and conflict of interests between the private, the public, and the IRI sector of the telephone industry has no sound justification from the point of view either of economic principles or sound business practices. It is a matter of record that the two private companies render less adequate telephone service, and that they have fallen far behind in meeting the legitimate demands for new telephone services.

In principle, all franchises granted in 1925 to the then five private companies expire in 1955, so that the opportunity for an over-all reorganization of the telephone system may be close at hand. A government committee has been studying the problem for some time, but no one has any inkling of the direction toward which the committee's work is moving. Unquestionably the threat of nationalization hangs heavily over the plans of the two private companies, and this is a factor which must be included among the causes of their poor showing. It is to be hoped that the government will reach the logical conclusion of buying out the two private companies and entrusting the management of the entire system to STET, which has proved the most efficient operator.

IRI also controls, to the extent of 98 percent of its stock, the

Italian Broadcasting Corporation (RAI), which occupies in Italy the position occupied by the British Broadcasting Corporation in the United Kingdom. At the beginning of 1952 the government entered into a new twenty-year convention with RAI, as a result of which RAI's exclusive franchise was extended to include television.

BANKING

Italy and France are the only two European countries in which the banking system is largely nationalized. Thus their paths have differed from that followed by Great Britain. IRI's most important banking assets are the three so-called banks of "national interest" (Banca Commerciale Italiana, Credito Italiano, and Banco di Roma), Italy's largest banking institutions. They have weathered the war and postwar storms quite successfully, and indeed have been a source of strength to IRI.

An important question was implicitly raised in 1945 by Luigi Einaudi, who was then governor of the Bank of Italy, when he outlined as follows the boundaries of public controls in the banking field:

If we bear in mind that postal savings banks are state agencies;—that the banks of public law, the banks of national interest, the ordinary savings banks are all public institutions, some of them depending directly from the Treasury, others controlled indirectly by the Treasury through IRI; —that cooperative and popular banks are of a semi-public nature;—and that therefore only the banks outside these categories are private banks, even though of course submitted to the general banking controls of the Bank of Italy;—we must conclude that of all commercial and savings bank deposits of the country, 30 percent is managed directly by the State, 49 percent by state-owned agencies, 8 percent by cooperative agencies, with only 13 percent managed by private banks.

These percentages deserve careful consideration. I call them to the attention of those who are pressing for the "nationalization" of the banks. In Italy the nationalization of the banking system is already an accomplished fact.[4]

[4] *Annual Report of the Bank of Italy* (Rome, April 18, 1945), pp. 58–59. This was the first report to be published after the collapse of fascism.

The last paragraph of the governor's statement points up one of the paradoxes in the Italian situation. In spite of the fact that about 87 percent of the deposits, and therefore of the credit facilities of the banking system, belonged to banks that were either state-owned or state-regulated, there was pressure then as there is now for "nationalization" of the banks. The governor of the Bank of Italy was, of course, quite right in saying that nationalization was already an accomplished fact. What the debate revealed, however, was the sense of public uncertainty and the belief that existing arrangements were at best provisional. Full nationalization in the judgment of the critics of the existing system meant more than maintenance of a "privatistic" solution, whereby the banks which had become government property continued to carry on their business very much as before and under the same old names.[5] What the appropriate solution was, no one could say with any precision. But the problem was felt to exist nevertheless (and, of course, it existed in all other IRI-owned industries as well) and to imply, perhaps above all, the need for a stronger assertion of governmental policies and directives.

OTHER INVESTMENTS

Apart from the five major areas we have examined so far in which IRI exercises a dominant role, there are other assets of a scattered nature; some of them are not very significant, others are potentially so.

Among the minor IRI investments are African phosphate mines, Sicilian hotels, as well as other industrial enterprises, the remnants of the Fascist policy of self-sufficiency.

IRI also manages on behalf of the Public Domain the two domestic and international Italian air lines. The domestic company, Alitalia, is 30 percent owned by the British European Air-

---

[5] France did the same when she nationalized the commercial banks, and Great Britain experimented with the same technique during the short-lived nationalization of the iron and steel industry, when the historic names of the steel producers and their separate identities were maintained so as not to disturb national and international trade relationships.

ways Corporation. The international company, LAI, is 40 percent owned by Trans-World Airlines.

IRI and the Public Domain jointly control Monte Amiata, a monopoly producer of quicksilver. Finally, and most importantly, IRI owns directly 8 percent, and indirectly probably a similar amount, of the shares of Montecatini, Italy's largest chemical enterprise. It has been suggested that were IRI to vote as one unit all its stock, both direct and indirectly owned, it might acquire a controlling voice in the management of Montecatini.

Since this policy has not in fact been followed, some observers have charged IRI with a total lack of direction and purpose in one of the most important areas of national economic life. Undoubtedly, the role of Montecatini in Italy is comparable to that once played in Germany by I. G. Farben. It is indicative of the present muddled state of public thinking on matters of government economic policy that the question has so far not been raised and made the object of open and full discussion in all its implications.

XIV

Problems for the Future

A RETURN TO PRIVATE ENTERPRISE?

The Italian government appears to be in business for good. There are no private business interests in the country with sufficient financial strength to acquire all, or most, of the enterprises which are at present owned by IRI and to do so under conditions that would guarantee their continued operation. But, even supposing that the contrary were true, there are many reasons why a total transfer from public into private hands should be resisted.

It should be stressed that all official announcements originating either in the legislative or the executive branch have opposed the sale of IRI's assets. Thus a Senate report favored the strengthening of IRI as an instrument of control and economic policy. And in the most painstaking review of the whole matter undertaken by any of the postwar governments,[1] Minister La Malfa in 1951 stated that the issue of the sale of public industrial assets can be raised only for those marginal firms that are not clearly part of the more important publicly controlled sectors or for those in which the government's share of ownership is limited.

It is interesting, on the other hand, to note that the Stanford report on the engineering industries concluded by suggesting the possibility of a program whose principal aim would be the return to private business of the greater part of IRI's assets, such return to be accompanied by the liquidation of IRI and of its subholding companies. This liquidation would be the task of a special

[1] See below, pp. 236–237.

committee, made up of representatives of the government, the workers, and private business and presided over by someone drawn, preferably, from private industry. A suggestion of this type, including as it does banks and public utilities as well as industrial assets, shows an inadequate awareness of the nature of the problem and of the over-all legal and industrial conditions of Italy.

We could approach the issue by looking at each of the major IRI-owned sectors, which account for about 90 percent of the total IRI assets (the remaining 10 percent is made up of small and scattered commitments which could indeed be liquidated and sold to private enterprise without raising any question of policy and with undoubted benefit to the public exchequer).

As far as the Big Three banks are concerned, the relative smallness of their capital funds (less than 1 percent of their total deposits) might conceivably make their purchase by private financial groups a fairly simple matter. But these groups would represent only industrial interests. Therefore it would seem difficult to prevent the banks from becoming once more entangled with the kind of industrial commitments from which they were cut off in 1933. The problem would again be created of a privileged position for the business groups controlling the banks, with subsequent costly public interventions probable—interventions of which the taxpayer would, as usual, bear the burden.

It is not enough to say that the new banking laws of 1936 would be adequate to prevent a tie-up between banks and industry. In the present state of weakness of administrative agencies, no outside control would be adequate, regardless of the sternness of banking laws.

Among the engineering firms controlled by Finmeccanica it would not be difficult to find several which could be sold to private business. This might be true in particular in the automobile, textile machinery, and machine tool fields, for these are types of economic activities which cannot be included in any program of government intervention in industry seeking to justify itself by appeals to the collective interest. These are the areas which even socialist Britain reserved to private ownership.

On the other hand, it will not be reasonable to suggest the return to private enterprise of industries which perform public services under monopoly conditions (power and telephone companies); or which are subsidized (shipping lines); or which are kept alive for defense purposes with production premiums, favored contracts, import quotas, or high tariff duties (iron and steel and shipyards).

In the iron and steel industry and the engineering and ship-building industries, particularly, it cannot be forgotten that many of them are of an extremely cyclical nature and that they still require a continuing flow of investments for modernization purposes. Even if a favorable production climate because of armaments or other causes were to make it possible to find someone ready to pay IRI an adequate price for these industries, the experience of the last decade shows that private purchasers would be most unlikely to risk the substantial capital and effort still needed everywhere, except perhaps in steel, to restore a semblance of rational operations. Private business would undoubtedly seek to realize the highest possible immediate profit without new investments, while bringing pressure to bear on the government in order to obtain favorable contracts. These would be easy to get since the threat of large-scale manpower curtailment would be used. But as soon as the cyclical benefits were reaped, the "private" owners would seek to get rid of their profitless plants once more, and the government, for the usual social reasons, would again take them over.

Nor are these forecasts fanciful ones. As the CISIM report points out, in 1935 IRI did sell to private enterprise two of its largest engineering firms, Breda and Reggiane. But both of them have had to be taken over for the second time by the government (not by IRI but by a separate public body, FIM). As the CISIM report points out:

This means that private business retained control of these two important engineering firms only during wartime and during the time required for the reconstruction of the railroad network. Twice within fifteen years the government has had to take over the burden of reconversion. Private enterprise got the benefits of exceptional economic circumstances, but did not contribute anything to the solution of the difficulties of normal peacetime production.

There is a further issue to be considered. It is pointed out that many of the nonengineering holdings of IRI have been able to pay dividends as well as to finance themselves in the open market. The question arises, however, whether the payment of dividends can always be taken as an index of normal conditions, of administrative efficiency, and of economic soundness. It must be remembered that the banks belong to a cartel set up and regulated by law; that the iron and steel industry has hitherto operated under the protection of heavy tariff barriers; that the shipping lines have enjoyed the benefits of subsidies; and that public utilities perform monopoly functions at prices fixed by government decision. It would therefore seem necessary, before conclusions can be reached as to the profitability of the nonengineering IRI holdings, to determine what advantages their industrial operations have derived from one or the other of many forms of state support. Such an analysis has never been made.

It should be added that similar subsidies, protective tariffs, and monopoly benefits are of course enjoyed by private firms too, so that perhaps one should express satisfaction over the fact that, at least, some of IRI's enterprises are not causing the state any additional losses but are in a position to return to it, in the form of dividends, some of the monies paid out earlier by the Treasury.

BUREAUCRACY AND ECONOMIC POWER

To oppose the liquidation of IRI does not mean to accept the present structure of IRI as permanent or as satisfactory, or to consider today's boundary line between the private and public sectors of the economy the ideal one.

In 1950 the Italian Cabinet entrusted to one of its members, Ugo La Malfa, the task of undertaking an inquiry into all direct and indirect government holdings in economic enterprises. On April 9, 1951, La Malfa presented his report entitled, "The Reorganization of the Economic Participations of the State," to the Cabinet. The report has not yet been officially released, and it remains, therefore, no more than a working paper for the guidance of the Italian government on the future reorganization of its economic activities.

In a subsequent statement made to the Senate on June 15, 1951, La Malfa declared that he had found a bewildering variety of relationships, jurisdictional issues, and types of enterprises. More than one thousand instances of public ownership had been found.

Enterprises performing the same economic function are set up under different jurisdictional controls and operate with different managerial systems. Some of them operate on the basis of appropriation from the general budget, others have a separate budget, some are public law bodies, others are commercial joint-stock corporations. Some belong to IRI, others to the Public Domain, many more to yet other public agencies. No discernible economic or other rational criterion exists to justify these arrangements. "Historical reasons" sometimes explain the more extreme incongruities of public policies. The shares of one economic enterprise may be owned by IRI, by the Public Domain, and by other government agencies, so that on their boards of directors the government is represented by different persons speaking with clashing voices and perhaps representing conflicting centers of political and administrative power.

Enterprises that boast of budgetary autonomy are in principle subjected to financial controls exercised by one or more Ministries. Such controls are not exercised with anything resembling uniformity. In some instances controls are merely formal, in others they extend to all managerial decisions. Nearly always the Ministries exercising such controls are several, so that among the controlling authorities continuous jurisdictional conflicts develop and even the simplest decision may be delayed for months and years, so that when finally taken it may often produce results which, because of shifting economic circumstances, are the opposite of those that were intended in the beginning.

One particularly unjustifiable form of government intervention is the ownership by the Public Domain or the Treasury, of corporations which are described as joint-stock companies, but of which the sole stockholder is the state.[2] It is clear that in such instances the device of the private corporation is used by the controlling agencies as a way of escaping from the rigid rules that the General Accounting Office seeks to enforce in the spending of public monies. The freedom thus acquired is sometimes used to enter into agreements with private business, agreements which, being secret, may not always protect the public interest. Finally, these "private" corporations have a tendency to breed other "private" affiliated companies, or subsidiaries, a process which inevitably tends to extend the area of government economic activities. All this happens while Parliament is kept entirely in the dark, and no notice of any kind is printed even in the *Official Gazette*.

It is clear that the central government bureaucracy considers these techniques as ways in which its own strength and influence in private industrial quarters, as well as its own pecuniary advantages, can all be increased. Civil servants sitting on boards of directors receive special indemnities, fees, reimbursements of expenses, and other extraordinary financial compensations which tend to multiply, several times over, their salaries. In part this is the consequence of the generally unsatisfactory level of salaries among the higher government employees. But it is also a manifestation of a spirit of greed, manipulation, and protection of selfish private interests as a result of which no good management and no proper defense of the general welfare is possible. Private empires are built, with bureaucrats developing into powerful "operators" capable of influencing the course of industrial activity in a manner not subject to public controls and often intended to protect similar positions of fellow bureaucrats or to satisfy the private interests of businessmen and politicians, from whom, of course, bureaucracy expects protection, in case of need.

[2] The more important examples are the three largest firms in the movie industry, two natural gas and oil corporations, and the Banca Nazionale del Lavoro.

A good example is that of Cogne, the steel-making concern in Val d'Aosta, which the Public Domain took over soon after World War I from the Ansaldo works of Genoa, which themselves became the property of IRI about ten years later. When that happened, Cogne should have been turned over to IRI. But the Public Domain successfully fought for the retention of its prize, even under the Fascist regime. No one has yet succeeded in forcing the Public Domain to give up the management of an enterprise entirely outside its traditional sphere of competence. The Public Domain obviously considers Cogne as a juicy plum, in spite of steady deficit operations, and refuses to surrender it.

The dominance of bureaucratic interests over the interests of the community has so far stopped any serious reorganization effort. No Cabinet minister dares to infringe upon the privileges enjoyed by some of the most powerful civil servants in his Ministry. Therefore public ownership continues even where such ownership can be justified only within the framework of a Communist state (movies, hotels and cinemas, cellulose, and optical instrument industries). Nothing has been done to sell those minority stock holdings which fail to give the state any effective voice in the management of a particular industry but yet compel the state to share in the commitments entered into by private owners.

Nor can the financial policies followed by the government toward IRI escape a substantial measure of criticism. The one constant policy seems to have been that of postponing as much as possible the granting of funds, needed by IRI, without making any distinction between funds needed for productive investment and those needed to meet operating deficits. In this way ultimate costs have been higher, while returns have been lower. This policy of delay has forced IRI to rely on unorthodox devices, such as expensive short-term borrowing. When at last funds are received, they are often needed to meet costs incurred in short-term financing.

Parliament shares responsibility with the Cabinet in this matter. When a bill was introduced by the government in October

1950 to increase IRI's endowment fund from 60 to 120 billion lire, Parliament did not act until August 1951, and then provided that the 60 billion increase was to be paid out in the two fiscal years 1951/52 and 1952/53. In the meantime, short-term borrowing by IRI had increased from 42 billion lire on December 31, 1949, to about 51 billions on December 31, 1952, while net interest charges increased from 4.2 to 4.6 billion lire. The Senate report on the bill frankly admitted:

Undoubtedly the current unsatisfactory financial position of IRI is the fruit of inadequate and fragmentary past policies. If IRI is to survive it must be guaranteed in timely fashion the funds needed to reach the goals assigned to it within the framework of the national economy. In this way IRI's managers will be able to devote their energies to the substantial tasks at hand, rather than waste their efforts in the search of a way out of the financial impasse in which they constantly find themselves.

REORGANIZATION PLANS

IRI cannot be appraised as a serious public experiment in industrial policy. It is rather an experiment in financial policy and, as such, one could describe it as a successful one, for, at relatively little cost to the state, it has at least put an end to the disastrous practices of the past which required the constant intervention of the government to sustain a banking system deeply involved in industrial commitments. In spite of the unsatisfactory developments and costly episodes narrated in the previous pages, one must say that IRI has created the preliminary conditions needed for a permanent reorganization on healthy foundations of Italy's banking system and for sound public decisions on the vast complex of industrial assets it has taken over.

It must also be clearly understood that the diseased areas in IRI's industrial empire are seldom the result of government mistakes. Such mistakes would presuppose a public policy, which in effect has never existed. Present difficulties are rather the consequence of past policies of private business, whose mistakes IRI has simply inherited. Rather than showing the bankruptcy of the

state as an industrial operator, the existence of IRI points to the
inadequacy of the legal and public policy framework applicable,
in the past as well as today, to the Italian private enterprise system
and shows the seriousness of the dangers run by the community
because of the absence of legislation capable of dealing with the
problems of a modern industrial society.

Once IRI was established on a permanent basis in 1937, it undertook a gradual and partial program of pruning and of reorganization, leading among other things to the establishment of the
iron and steel, shipping, telephone, mechanical and public utilities subholding companies into which IRI is now divided. This
reorganization has stood IRI in good stead in the years since the
end of World War II and has made the reconstruction of IRI's
iron and steel mills, passenger and merchant fleet, and telephone
system easier than it would otherwise have been. All this, however,
must be considered only as a preliminary step, beyond which it
is necessary to proceed if a more rational permanent arrangement
is to be achieved.

When Ugo La Malfa presented to the Council of Ministers his
report of April 9, 1951,[3] he made recommendations that can be
summed up as follows:

All public economic enterprises, including those controlled by
the Public Domain, should be regrouped in a series of holding
companies, according to types of activity, and all of them should
be placed under the effective control of an enlarged IRI, to be
headed by a Cabinet member. The minister would be responsible
both before the Cabinet and Parliament for the management of
all government-owned business. The minister would be assisted
by an adequate technical staff, capable of formulating over-all

[3] Upon receiving the La Malfa report, the Cabinet decided to review it
before presenting it to Parliament. Since then three years have elapsed and
the report has disappeared without trace. This appears to be the normal fate
of all government reports. Committees on the reform of the civil service, on
national accounting procedures, on control of government monopolies, and on
exploitation of natural resources have been appointed four, five, or six years
ago. No public announcement has ever been made of the outcome of their
deliberations.

programs and of carrying out periodic inspections at the operating level.

The minister would share his responsibility jointly with the Cabinet. A board of directors would develop financial policies and coordinate the management of the several subholding companies, and the managers of each separate enterprise would assume the technical, financial, and operating responsibilities appropriate to their jurisdiction.

The appointment of a Cabinet member to head IRI would make feasible the maintenance of political controls by Parliament. The assumption by IRI itself of all necessary powers for the effective and centralized control which today does not exist as scores of different government departments can all claim special roles, would make for both administrative inefficiency and open the way to interference by private interests.

Finally, no member of the staff of the General Accounting Office would be a member of any of the boards of directors or managers of IRI or of its subsidiaries. The same would apply to the Court of Accounts, which is the highest agency of administrative control over the activities of public bodies. This appears logical if the controlling agencies are expected to carry out effective and independent checks.

There is general and ready agreement with most of the points covered by La Malfa's plan. In order to sharpen the outline of the problem and to extend the discussion so as to include issues not raised by La Malfa, I shall conclude this essay with a six-point program, which appears to me essential in all its aspects if real progress is to be achieved in the area of public management of economic enterprises.

A SIX-POINT REFORM PROGRAM

Boundary Lines and Yardsticks

The establishment of a clear boundary line between private and public activities should be one of the main goals of public policy. In making this distinction, the government should take over in their entirety those economic sectors which it wishes to re-

tain under its control and give up the yardstick theory of competition of public and private industries in the same field. While
IRI should retreat in certain areas, it must also advance in others.

The yardstick theory, even though often defended, does not
appear capable of fulfillment. Competition between public and
private enterprises is not a healthy competition leading to improved techniques and modernization. It may very well develop
into a threat to the survival of even the soundest private enterprises, for no one can reasonably forecast the volume and rhythm
of future investments and production in the state-owned industries. The financing of state enterprises proceeds not from funds
freely underwritten by private investors but from funds forcibly
collected from taxpayers, or secured through public borrowings,
the repayment and interest of which are ultimately guaranteed
through taxation. Further, the managers running public enterprises can engage in the riskiest types of activity and continue to
manage them at a loss for a long time, without even damaging
their reputation in doing so, for responsibilities can easily be
shifted to politicians and higher public bodies, whose general directives the managers are supposedly bound to follow.

Public enterprises cannot be managed with the same criteria as
private enterprises. The profit motive must be the chief goal of
private business. The state, on the other hand, must seek to the
greatest possible extent those goals which in democratic countries
are fixed by parliamentary majorities. The failure of IRI to proceed on these assumptions was criticized by the left-wing Christian
Democratic party leader, Giovanni Gronchi, at a recent Christian
Democratic party congress:

Alone in Europe, the Italian government has so far shown its inability to
use for purposes of collective welfare its massive industrial assets, in spite
of the fact that they are of such size that they could exert a constructive
influence on key sectors of the national economy. . . . Indeed, IRI-
owned industries, which should defend the public interest, are managed
with a capitalistic outlook. This is so true, that managers of IRI feel it
to be entirely appropriate on their part to belong to the National Associ-

ation of Manufacturers. This is clear, even if indirect, proof of a complete lack of understanding on the fundamental difference of purpose
between public and private policies on industrial matters.[4]

Just like a private enterpreneur, the state must seek to produce
every unit of goods it turns out with the smallest possible use of
manpower, raw materials, and capital means. If at any point
there is waste, the community will suffer. But this does not mean
that the state should always pay—as private producers do—the
lowest possible compensation to the factors of production in
order to reduce, as much as possible, money costs. Not only should
the state refrain from exploiting its monopolistic position (by
forcing, for example, a reduction in the prices it pays for goods
and services) but, or so it might be reasonable to maintain, the
state ought to pay prices above the market (as for instance in the
case of wages paid to the least skilled workers, in order to lift
them up to a tolerable minimum level of subsistence). The state
would not be justified if it were to conclude agreements with
private producers in order to restrict and divide markets so as to
increase prices. But it might be justified, in certain instances, in
selling below cost, as when such sales were to encourage the consumption of certain types of services and commodities (transportation, health services, housing, essential foodstuffs).

Because of all these reasons it is difficult to compare the operating results of public and of private enterprises, nor is authentic
competition among them conceivable. If Italian big business toler-
ates the presence, within its fold, of state-owned enterprises, it is
only because it knows that in practice it will not suffer from
state competition, and it will always seek the support of government-owned industries when it engages in drives for higher tariffs
and bigger privileges. Private pressures for higher tariffs and
subsidies stand a better chance of success if they are supported, be-

[4] When these views were criticized in 24 *ORE*, a Rome daily representing
industrial interests, Gronchi replied as follows (same paper, issue of December
16, 1952): "IRI's activities should not be viewed from the point of view of
either profit or loss, but rather developed to realize the greatest collective
utility."

fore public opinion and responsible political bodies, by the managers in charge of public enterprises.

The "yardstick approach," which in other countries, as in the United States, may have led to the acceptance by private industries of the policies pioneered by the public sector of that industry (the example of the Tennessee Valley Authority is the clearest), has been construed by private industrial interests in Italy as leading to "neutralization" or "sterilization" of the public sector. One can see a candid admission of this in a statement made by the largest private public utility, the Edison Company of Milan, in answer to a questionnaire prepared by the Economic Committee of the Constituent Assembly in 1947:

We cannot say that the public utilities owned by IRI have initiated different policies, for they have kept to the path outlined by private public utilities. . . . Nor have they engaged in competition with us. . . . It is necessary that IRI be subjected to certain controls. These controls should be exercised not only by Parliament but also by trade organizations which possess more adequate technical skills than mere political bodies.

The calculated irony of the reference to the "trade organizations" that should be called to exercise controls over IRI can be savored only if we understand that those words were meant to designate the association of privately owned public utilities. In the United States this would be equivalent to saying that the Edison Electric Institute should be granted powers of control over the Tennessee Valley Authority.

Italy must face up to the same decisions that Great Britain and France have had to take: if public ownership is thought to be desirable for any particular industry, then the entire industry should be nationalized.

Regrouping of Nationalized Areas

Nationalized industries should be regrouped along sound economic lines in order to provide a series of industrial subholding companies, each one of homogeneous content. At the same time, by paying attention to the boundary lines established between private and public activities, they should be prevented from spreading their areas of operation surreptitiously.

The advantages of this approach will be many. An end will be put to the present confusion which permits the two firms producing almost all of Italy's coal and both owned by the Public Domain to continue to operate as wholly separate and uncoordinated enterprises; which allows Cogne to produce steel without reference to what Finsider, the IRI-owned steel subholding company is doing, merely because Cogne is owned by the Public Domain; which permits the planning of power production by Larderello, owned by the state railways, to proceed without regard to the planning of Finelettrica, the IRI public utility subholding company.

It would also terminate the present practice of asking IRI to shoulder the responsibility of taking care of an endless stream of bankrupted enterprises, taken in tow by weak governments yielding to business and labor pressures.

Civil Service or Private Management of Nationalized Industries

The question should be frankly faced as to whether, under appropriate guarantees, private entrepreneurial groups should not be given the task of managing some of the nationalized industries. The dilemma is this: on the one hand there is the impossibility or inadvisability of private ownership and, on the other, the shortcomings of public management. The inadequacy and weakness of the bureaucracy are such that direct state management is justified in Italy today only when the alternative of private management of nationalized industries is clearly not feasible. It is obvious, however, that no operating license to private groups should be made without the fullest open competition and in the absence of the most stringent guarantees concerning managerial, operating, financial, bookkeeping, wage, salary, and publicity procedures that would have to be followed by those entrusted with public assets.

Public Accounting

The war and its aftermath have tended to make worse the traditional delays in the rendering of accounts. The requirements of public disclosure have been forgotten. Not only are balance sheets set up in defiance of sound economic practice, but they are issued with appalling delays or not at all. The annual presentation of full and informative balance sheets should become compulsory. More than that, the balance sheets themselves ought to be based upon a drastically modernized set of procedures. It is difficult to assess the chief responsibility for the present unsatisfactory state of affairs—whether the bureaucrats, seeking to hide an unfavorable picture, or the government, anxious to avoid direct responsibility for policies which are not economically justifiable, is at fault. In the future, the political costs of the activities of public enterprises ought to be revealed in full, so as to appraise the country of what is involved. Otherwise, no rational calculation of costs, no real profit and loss accounts, no authentic measuring of the worth of individual managers will be possible.

The Training of a Modern Administrative Class

No plan of reform will ever be successful so long as the Italian government does not succeed in training a modern administrative class with the skills necessary to manage nationalized industries.

Today most of the managers of public enterprises are chosen by the ministers either to pay patronage debts or to satisfy the demands of private business groups anxious to maintain their own emissaries in the vital centers of national economic life. This is the worst of all possible systems, for it brings to positions of command individuals who are either incompetent or who consider themselves on leave from private industry, to which they obviously intend to go back in short order, having in the meantime developed the policies most favorable to their real masters.

IRI should proceed to the training of its own managerial cadres with the same care with which the armed forces provide for the training of their officers. Young university graduates should be hired and sent to special business and industrial schools as well as on training trips abroad. In-training programs should be more fully developed and a clear chance offered to the younger technicians and managers to rise to the top. Finally, salaries should be sufficient to keep in the public service the best men, who today are almost always lured away by private industry.

The Public Corporation

As things stand at present, most of the enterprises controlled by IRI or by the Public Domain are largely organized under the code provisions regulating private joint-stock companies. The question arises as to whether a shift in their legal structure should occur, and whether the corporations controlled in one way or another by the state should become public corporations.

In some of these enterprises the state is sole owner. In others the state owns only a majority, or even a minority, of the stock. In still others, the state owns such a small proportion of the stock that it cannot be said to possess effective control. When state ownership is total, the fiction of "the private corporation" offers bureaucracy important advantages of freedom of decision and of manipulation. When the state shares ownership, in varying degrees, with private investors, the state lays itself open to the pressures of the private owners, who all too frequently use partial state control as a screen behind which they try to achieve more readily their own private ends. It is difficult therefore to justify the present legal structures when they are used either to strengthen the hold of obsolete bureaucratic power or to favor private interests.

A better defense might be made for the mixed corporation in which the state owns a majority, or a controlling part, of the stock, with private investors owning the rest. The supporters of the mixed system maintain that it enables the state to draw upon the experience of private businessmen, who are members of the boards of directors of the mixed corporations; that it possesses a flexibility in the management of affairs which leads to successful operation; and that it draws partially upon private sources for the supply of needed capital funds.

It is true that, as a whole, businessmen show a greater understanding of business than civil servants, even though in their dealings with the state they have always shown a serious lack of public responsibility, and the mixed corporation is supposed to bring together private business interests and public representatives who have the controlling voice. Even so, we must raise the question of whether the influence of the private owners would not be directed toward the realization of the highest possible profits, a goal which would not necessarily coincide with the highest public good. Therefore, if publicly controlled enterprises are anxious to exploit the greater skills of businessmen, the choice must be based on the businessmen's qualifications to carry out the public mission with which they are to be entrusted.

It is also said that the mixed corporation, by comparison with the public corporation, has a greater freedom of action. Such freedom may, however, be purchased at too high a price if it entails the loss of all effective controls for the protection of the public interest. In practice, the civil servants who today are running private or mixed corporations are not answerable for their activities before any administrative tribunal, not to mention Parliament. The public-spirited and devoted manager may presumably derive certain advantages from this freedom, but it is absurd to build a system of public management of economic enterprises on the assumption of the widespread availability of such outstanding individuals.

With reference, finally, to the contention that the mixed corporation can rely both on public and private funds for the satisfaction of its capital requirements, it should be said that the advantages are largely fictitious. First of all, the state can always borrow at lower costs than private borrowers. In the second place, even if in theory bonds issued by state-controlled corporations that are set up under the "private" or the mixed "formula" are not part of the public debt, as would be bonds of public corporations, this is surely an illusory bookkeeping advantage, for ultimately all indebtedness of state-controlled corporations, whether private, mixed, or public, becomes a charge against the Treasury.

The truth is that the present legal structure of the private corporation, far fram being acceptable as an instrument adequate for the realization of public policy, is not even adequate for the realization in the twentieth century of the purposes of private business. The private corporation in Italy is still based on nineteenth-century institutions. Since that time its functions and responsibilities have drastically changed. And yet, unlike the United States, Italy does not have any legislation to protect the interests of the stockholders, to control the activities of corporation directors, to prevent concerted action in restraint of trade, and to force full and authentic disclosures of the affairs of business corporations. The control exercised by Italian courts over joint stock companies is purely formal and is not even adequate to guarantee the authenticity of the few figures which must be revealed in annual statements. As La Malfa said in his 1951 report:

As a rule the published capital and operating accounts of Italian joint stock companies provide figures which are far removed from the real ones. . . . Tax evasions as well as other reasons have led to these practices, which must certainly be counted as one of the evils, and not a minor one, from which Italy's public life is suffering.

The mixed corporation may represent a useful bridge between public and private ownership, whenever the state is in the midst of liquidating its economic assets. But when no such liquidation is being carried out or contemplated, and when the problem is in effect that of finding the best possible administrative arrangement for the industries that are to be kept permanently under state ownership, the mixed corporation is a very dubious solution. All relevant and positive experience seems to point instead to the autonomous public corporation, wholly state-owned, freed from too rigorous civil service procedures but effectively controlled by government and Parliament in the interest of the general welfare. The best Italian example of this approach is to be found in the fifty-year-old public corporation that manages the national railroad network. Even better examples are to be found in the modern public corporations through which Great Britain manages the vast range of its nationalized industries and public utilities.

Obviously the statutes governing the public corporations ought to take into account the different natures of the industries coming under their control, and flexible arrangements should be made for the selection of the members of the boards of directors, the fixing of varying degrees of control by the Cabinet and other administrative bodies, and the preparation of balance sheets. Nor should it be forgotten that the overriding consideration in any case must remain that of an adequate reform of the civil service, for without it no system for the management of nationalized enterprises, no matter how well conceived, will yield satisfactory results.

Bibliographical Note

PART I. A COMPARATIVE STUDY OF NATIONALIZATION POLICIES

A bibliography of nationalization in Great Britain, France, and Italy is to be found in Mario Einaudi, "Nationalization of Industry in Western Europe," *American Political Science Review*, March 1950.

On the British public corporation, see D. N. Chester, *The Nationalized Industries: An Analysis of the Statutory Provisions* (2d ed.; London, 1951); William A. Robson, *Problems of Nationalized Industry* (Oxford, 1952); Herbert Morrison, *Government and Parliament* (Oxford, 1954), in particular Chapters 12, 13, and 14; and the twelve pamphlets published by the Acton Society Trust, *Nationalized Industries* (London, 1950–1953). See also the unpublished Cornell dissertation by Gerhard Loewenberg, "The Effects of Governing on the British Labour Party" (Ithaca, 1955), especially Chapter III and the bibliography.

On nationalization and planning, see B. W. Lewis, *British Planning and Nationalization* (New York, 1952); and S. H. Beer, "British Planning under the Labour Government," *Social Research*, March 1950. For a different point of view on the relationships between public economic intervention and political dictatorship, see Friedrich von Hayek, *The Road to Serfdom* (Chicago, 1944). Underlining Soviet influence on the West, is E. H. Carr, *The Soviet Impact on the Western World* (New York, 1947).

For the compatibility between socialism and democracy, see the classic work of Joseph A. Schumpeter, *Socialism, Capitalism*

247

and Democracy (New York, 1942). Later editions include a discussion of the consequences of World War II.

References to Barone and Rathenau are to Enrico Barone, "Il Ministro della Produzione nello Stato Collettivista," *Giornale degli Economisti,* 1908 (an English translation of this essay has now been published in *Collectivist Economic Planning,* ed. by Friedrich von Hayek [London, 1935]); and Walter Rathenau, *Die Neue Wirtschaft* (Berlin, 1919).

Charles Morazé has dealt with the problems of French economic society in *La France Bourgeoise* (Paris, 1947), written during the war. For the views of the Resistance, see H. Michel and B. Mirkine-Guetzévitch, *Les Idées Politiques et Sociales de la Résistance, Documents Clandestins, 1940–1944* (Paris, 1954).

A number of French magazines in recent years have devoted a great deal of attention to the stagnation of French economy. Among those writing from a non-Communist point of view, *La Vie Intellectuelle, Esprit,* and *L'Express* may be mentioned. The Fondation Nationale des Sciences Politiques has been interested in the political implications of French economic developments. Published among its "cahiers" is Jean Chardonnet, *La Sidérurgie Française: Progrès ou Décadence?* (Paris, 1954). A lively analysis of French difficulties has been written by a Swiss journalist, Herbert Lüthy, *À l'Heure de Son Clocher* (Paris, 1955).

On the 1953 French decrees, see Jacques L'Huillier, "Les Nationalisations en Danger," *Terre Humaine,* 1953.

The works of Pierre Mendès-France are all relevant to the issue of proper public management of economic assets: *Gouverner, C'est Choisir* (Paris, 1953), the investiture speeches of June 1953; *Gouverner, C'est Choisir,* vol. II, "Sept Mois et Dix-sept Jours" (Paris, 1955), the principal speeches of Mendès-France as Prime Minister from June 1954 to February 1955; *Dire la Vérité, Causeries du Samedi* (Paris, 1955), Mendès-France's radio addresses; and, in collaboration with Gabriel Ardant, *La Science Économique et l'Action* (Paris, 1954).

The first published report of the Italian government oil monopoly, ENI (Ente Nazionale Idrocarburi) was issued at the end of 1954 as *Relazioni e Bilancio al 30 Aprile 1954*. Reports and balance sheets of all ENI's subsidiaries are included.

The most up-to-date and authoritative book on TVA is by Gordon R. Clapp, *The TVA: An Approach to the Development of a Region* (Chicago, 1955).

The most deliberate and careful expression of the British Trade Unions' point of view on the future of nationalization is to be found in *Public Ownership: An Interim Report Presented to the 85th Annual Trades Union Congress of September 1953*. The text of the report is to be found in the *Proceedings* of the Congress and is also available in a separate reprint. See also H. A. Clegg, *Industrial Democracy and Nationalization* (Oxford, 1951), and H. A. Clegg and T. E. Chester, *The Future of Nationalization* (Oxford, 1953).

The work of the European Coal and Steel Community can best be followed through its official documents, of which the most important ones are the reports submitted by the High Authority to the Common Assembly on the situation of the Community. So far four have been issued: in January 1953, in April 1954, in November 1954, and in April 1955.

For a juridical discussion of the European Coal and Steel Community, see Paul Reuter, *La Communauté Européenne du Charbon et de l'Acier* (Paris, 1953). The socialist leader André Philip has been an articulate political defender of supranationalism. Among his many books, see *L'Europe Unie et Sa Place dans l'Économie Internationale* (Paris, 1953). André Philip is also editor of *Nouvelles de l'Europe*, a monthly of the Mouvement Européen. The January 1955 issue is devoted to the Coal and Steel Community.

The *Annual Reports* issued in Paris since 1948 by the Organization for European Economic Cooperation should also be consulted. The fourth, December 1952, and the sixth, 1955, are especially valuable.

The most eloquent and vigorous criticism addressed to the principles upon which the efforts and planning of European supranational integration rest is to be found in François Perroux, *L'Europe sans Rivages* (Paris, 1954).

PART II. NATIONALIZATION IN FRANCE

Only works published in France (Paris is the place of publication unless otherwise given) are listed here. For a complete bibliography covering the period prior to 1949, see René Gendarme, *L'Expérience Française de la Nationalisation Industrielle et Ses Enseignments Economiques* (1950). *Droit Social* has published, since 1945, many articles on nationalization and should be consulted as a primary source of information.

On nationalization problems in general, see—

Marcel Armengaud and others, *Vingt Ans de Capitalisme d'État* (1951).
Buttgenbach and Robert Jacomet, *Le Statut des Entreprises Publiques* (1947).
Pierre-Marie Delesalle, *Le Statut du Personnel des Entreprises Nationalisées* (1954).
L. Julliot de la Morandière and Maurice Byé, *Les Nationalisations en France et à l'Étranger*, Vol. I, "Les Nationalisations en France" (1948), issued by the Institut de Droit Comparé of the Faculté de Droit de Paris, with essays by Bernard Lavergne, Simon Gueulette, Jean-Marie Auby, Georges Thomas, Maurice Picard, and Paul Reuter.
E. S. Kirschen, *Conduite Financière des Entreprises Privées et Publiques* (1952).
Henri Laufenburger, "Quelques Aspects Inattendus des Nationalisations," *Revue de Science et Législation Financière*, 1952.
Bernard Lavergne, *Le Problème des Nationalisations* (1946).
Marcel Pellenc, *Le Bilan de Six Ans d'Erreurs* (1950).
François Perroux, *Les Nationalisations* (1946).
Marcel Ventenat, *L'Expérience des Nationalisations* (1947).
Jean Rivero, *Le Régime des Nationalisations* (Juris-Classeurs Civil, 1948). This study, which is the most complete from the juridical point of view, is kept up to date by the Juris-Classeurs.
B. S. Chlepner, "Reflexions sur les Nationalisations," *Revue de l'Institut de Sociologie*, 1949.
Jean Rivero, "Le Régime des Entreprises Nationalisées et l'Évolution du Droit Administratif," *Archive de philosophie du droit*, 1952.

XXX, "Connaîtra-t-on les véritables résultats des nationalisations?" *Revue Administrative*, 1951.

Ministère des Finances, *Inventaire de la Situation Financière (1913–1946)* (1946). This volume contains a complete list, as of its date of publication, of the public enterprises and mixed corporations, as well as financial data which summarize a great deal of French economic history since 1913.

An up-to-date inventory and catalogue of all public and semi-public enterprises was published as part of the 1954 Loi de Finances: *Nomenclature des Établissements Publics et Semi-Publics de l'État, des Sociétés d'Économie Mixte et des Fondations et Associations Subventionnées d'Intérêt National* (Assemblée Nationale, Document No. 6748, 1954, 257 pp.).

On questions of price policies, see—

Maurice Allais, *Économie Pure et Rendement Social* (1945).

Marcel Boiteux, "La Tarification des Demandes en Pointe," *Revue Générale de l'Electricité*, 1949.

René Courtin, *Cours de Théorie Économique, 1949–1950* (1950).

Roger Hutter, "La Théorie Économique et la Gestion Commerciale des Chemins de Fer," *Revue Générale des Chemins de Fer*, February, July, and October 1950.

The Monnet Plan extended to such nationalized enterprises as coal, electricity, gas, and railroads. The Plan's operations can best be followed through the reports issued by the Commissariat Général:

Commissariat Général au Plan, *Rapport Général sur le Premier Plan de Modernisation et d'Équipement* (November 1946).

——, *Rapport du Commissaire Général sur le Plan de Modernisation et d'Equipement de l'Union Française: Réalisations 1947–1949 et Objectifs 1950–1952* (December 1949).

——, *Quatre Ans d' Exécution du Plan de Modernisation et d'Équipement de l'Union Française: Réalisations 1947–1950 et Programme 1951* (1951).

——, *Rapport sur la Réalisation du Plan de Modernisation et d'Équipement de l'Union Française: Année 1952* (1953). This is a volume of 326 pages which gives the final account of the results of the first "Monnet

Plan." As such it is the basic document to be consulted on the scope of public investment in nationalized enterprises.

The same activities can also be followed through the series of reports prepared by the Commissariat Général and issued by the National Assembly as annexes to the finance bills. The most recent ones are:

Projet de Loi de Finances pour l'Exercice 1954. *État des Operations du Plan de Modernisation et d'Équipement* (Assemblée Nationale, Document No. 6748).

Projet de Loi de Finances pour l'Exercice 1955, *État des Operations du Plan de Modernisation et d'Équipement* (Assemblée Nationale, Document No. 9414).

Other important parliamentary documents include the following:

Assemblée Nationale, *Projet de Loi relatif au Développement des Dépenses d'Investissements Économiques et Sociaux pour l'Exercice 1952* (Document No. 2053).

——, *Rapport Présenté au Nom de la Commission des Finances sur le Projet de Loi relatif aux Finances d'Investissements de 1950 par M. Barangé* (Document No. 9717).

Conseil Économique, *Avis et Rapports du Conseil Économique sur les Dépenses d'Investissement pour 1951* (Études et Travaux du Conseil Économique, No. 17, 1951).

Conseil de la République, *Avis Présenté au Nom de la Commission de la Production Industrielle sur le Projet de Loi relatif aux Finances d'Investissements de 1950 par M. Armengaud* (Document No. 347).

——, *Rapport Présenté au Nom de la Commission des Finances sur le Projet de Loi relatif aux Finances d'Investissements de 1950 par M. Pellenc* (Document No. 326).

In 1954, a second Plan of Modernization and Equipment was launched. The Economic Affairs Committee of the National Assembly issued a comprehensive report in three volumes analyzing the plan: Assemblée Nationale, *Rapport Fait au Nom de la Commission des Affaires Économiques sur le Projet de Loi (No. 8555) Portant Approbation du Deuxième Plan de Modernisation et d'Équipement,* Vol. I, "Les Données Fondamentales de la Situation Économique de la France," Vol. II, "Exposé du Plan," Vol. III, "Decisions de la Commission" (Document No. 9133, August 11, 1954).

Until 1953 the over-all administrative control of nationalized industries was in the hands of the Committee on Verification of Accounts. It prepared three reports which are primary source materials. They were published in the administrative annexes of the *Journal Officiel* as follows:

Commission de Vérification des Comptes des Entreprises Publiques, *Rapport d'Ensemble,* August 21, 1949.
——, *Deuxième Rapport d'Ensemble,* January 26, 1951.
——, *Troisième Rapport d'Ensemble,* October 3, 1952.
This is the last of the reports published by the Commission.

Annual reports on the operating results and the accounts of nationalized enterprises are now published with fair regularity. Since 1947 the reports are usually available for the following public enterprises: Charbonnages de France and Houillères de Bassin, Électricité de France, Gaz de France, Société Nationale des Chemins de Fer, Régie Renault, Air France, and Conseil National du Crédit.

On coal, see—

M. Allais, *La Gestion des Houillères Nationalisées et la Théorie Économique* (1953).
Étienne Audibert, *Cinq Ans de Nationalisation* (1950).
——, *Tribulations et Perspectives des Charbonnages Français* (1949).
J. Personnaz, "La Mise en Application de la Nationalisation des Houillères; Les Biens Remis aux Actionnaires des Anciennes Sociétés Minières," *Droit Social,* 1952.
Charbonnages de France, Service du Contentieux, Textes Législatifs et Règlementaires: *Nationalisation des Houillères: Statut des Charbonnages; Statut du Mineur.* These official documents are kept up to date.
Conseil de la République, *Rapport Annuel au Nom de la Sous-commission du Conseil de la République Chargée du Suivre la Gestion des Entreprises Nationalisées* (Document No. 824, 1950).

On electricity and gas, see—

Électricité de France; Gaz de France, *Cahiers de Documentation Juridique.*

Cahiers de Documentation Juridique, *Recueil des Lois et Règlements Interessant la Nationalisation du Gaz et de l'Électricité* [et textes règlementaires d'ensemble sur les entreprises publiques] *1946–1950* (1951).

On transportation, see—

L'Année Ferroviaire. Published once a year.

Le Déficit d'Air France: Comment y Remédier? (1951). Preface by Marcel Pellenc.

Lécrivain-Servoz, *Pour le Redressement Financier des Chemins de Fer Français* (n.d.).

Marcel Pellenc, *La Réforme de la SNCF* (1951).

Boyaux, "Le Problèm du Chemin de Fer," *Revue Politique et Parlementaire,* 1951.

Henri Peyret, "La Situation Économique et Financière de la SNCF," *L'Économie,* Supplement No. 322, 1951.

Christian Pineau, "Le Déficit de la SNCF," *Banque et Bourse,* 1950.

Air France, *Air France: Service Public* (1951).

SNCF, *L'Évolution de la Productivité de la SNCF* (January 1951).

On banks, see—

J. M. Fourier, "Bilan de la Nationalisation des Banques," *Droit Social,* 1952.

François Mierse, "La Nationalisation des Banques," *Esprit,* 1954.

The following is a list of the more important parliamentary documents relating to the reorganization of nationalized industries in the years from 1947 to 1950, when the issue was under active consideration by the National Assembly:

Assemblée Nationale, *Projet de Loi Portant Statut Général des Entreprises Publiques Présenté par Henri Queuille* (No. 6027, 1948).

——, *Proposition de Loi* (No. 1289, May 9, 1947). The Thorez bill.

——, *Proposition de Loi* (No. 1522, May 30, 1947). The Schneiter bill.

——, *Proposition de Loi* (No. 2044, July 17, 1947). The Bardoux bill.

——, *Proposition de Loi* (No. 9091, 1950). The Pellenc bill.

——, *Proposition de Loi* (No. 11403, 1950). The Armengaud bill.

——, *Rapport Présenté au Nom de la Commission des Finances sur le Projet de Loi No. 6027 par M. Guérin* (No. 8572, 1949).

PART III. NATIONALIZATION IN ITALY

The Institute of Industrial Reconstruction publishes annual reports. They are useful, even though limited in the information they offer; the last one appeared in 1954 and contains summary operating and financial accounts for 1953. In recent years an English version has been published, with graphs and statistical tables, *1953 Annual Report* (Rome, 1954). Each of the great subholding companies into which IRI is divided publishes annual reports as well.

A number of Italian weeklies have frequent articles on IRI. Among them can be mentioned *Il Mondo* (Rome) and *Il Mercurio* (Milan).

Important source materials can be found in the four volumes on Italian industry prepared under governmental auspices in 1946 and 1947 for use by the Constituent Assembly and published as *Rapporto della Commissione Economica Presentato all'Assemblea Costituente* (Rome, 1946–1947).

The parliamentary discussions for the increase of IRI's capital funds centered around a government report presented to the Senate on October 13, 1950 (Senate Document No. 1327) and the report of a Senate committee on the government bill on April 12 1951 (Senate Document No. 1327A). The Senate debates of May 23 and June 12 and 13, 1951, are especially noteworthy.

The government-sponsored committee of inquiry into the engineering industry (Commissione Indagini e Studi sull'Industria Meccanica—CISIM) published in 1952 a number of reports which are valuable for an appraisal of one of the areas of Italian industry in which governmental commitments have been both important and the source of much difficulty. The two chief reports are *L'Industria Meccanica Italiana alla Fine dell'Anno 1951* and *Rilievi e Proposte sulla Industria Meccanica Italiana* (Rome, 1952).

CISIM enlisted the assistance of the Stanford Research Institute as part of the ECA technical assistance program. The Stanford group produced a massive report of 343 pages available in English as *Economic and Industrial Problems of the Italian Mechanical Industries* (Rome, 1952). The Stanford report includes a chapter on government participation in Italian industry which is devoted to IRI and has suggestions for a drastic program of reorganization and liquidation which evoked much criticism.

The La Malfa report presented to the government on April 9, 1951, appeared under the title *La Riorganizzazione delle Partecipazioni Economiche dello Stato* (Rome, 1952). But the publication was for official use only. Together with earlier and subsequent reports on IRI, it is now about to be released for general use in a volume which is due to appear in the spring of 1955.

The author of this section, Professor Ernesto Rossi, has been able to consult in the IRI archives a number of unpublished reports concerning various phases of IRI's activities. The chief ones were: "Le Origini dell'IRI e la Sua Azione nei Confronti della Situazione Bancaria" (1944); "L'IRI nel Primo Quinquennio di Vita" (1944); "L'IRI Ente di Carattere Permanente" (1944); "L'IRI e la Sua Funzione nell'Economia Industriale Italiana" (1948); "L'IRI nel Quadro dell'Industria Meccanica Italiana" (1948); and "Notizie sull'Istituto per la Ricostruzione Industriale" (1951).

A spirited running commentary on Italian industrial problems is to be found in Ernesto Rossi, *Settimo: Non Rubare* (Bari, 1952). The volume is a collection of essays and articles, nearly all of them published in *Il Mondo* in the years from 1949 to 1952.

Index